PENGUIN BO

AMERICAN HEA

Mick Brown was born in London in 1950. He wrote for the *Sunday Times* for ten years as well as for national and international magazines. He is now a regular contributor to the *Telegraph Magazine* and a freelance writer. His last book was a biography of Richard Branson, *The Inside Story*. He lives with his wife Patricia and their three children in London.

MICK BROWN

———————

AMERICAN HEARTBEAT

TRAVELS FROM WOODSTOCK TO
SAN JOSE BY SONG TITLE

PENGUIN BOOKS

For Patricia and Celeste, Dominic and Clementine

PENGUIN BOOKS

Published by the Penguin Group
Penguin Books Ltd, 27 Wrights Lane, London W8 5TZ, England
Penguin Books USA Inc., 375 Hudson Street, New York, New York 10014, USA
Penguin Books Australia Ltd, Ringwood, Victoria, Australia
Penguin Books Canada Ltd, 10 Alcorn Avenue, Toronto, Ontario, Canada M4V 3B2
Penguin Books (NZ) Ltd, 182–190 Wairau Road, Auckland 10, New Zealand

Penguin Books Ltd, Registered Offices: Harmondsworth, Middlesex, England

First published in Great Britain by Michael Joseph 1993
Published in Penguin Books 1994
1 3 5 7 9 10 8 6 4 2

The acknowledgements on p. viii constitute an extension of this copyright page
Maps by Ken Cox, illustrations by Steve James

The moral right of the author has been asserted

Printed in England by Clays Ltd, St Ives plc

Contents

	Map	vi
	Acknowledgements	viii
	Lyric Acknowledgements	ix
one	'Woodstock'	1
two	'Chattanooga Choo-Choo'	33
three	'Memphis, Tennessee'	49
four	'Meet Me In St Louis'	70
five	'What's Made Milwaukee Famous (Has Made A Loser Out of Me)'	86
six	'Twenty-four Hours From Tulsa'	119
seven	'El Paso'	133
eight	'By The Time I Get To Phoenix'	152
nine	'Do You Know The Way To San Jose?'	167
ten	'Baltimore'	184
eleven	'Nashville Cats'	211

Ken Cox

Acknowledgements

This book would not have been possible without Nigel Horne, the editor of The **Telegraph Magazine**, London, whose telephone call first set me on the road across America. I am deeply indebted to Nigel for his belief, his editorial skills and judgement, and his friendship.

Some parts of this book first appeared, in abbreviated form, in The **Telegraph Magazine**, and I am particularly grateful to the deputy editor George Darby whose sagacity, wit, compendious knowledge of vintage pop music and a cappella stylings of the same, made such an invaluable contribution. Thanks are also due to Raymonde Watkins, Mariana Asprey, Deanne Elliott, Fiona Crawford and to Paul Burgess.

I am also grateful to the following: D'Army Bailey, John Bickerton, Eileen Bickerton, Tony Byworth, John Cassady, Carolyn Cassady, Robert Chalmers, Hal David, Linton Deskins, Bobbie Deskins, Don Dooley, P. J. Erickson, Vince Fitzpatrick, Vic Garbarini, Ray Hartmann, Leon Metz, Dub Nell, Therol Nell, Randy Newman, Jon Philibert, Mary Schmitz, Roger Sovine, Mitch Walking Elk, Carolyn Whitaker, Timothy White, Richard Wooton and Chuck Young. Grateful thanks to Caroline Dawnay, and to my editor Louise Haines, for her patience and advice.

Several books have proved particularly informative, and may be of further interest to readers. They include:

Woodstock: History of an American Town by Alf Evers. Woodstock: The Overlook Press.
The Shooters by Leon C. Metz. El Paso: Mangan Books.
Border by Leon C. Metz. El Paso: Mangan Books.
The Holy Goof by William Plummer. New York: Athena Books.
Off The Road by Carolyn Cassady. London: Black Spring Press.
Storming Heaven by Jay Stevens. London: Heinemann.
Elvis by Jerry Hopkins. London: Open Gate.
Good Rockin' Tonight by Colin Escott with Martin Hawkins. London: Virgin.
This Is Milwaukee by Robert Wells. Milwaukee: Renaissance Books.
Bearing The Cross by David J. Garrow. London: Jonathan Cape.
The Future South, edited by Joe P. Dunn and Howard L. Preston. Chicago: University of Illinois Press.
Situationist International Handbook, edited by Ken Knabb. Bureau of Public Secrets, Berkeley, California.

Lyric Acknowledgements

The author and publishers would also like to thank the following companies for their kind permission to quote from lyrics:

'Woodstock' from the album *Ladies Of The Canyon* by Joni Mitchell, 1970. Reproduced by permission of Warner Chappell Music Ltd, Woodford Green, Essex IG8 8HN.

'Chattanooga Choo-Choo' by Harry Warren and Mack Gordon, 1934. Reproduced by permission of Warner Chappell Music Ltd, Woodford Green, Essex IG8 8HN.

'Memphis, Tennessee' by Chuck Berry, 1949. Reproduced by permission of Jewel Music Publishing Company Ltd, London WC2H 8NA.

'Meet Me In St Louis' by Kerry Mills and Andrew B. Sterling, 1904. Reproduced by permission of Redwood Music Ltd, London NW1 8BD.

'What's Made Milwaukee Famous (Has Made A Loser Out Of Me)' by Glenn Sutton. © 1968, Al Gallico Music Corporation, USA. Reproduced by permission of EMI Music Publishing Ltd, London WC2H 0EA.

'Twenty-four Hours From Tulsa' by Burt Bacharach and Hal David, 1964. Reproduced by permission of CPP/Bellwin United/EMI Partnership Ltd.

'El Paso City' by Marty Robbins, 1976. Reproduced by permission of Acuff-Rose Opryland Music Ltd and Music Sales Ltd, London W1V 5TZ.

'By The Time I Get To Phoenix' by Jim Webb. © 1967, Koppelman-Dandier Music/ Jonathan Three Music, USA. Reproduced by permission of EMI Songs Ltd, London EC2H 0EA and Island Music Ltd, London W6 0RA.

'Do You Know The Way To San Jose?' by Burt Bacharach and Hal David, 1968. © Blue Seas Music Inc/Jac Music Co. Inc. Reproduced by permission of MCA Music Ltd, London W6 8JA.

'Baltimore' by Randy Newman. © 1977, Six Pictures Music, USA. Reproduced by permission of EMI Music Publishing Ltd, London WC2H 0EA.

'Nashville Cats' by John Sebastian. © 1966, Hudson Bay Music Co. USA. Reproduced by permission of Robbins Music Corporation Ltd, London WC2H 0EA.

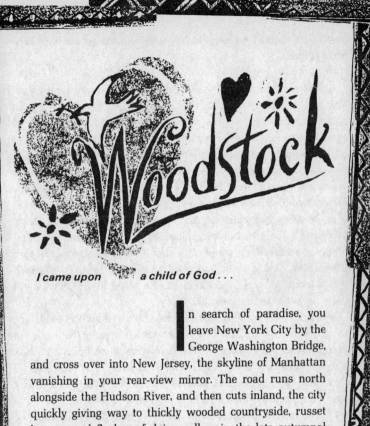

I came upon a child of God . . .

In search of paradise, you leave New York City by the George Washington Bridge, and cross over into New Jersey, the skyline of Manhattan vanishing in your rear-view mirror. The road runs north alongside the Hudson River, and then cuts inland, the city quickly giving way to thickly wooded countryside, russet browns and flashes of dying yellow in the late autumnal sunlight.

On the weekend of 14/15 August 1969, there was a 30-mile traffic jam on the New York Thruway. Stuck in it, as she was, the singer Joni Mitchell was therefore obliged to improvise, or rely on hearsay, for her description of the arcadian idyll in 'Woodstock'.

I came upon a child of God, he was walking along the road/ When I stopped and asked him where he was going, this he told me/We're going on down to Yasgur's farm, gonna get back to the land/Gonna listen to a rock and roll band/Gonna set our souls

free/We are stardust, we are golden/And we've got to get ourselves back to the garden.

In fact, the very name of the Woodstock Festival was a misnomer. The garden of Mitchell's song – a dairy farm owned by a man named Max Yasgur – was actually 60 miles from the town of Woodstock, close to a village named Bethel. The organisers expected 50,000 people. Some 400,000 turned up. The site was officially designated a national disaster area. Lavatories overflowed. There were three deaths, two births, four miscarriages. *The New York Times* described it as 'outrageous'. And yet, miraculously, the mood was beatific, harmonious. And some great myth was born. Woodstock. It meant innocence, idealism, good vibes, man. Or, that hippie nonsense. Some people talked of it for years afterwards, as if it were the only moment they had truly been alive. To others it would come to mark a nadir in human absurdity. Either way, it begat an industry that grew like topsy.

Woodstock the town might have had little to do with Woodstock the festival, but it was the town that was left to carry the burden of its mythology. Few people made the pilgrimage to the site of Max Yasgur's farm. But every August the main street of Woodstock still filled with sightseers and sentimentalists for whom Woodstock meant something more than a loud noise in a big field.

But August was high season, and I – thankfully – had missed that. The road that carried me into Woodstock was all but deserted; the countryside dressed in rich shades of brown and orange in the autumnal afternoon sunlight. The main street – Tinker Street – was lined with timber houses, painted white, in the colonial style; an old fire-engine house; a lovely white wooden church, Dutch Reformed, with an obligatory dreaming spire. There were shops selling beeswax candles and tie-dye T-shirts, rustic antiques and handicrafts by local artists. It bore the affliction of all places that the accident of history, the accumulated weight of years of flattery in travel books, and the attentions of tourists, have designated as 'pretty', in that it no longer resembled a place where people lived so much as one that people visited.

Yet curiously, there seemed to be a chronic shortage of places where a visitor to Woodstock could stay. A poker-work welcome sign hung on the door of a rooming house on Tinker Street. I rang the doorbell; there was no answer. I pushed the door open and stepped inside. The interior was suffocating in chintz and self-conscious folksiness. It looked like the kind of place where you could be found dead in your bed having expired quietly from a surfeit of politeness. I tiptoed out.

The Mill Stream Motel was a collection of timber shacks, set down a pretty wooded track, beside a river. The office and 'coffee shop' was equipped with a desk, a creaking plastic sofa and a broken refrigerator standing in the middle of the room. The cabins were minute and sparsely furnished. The small black and white televisions in each one offered six channels of migraine haze. There was no heating. It felt like the kind of place where lonely people checked in to bid farewell to the world with an overdose of sleeping tablets or a single gunshot through the mouth.

Woodstock was seeming less and less like paradise by the second. The sky was growing dark, my temper more irritable, and my circumstances more desperate.

At last, 6 miles out of town, at the junction of the expressway back to New York, I found a Howard Johnson's chain motel – a study in bland anonymity. It was the start of the deer-hunting season, and the car park was full of pick-up trucks, the bar loud with men in jeans and caps and hiking boots, yakking over the drone of a television ball game. I went to my room, and watched the local news on television. An elderly couple had been found murdered, barely 2 miles away. I fell asleep to the sound of car doors banging, voices raised in dispute, footsteps in the corridor outside. It was the kind of place where by the time your body was found the murderer would already be out of the state.

Like Joni Mitchell, I missed the Woodstock Festival. She was stuck in a traffic jam. I was stuck in an office in London, working on a newspaper devoted to selling property, where stardust was conspicuous by its absence.

The news of the world's biggest traffic jam impinged on my consciousness hardly at all. It would be another year before I would experience *Woodstock*, the film, sitting in a cinema in, of all places, Rotterdam, Holland. The film made the festival look like somewhere you wished you'd been. Young girls taking off their clothes and frolicking in the long grass; people ostentatiously brandishing joints at the camera, banging bongos and finger-cymbals. On a wet Wednesday night in Rotterdam, it all had the unreal air of some exotic tribal ritual recorded for posterity by anthropologists.

I missed the Woodstock Festival, but I inherited its legacy; days sitting in damp, windblown fields, queuing for hours at chemical latrines, eating inedible food and listening to announcements telling you not to buy the blue tablets, and for Dave to meet Shagger at the bad trips tent. By then the daffy Utopianism of Woodstock had already dissipated in the festival which immediately followed it, at Altamont, California, where a young man was beaten to death by Hells Angels. That too I saw in the cinema. These cultural shifts sounded in Britain like ricochets of gunfire, messages I had been hearing since adolescence.

My first great love was rhythm and blues. I had an older friend, with whom I had grown up collecting football cards, and standing in the rain at the popular end at Crystal Palace. His elder brother frequented Soho nightclubs. He wore a pork-pie hat; owned a complete set of *Downbeat* magazine, and records by Theolonius Monk, 'Sonny Boy' Williamson and Chuck Berry. The connection was made. At the age of fourteen I took a bus journey across London, to Walthamstow, to see James Brown perform for the first time on an English stage. It was the most exciting, the most exotic, thing I had ever seen. He was living mercury, a blur of rhythm and colour. Nobody had ever sounded like that before, dressed like that, moved like that.

Brown had come from Augusta, Georgia. I found it on the map, secreted it in my imagination. A hot, dusty place, surrounded by cotton fields, I decided. Cars with huge fins and wraparound bumpers nosed along the streets, and there were bars on every corner, blaring out party music, and inside, men with pompadour haircuts and scarlet slubbed-silk suits – like James and his backing singers the Famous Flames – and fabulous, serpentine women, shimmying up close. An English accent, I felt sure, would go far in such a place.

Brown's claim to be 'the hardest working man in show business' was no exaggeration. At the height of his success through the Sixties, Brown was working 364 days a year, travelling across America by train and show-bus from date to date. Brown had a song called 'Night Train', an instrumental which rocked and clattered like an express train, with Brown the conductor, taking note of the stops along the way: Miami, Florida; Atlanta, Georgia; Raleigh, North Carolina; Washington DC, 'oh, and Richmond, Virginia too . . .' The song was so successful, he followed it with another called 'Mashed Potatoes USA', which repeated the same trick with a new set of names: New York City, Boston, Buffalo, 'going straight down the road, gonna stop at Cleveland, Ohio . . .' These songs struck me as more than just lists. They were calls to communion, a way to embrace the audience, make them part of the mystery and excitement of what Brown sang about.

Pop music is a language of hidden codes and meanings. It speaks to those who have ears to listen. It draws maps of emotional landscapes, and sometimes geographical ones too. It plants ideas, dreams, to incubate in the imagination, to be tested and proved. I drew a map of America from songs, came to it like a blind man reading Braille.

Memphis, Tennessee, was where Chuck Berry was trying to contact his girl Marie. Memphis was also the home of the blues. In Kansas City there were crazy little women, and Wilbert Harrison was going to get him one. Abilene was 'the prettiest town I've ever seen'. In Surf City there were two girls for every boy. I couldn't be sure where Surf City was – a mythic heaven in Brian Wilson's imagination, shaped from that Californian triumvirate of surf and sand and sex – but I knew I wanted to go there.

Natchez was a town in Mississippi where a dance hall burned down, killing 200 revellers. Howlin' Wolf had sung a song called 'Natchez Burning'. These songs could be a political education too. My first understanding of the evil of segregation was learning that when the Motortown Revue played theatres in the American South, the whites would sit downstairs, the blacks upstairs. Motortown was Detroit, and when Martha and the Vandellas sang 'Dancing In The Street', I could hear the roar of the auto-industry production lines and smell the exhaust fumes on the freeway.

These songs were pieces of American heaven, describing a vista of possibilities that found no equivalent in English music. They hinted at a vastness, a variegated landscape and range of experiences that demanded to be celebrated, made sense of. Even to the Americans, it seemed, America was exotic. They believed in its own mythology; they got excited about just being there, and if they were excited, how could I fail to be? Once you had heard 'Route 66!', you knew with a certainty that you seldom felt about anything else, that one day you would drive it, and when you did it would be fun. And so it is. This was indoctrination masquerading as infatuation, perhaps. I felt, in a sense, American; my culture more of that country than my own. Now it is called Coca-Colonisation, but it felt like missionary work, and I was an eager convert.

When I first visited America in 1972, I experienced the feeling of *déjà vu* common to almost everyone when they first set foot in that country. Those buildings, those places, those voices – so familiar did they seem from films and television programmes as well as songs. It took some time to realise that this was actually an alien landscape whose first appearance of familiarity disguised a deeper sense of the unknown.

In the intervening years I had visited some of these songs, but curiously not the interesting ones. New York, New York, and Chicago ('that wonderful town . . .') were as braggadocio as the songs which described them. But these weren't stories, they were advertising slogans, film sets with which we were already over-familiar. But what of San Jose, Phoenix and El Paso? What lay Twenty-four Hours From Tulsa? Like Joni Mitchell, I wanted to get myself back to the garden, and I took the road out of New York City, heading north.

To the Indians who had lived and hunted there since before the time of Christ, the land around what would come to be known as Woodstock must have seemed a kind of Utopia. The forests were thick with game; the broad river that would later be named the Hudson filled with fish; the land beautiful and abundant. To the first white settlers who bought land from the Indians in the seventeenth century, the attractions were partly mercantile; their eyes were on the unlimited supply of timber for logging. By the end of the nineteenth century, Woodstock had begun to take shape; a small, rural hamlet – typical of dozens in the area which had been by-passed by the railroad – with a legacy of old Dutch, German and New England families, and small local industries of glassworks and saw-mills. Such notoriety as the town enjoyed grew from an enduring belief among many of the local people in witchcraft, and a reputation for good air and clean water, which made it reputedly the healthiest town in the whole of New York State. 'Woodstock Where People Seldom Die', said the headline in a local paper of 1907, pointing out that of the town's population of 1,700 people, one in sixteen was aged between seventy and eighty; one in thirty-two was aged over eighty, and half a dozen had passed the age of ninety.

It was this air of bucolic serenity that first attracted Ralph Whitehead to Woodstock in 1902. Whitehead was the heir to a Yorkshire mill-owning family fortune, a scholar and aesthete who as a student at Balliol College, Oxford, had come under the spell of John Ruskin, the English author, critic and Slade professor of art at Oxford. Ruskin was a Utopian prophet who saw a polemical purpose to art. He lamented the social injustice and squalor arising from unbridled capitalism and industrialisation – the beginnings of mass-production – and saw craftsmanship as a way for the working man to regain control of his own life, realising dignity and self-esteem through creativity.

As mill-owners, Whitehead's family were responsible for their fair share of exploitation and pollution. Whitehead resolved that when he inherited the mills they would be run as workers' co-operatives. He quarrelled with his father, left Oxford and went to Paris to work as a carpenter. The quarrel was eventually mended

7

and Whitehead came into his family inheritance, although he was to play no part in Yorkshire mill-owning life. Instead, he travelled extensively throughout Europe. He studied Plato and Kant, and took a scholarly interest in the works of Dante, editing and publishing an edition of *Vita Nuova*, and accumulating an extensive library of Dante's works. Above all, he dreamed of starting a community that would unify his two abiding passions, of aesthetics and social reform.

By 1890, Whitehead's enthusiasm for ideas of social reform led him to the New World, America, where the fulfilment of his dreams seemed more a possibility. William Morris, the English craftsman, poet and Utopian – and another influence on Whitehead – had written that beautiful work could only be done in beautiful places, and in 1901 Whitehead and his new American wife Jane Byrd founded a school for arts and crafts called Arcady, in Santa Barbara, an idyllic spot on the Californian coast north of Los Angeles. At Arcady children were taught weaving, wood carving, modelling and music, in surroundings that echoed the genteel propriety of an English country house party. But Whitehead dreamed of something more – a colony where artists of all kinds could come together, comfortably isolated from the dehumanising and degrading life of the city, agreeably in touch with nature.

Scouts were despatched to the mountains of Virginia and the Carolinas in search of sites. When a friend suggested Woodstock, in the heart of the Catskill Mountains, Whitehead expressed reservations. The great humanitarian and social reformer also happened to be a virulent anti-Semite, and the Catskill Mountains were a traditional retreat for Jewish people, escaping the sweltering New York summers.

But in every other particular, Woodstock perfectly matched the criteria John Ruskin had laid down in his great work *Modern Painters* for sites most propitious for good work in the arts: elevations of around 1,500 feet, near land where grapes and grain could be grown and within reach of centres of population.

In 1902 Whitehead bought 1,200 acres of land, thickly forested with pine, elm and birch, on a hillside overlooking the town. He built himself a home, White Plains, in the Swiss chalet style, and work began on constructing a small village of chalets, studios, meeting rooms and a theatre in the woods around. Whitehead called his community Byrdcliffe. In the manifesto which he issued to proclaim its opening he expressed his belief that 'living in peaceful country places', pursuing a life dedicated to the arts and crafts, would help to reverse the dehumanising rush of city life. He might have been writing the script for what would happen on Max Yasgur's farm almost seventy years later.

For all his idealistic principles, Whitehead was regarded by some of his fellow colonists as despotic; his vision of Utopia rigidly hierarchal. Almost before the community had begun, rifts began to appear. One of Whitehead's colleagues, Harvard Hervey White, nursed ambitions to buy out Whitehead and take over Byrdcliffe himself. Curiously, one of the main obstacles to White's plan was Byrdcliffe's plumbing. Whitehead was fastidious about personal hygiene, and a disproportionate share of the cost of developing Byrdcliffe had gone into laying plumbing and sewerage outlets, and installing a bath, in every house and cottage on the estate. White was more indifferent to personal hygiene, but acknowledged that it was the astronomical cost of the plumbing which ultimately put Byrdcliffe at a price beyond his reach.

In 1904, however, Hervey White had left Byrdcliffe, to found his own Woodstock Art League, an arts-and-crafts community on a farm which White christened the Maverick, in the neighbouring town of Hurley. There, White inaugurated the Maverick Festivals, Dionysian revels with music, costume drama, acrobats and players, which enlivened Woodstock life through the 1920s.

By the time of Ralph Whitehead's death in 1929, the Utopian ideals of Byrdcliffe had all but evaporated, and it had settled into the role it occupies today – less a brave social experiment than a genteel retreat for painters and craftsmen, suffering the indignity of being dependent on a combination of tourism and grants for its survival. The Tinker Street premises of the Woodstock Guild, which now administered Byrdcliffe, was offering souvenir tea towels alongside the art works; and the pleasant lady who runs the office told me ruefully that the Guild had recently had its state funding cut by 65 per cent.

Byrdcliffe's most enduring legacy was to put Woodstock on the map, and to establish irrevocably a certain artistic tone for the town. By the early Sixties, the old painters and potters had been joined by a younger generation of folk musicians. Peter Yarrow, of Peter, Paul and Mary, was one of the first to move to the town. Woodstock became the rural outpost of the New York Greenwich Village folk scene, centred on the 'Sound Outs', or hootenannies staged regularly in the town. The torch of social reform first lit in Woodstock by Ralph Whitehead passed into new hands.

By 1964, the nascent bohemia was sufficiently developed in Woodstock for a local newspaper columnist seriously to float an idea being bandied around by some Woodstock businessmen to turn Tinker Street into a replica of Paris' Left Bank as a tourist attraction – presumably complete with pavement cafés with check tablecloths and candles in chianti bottles, and colourfully impoverished artists sketching passers-by.

In fact, Woodstock already had a tourist attraction to rival almost anything that Paris had to offer. It was named Bob Dylan. Dylan had first been brought to Woodstock by his manager, the New York impresario Albert Grossman. Grossman had taken a house in the neighbouring village of Bearsville, and then started quietly acquiring properties: he opened a restaurant, the Bear Café; then the Bearsville recording studio, and later a performing arts theatre. When he first came to town, Dylan lived in Grossman's home, and then for a short period in a room above the Café Espresso on Tinker Street, where he, Joan Baez and Peter, Paul and Mary sometimes performed, while patrons played chess on check tablecloths (some of the Left Bank atmosphere had taken hold). Later, Dylan bought his own home in the Byrdcliffe community, then moved again to a more secluded estate outside town on the Ohayo Mountain. It was riding through the hills above the town that Dylan had the motor-cycle accident that marked a turning point in his career.

Somewhere along the way, the Café Espresso had changed its

name, to the Tinker Café. Dylan's 'Just Like A Woman' was playing on the jukebox on the night I visited. It still featured live music as well, but the chessboards had been replaced by electronic videogames. I was told that the house Dylan had lived in at Byrdcliffe was now owned by Donald Fagen, of the group Steely Dan. I followed the rough track from the Byrdcliffe Theatre, past the No Trespassing signs. The track petered out at a set of gates, through which could be seen a pretty house in a quasi-Chinese style, half hidden behind a screen of pine trees. There was no sign of life, or of ghosts.

Dylan's presence conferred a sort of benediction on Woodstock as a musicians' town. His backing group, The Band, took a house called Big Pink, in the nearby town of Saugherties, and it was here, in the period of recuperation after his motor-cycle accident that Dylan recorded the material that would subsequently be released as *The Basement Tapes*.

Van Morrison came to town; Paul Butterfield; the folk singer Tim Hardin. Janis Joplin, who like Dylan was managed by Albert Grossman, was a frequent visitor. Woodstock's reputation as a music centre of the dawning hippie movement – Haight Ashbury in the woods – began to grow, drawing into its orbit the inevitable caravan of sightseers, backpackers, freaks, dreamers, the dispossessed. Ralph Whitehead's vision of Utopia had returned in mutant form, parading along Tinker Street in fancy dress.

For Dylan, the attractions of Woodstock began to pall in direct proportion to the invasion of his privacy, and in 1969 he finally left the town for good, driven out by the persistent attentions of sightseers and autograph hounds. Woodstock, he told his biographer Robert Shelton, had become 'a joke'; his home a shrine for people 'trying to pick up a piece of earth, a piece of lawn or the shrubs'.

Dylan wasn't the only one who rued the changes that had come over the town. Woodstock's traditional tolerance to artistic nonconformity was stretched to breaking point by the growing numbers of people ostentatiously rolling joints on the village green and bathing nude in a local pond known as the Big Deep. By 1969, the anti-hippie hysteria had reached epidemic proportions. A local dignitary described the typical hippie thus: 'a creature who walks on two legs, full of lice of the head and pubic section, full of communicable diseases, who speaks an illiterate language.'

Arrests for vagrancy in the town were running at fifteen a day, and a campaign gathered steam to run the invaders out of town. Woodstock, the local town justice raved, 'is being rapidly overrun with hippies during the day and into the night. They sit everywhere, ignore cars on the streets and insult those who ask them to move. Our citizens are afraid to go shopping in the village and our children are intimidated or corrupted by them.'

The Chamber of Commerce sponsored a meeting in the town hall to discuss 'The Hippie Impact on Woodstock as a Community'. Among those taking part in the debate was a man named Michael Green, who had established a small commune and meditation centre on the outskirts of town. Seated yoga-fashion, with one foot in his lap, Green addressed the meeting on the principles of non-violence and the dawning of a new age of tolerance and harmony. The following week, his meditation centre was burned down in an arson attack. True to his principles, Green refused to co-operate with the police in finding the arsonists.

Given the prevailing atmosphere, it was hardly surprising that when a local promoter called Michael Lang announced plans for the first 'Aquarian Exposition' of music and arts in Woodstock, the shutters came down with a resounding crash. Lang was obliged to cast around for another site. The first choice – in a town called Wallkill, some 40 miles from Woodstock – was thwarted when local residents applied for an injunction to keep the festival out. Which is why the Woodstock Music and Arts Festival ended up on Max Yasgur's 600-acre dairy farm in the sleepy hamlet of Bethel.

Twenty-two years on, Woodstock, the town, displayed a marked ambivalence to its residual association with Woodstock, the Festival. In the aftermath of the Festival, the numbers of homeless and penniless people descending on the town had been so great that a 'rescue mission' called The Family had been set up to provide help, food and support for the lost and bewildered. Founded in a time when the spirit of free goods, free love, free everything was still abroad, it had now become a rather sorry adjunct of the social services, dependent on state subsidy for its survival.

Even now, Japanese tourists and straggly-looking backpackers would turn up in town on the anniversary, asking for directions to the Festival site. People complained it was a bore having to keep directing them 60 miles south-east, but the inconvenience could be partly mitigated by selling them a Woodstock Festival T-shirt, poster or badge. The shops along Tinker Street were full of them. Tinker Street retained an element of stylistic déjà vu, with its shops selling tie-dye shirts, scented candles, joss sticks, Tibetan wind-chimes and Indian prayer mats. Yet bourgeoisification had settled comfortably on the town. Many of the generation of artists who had come to Woodstock in the Thirties and Forties lived there still, along with the musicians who had drifted in during the Sixties and Seventies. But during the Eighties Woodstock had become fashionable among New York professionals – the commodity brokers, arbitrageurs and lawyers – as a weekend retreat. Property values assumed Himalayan altitudes (one real-estate office on Tinker Street was advertising 'Surreal estate' – as much a description of the prices as the properties themselves).

One night I had dinner at the Bear Café. There was a performance in the theatre next door – a girl singer whose name I didn't recognise, but evidently a local favourite: the car park was full of Jeeps and Volvos, the audience the embodiment of well-heeled, casual chic. The temperature had suddenly dropped, and I sat in the restaurant while the beginnings of a snowfall agitated the air outside, and melted into the stream gurgling past the window. The restaurant was full of couples, animated, laughing groups, in tweeds and cashmere, drinking champagne. There did not seem to be an artist – certainly not an impoverished one – in sight.

Woodstock could, however, boast its own chapter of the Rainbow Family.

The Rainbow Family were, perhaps, the true offspring of Woodstock, the Festival. They were the last of the hippies: tepee-dwellers, communards, Grateful Dead fans, blitzed-out keepers of the faith. People talked of them as naturalists had once talked of the buffalo, gentle and unassuming creatures, whose grazing grounds had been parched almost dry by the meretricious greed ethic of the Eighties. But they had clung on tenaciously and, like the buffalo, were even staging something of a comeback.

'How would you describe the Rainbow Family?' I asked the lady who ran the Woodstock Guild.

She gave it some thought. 'Idealists,' she replied.

There was a carpenter fitting shelves in her office as we talked. How would he describe them? He thought about it too. 'How about assholes?' he said.

The nominal leader of the Rainbow Family in Woodstock was a man named Day, his 'headquarters' a barber's shop on the edge of town, the last in a row of wooden buildings that also included a liquor store and a car mechanic's workshop. An image of the earth, as seen from space, had been painted on the front of the barber shop, with a sign above saying Save The Earth. Inside, two old-fashioned barber's chairs, sculpted in chrome and leather, stood in front of a mirrored wall; but most of the space was given over to racks of clothes – tie-dye T-shirts, trousers in crushed velvet, beaded dresses, fringed jackets, batik kaftans; the staple elements of hippie costume had remained remarkably consistent over the years, and it was hard to tell whether these clothes were relics from the Sixties, or newly manufactured to capitalise on the renaissance of hippie style as high fashion.

Day was of indeterminate age. His eyes twinkled above a greying moustache and beard; his hair fell untidily on his shoulders (not the best advertisement for his skills as a barber, I thought); he wore a woollen hat, studded with peace badges, topped with a knitted mushroom stalk, lending him the appearance of a dishevelled garden gnome.

'My name is Day . . .' He had worked up a particular mode of introduction, a manifesto, a regular little performance. 'My name is Day, I shine God's light along the way, in colour and line and in rhythm and rhyme – that's what I do for you . . .' The last line, I noticed, did not scan. No matter. He executed an awkward pirouette in the centre of the room. A drum roll sounded somewhere offstage.

'Can't you see, you and me, there really ain't no mysteree, everything you can see is in harmony, thanks to the divinitee. Endlessly, you and me in harmonee, poetry unravelling the mysteree, you're already free to be, you be you, let me be me, let's enjoy the diversitee, endlessly, can't you see, there really ain't nothing to say, that love is the way, can you do it today . . .'

This was how Day spoke; in rhyme and parables; his grasp of the everyday, mundane requirements of conversation – meaning, exposition, chronology was haphazard.

He had once been a businessman, the owner of five barber shops and boutiques, between Boston and New York City, employing eighty people. 'I was busy seeking happiness in materialism,' he said, 'but I never found it there.' He made materialism sound like a place – Materialism, Illinois – a bustling metropolis, thronged with people in button-down shirts and wing-tip brogues. That was in the Sixties. By the end of it, the conversion had begun. 'Realisations, divinations . . . let's just say the scales fell from my eyes.' He breathed deeply. 'God gave me a vision in which he was merciful, and the Family as a vehicle to serve. That became my ministry.'

He set out for the Woodstock Festival, but like Joni Mitchell – like so many others – was delayed in traffic. He finally arrived in town two years after the Festival had finished – sent, by the Family elders, he said, to take the role of 'communications specialist, to communicate to the mainstream dream that life wasn't what it seemed.'

Who were these elders, I asked?

Day grew vague. 'People . . .' He pointed to a picture on the wall, a sepia photograph of an American Indian. 'The chief of the dog soldiers. We had our own chief. Bob Reynolds – he was the security officer at the Woodstock Festival; Bob was to the Rainbow Family both the peyote priest and the leader of the brothers who defend the family, and are willing to lay down their lives for that.'

It was Reynolds, said Day, who tore down the fence at the Woodstock Festival, who liberated it from commerce, and delivered it to the people. 'Bob had the power to sound the conch . . .'

And where was he now, I asked.

'He's gone home,' said Day.

Home?

'To his mansion.'

Mansion?

'In the sky . . .'

Aha! Like, return to sender?

Day was stroking his beard contemplatively. 'Right, right.'

Another presence had materialised in the shop, a wraith-like figure with a wispy beard and dreamy eyes blinking out from under an Australian bushman's hat.

'Ah, welcome home,' breathed Day, dispensing with introductions. The man simply nodded and sat down on the floor, cross-legged.

Day saw the Woodstock Festival as an epiphany, a new beginning, a time and a place where the world had mysteriously, ineluctably changed. 'Woodstock was the birth of a new spirit,' he said. 'It manifested there collectively, in that the spirit moved us together on a site called Bethel – which means the House of God in Hebrew. Nothing is coincidence, you see.

'And there across many fires we saw each other and realised that we were already the seed of a planetary culture, one that was looking towards a spirit-filled life that was technologically sound and ecologically adaptable.

'Out of this grew an embryo. We realised we had gone beyond authority, that we ourselves were perfectly capable of controlling ourselves. We saw that peace, love and music would heal us. That an event where money was not relevant was a way of coming together that would make us better. Out of that came the vision of a new Jerusalem.'

He lit a cigarette. Inhaled deeply. His friend was sitting quite still on the floor, nodding encouragement. A year after the Woodstock Festival, said Day, the Rainbow Family held its first gathering at Vortex, California. I had never heard of Vortex. It sounded too good a name to be true. 'That's where we came together in a new style – spirit-filled, no money, give it all away, that's all we've really got to say.'

There had been Family gatherings every year since then, all over

America. But what, I couldn't help asking, did the Rainbow Family actually *do*?

'Do?' Day's expression examined the word as if he'd never heard it before. 'What do you mean, do?'

I meant, what were its activities, its objectives, its reason for existence?

'Family is a *style*,' said Day. 'It's a way of being together to reach consensus; a way of communicating from the heart of the people. We do things by consensus that have gone way beyond democracy, which means that *everyone* has to agree on something before we do it.'

Everyone? Did that ever happen – everyone agreeing on something?

'We've done it for twenty years,' said Day. 'Serious counsels lasting eight or nine days, hassles, working it out by factions – one man left blocking the consensus, the rest of us working on him till he comes round . . .'

But what, I asked, did the Family vote on?

'Where the next national gathering will be; the next international gathering; whether to go forward with a regional gathering. Just recently, we've developed the idea of a whole second bio-regional happening. Right now you are in the second bio-region – from the Tapanzee to Albany. Some bio-regions are much bigger than others. They will have established a complete network of focalisers like myself who exchange information, post things on the wall to tell you about Family Business.'

This was bizarre and somewhat confusing. The surviving legacy of Woodstock Nation seemed to be a party-planning service, run on lines of bureaucracy to rival the Inland Revenue. But Day was an incorrigible idealist, and there was something touching about his dream of building Jerusalem in a barber's shop. 'They haven't been able to get rid of us,' he said. 'They have tried very hard to eliminate us as a species all over America; they pull down our tepees, debase us, make fun of us. We are at the bottom of the social/economic pool, as usual. This is not unusual for us. But we take the vow of poverty when we begin to walk this road anyway. We live on minimal survival.'

Woodstock had changed, he said. Where once there were freaks, now there were 'yups'. Here, on this sacred soil, the cradle of the new beginning, temporarily postponed.

'The other people here in Woodstock come and go, buy their houses, raise their kids. Some are transformed by being here; others maintain the reality they bought here with them. We love them, regardless of what they are. Let the yups come home, may they grow in the light. We're praying for them . . .'

Day gave a beatific smile and glanced around for somewhere to put out his cigarette. His eyes lighted on a cactus plant, struggling for life in a small pot of parched earth. He leaned over and ground out his cigarette in the earth.

'I've raised two kids here,' said Day, 'been here twenty years and I'm still not accepted as local. You are not Woodstock until you die, and if you die a success, on their terms, they'll claim you.' Day agreed that for him this was not a likely prospect. 'And they don't take you home either,' he said.

The road to heaven in Woodstock came in three distinct stages. The Dutch Reformed Church stood on the village green, white clapboard and a steeple; a picture postcard of the stolid faith of the founding fathers. Climbing the steep road that ran to the top of Overlook Mountain, one came to the Church of the Sermon on the Mount, a quaint, wooden building, set in a clearing in the woods. The church had been founded in the Twenties by a priest named Father Francis, a member of the Nonconformist Old Catholic movement. In the Sixties, until Father Francis' death, it had been a popular place of worship among artists and musicians.

A short walk further up the hill was the most recent addition to the spiritual panoply – a Buddhist retreat, occupying an old summer lodging house, known as Meads. The retreat had been founded in 1978, by a Tibetan abbot named Khenpo Kharthar Rinpoche. In Buddhism, a Rinpoche is from 'beginless time', and has chosen the time and manner of his reincarnation to best suit his work to lead all sentient beings towards enlightenment. Meads had been chosen as a particularly propitious site for the retreat, set in mountains, close to a stream, facing the East.

The administrator of the retreat was Miles Deutsch, an earnest, bespectacled man in his early forties. Miles, who had trained in engineering and once made bio-medical scanners, had been a practising Buddhist for the past fifteen years. Now he had given up his career to concentrate full-time on his religious studies.

The retreat was the American seat of a Buddhist abbot, his High Highness Gyalwang Gwyla Karmapa, who had died in 1981, announcing that he would return in another incarnation in due course. But his successor, the reincarnated lama, or tulku, had yet to be recognised and formally enthroned. 'We're waiting hopefully,' said Miles.

Did he have any idea when this might be?

He gave a faint smile. 'These things don't work on a timetable.'

A handful of Americans and ten Tibetans lived permanently in the retreat, and on any weekend there were some fifteen or twenty people visiting, for talks and meditation. Holy observances were conducted in what had once been the lounge of the summer house, but for the last ten years the monks and residents had been building a temple in the grounds, which was now nearing completion. It was a large building, austerely beautiful in white stone and crowned by an enormous golden cupola. A Tibetan monk had come from the order's community in Sikkim to paint the temple in traditional style. Fantastically ornate geometric designs in vivid, primary colours embroidered the doors and windows and seemed to dance on the walls. Inside the air was perfumed with the smell of fresh paint, newly sawn timber and yak butter candles, flickering at the shrine. Brightly coloured banners hung from the ceiling, depicting the Buddha in his various manifestations, and at the end of the room sat an imposing brass Buddha, 11 feet tall. It had been brought from Nepal, and was the largest in America.

Miles walked me across the grounds to the cabins where monks and novitiates conducted their private retreats. These were carried out in complete solitude, he explained, entailing sixteen hours of religious practice, study and meditation each day. The novitiate was expected to learn the relevant texts in Tibetan, and was not allowed to speak to, or even see, another person. Food was left outside the cabin on a tray. The duration of the retreat was decided on by the abbot, according to the novitiate's spiritual discipline and progress. Miles had been a student of Buddhism for ten years when he first went into retreat. His abbot had instructed him to remain in solitude for a year. After eleven months, the abbot told him he was doing so well he should stay in the cabin for another two years. Miles had accepted this without question. 'It's pretty frightening,' he said. 'You face yourself all the time. That's the major difficulty, because all you're left with is your own mind. The first year in particular seems awfully long.' As a special concession, he said, the novitiate did have some say in the menu. 'I'd send out notes asking for Rice Krispies.'

It was not unusual to have your retreat extended, said Miles. An American Buddhist nun from Phoenix, named Ani Wang Mo, had begun a three-year retreat here in 1978. Halfway through, after consultations with the abbot, her stay had been extended. She finally emerged after twelve years in silent contemplation on 15 December 1990; she now lived at the order's monastery in Sikkim. An overgrown footpath led through the woods to the cabin where she had lived, some 200 yards from the retreat. It was a small, unbelievably ramshackle, two-storey wooden building. Downstairs was a wash-room and wood-burning stove. A narrow ladder led to the upstairs room. It measured no more than 10 feet square and was furnished with only a small table, a chair and a Tibetan box – a cross between a chair and a shortened bed – for sleep and meditation. Ani Wang Mo's presence was as palpable a thing in the room as these few pieces of rudimentary furniture. From a rickety balcony, one could look down the hill, and through the trees see the old Church of the Sermon on the Mount – Father Francis' church. Down in the valley were supermarkets, Exxon signs, people going about their daily business. Yet here was perfect serenity, the only sound birdsong and the wind sighing in the trees.

A Rinpoche, the Venerable Dozgchen Ponlop, was visiting from Sikkim that weekend to give a series of talks, and that evening I drove back up the hill to the retreat to hear him. Dozgchen Ponlop, I was told, was a lama of the Nyingma order – the third highest

Nyingma lama alive. In a previous incarnation he had been the brother of his High Highness Gyalwang Gwyla Karmapa, the founder of the order. Some thirty people were seated, cross-legged, in the prayer room of the retreat, awaiting his arrival. I guessed from their nods and whispered greetings that most were local people, living either in the retreat, or in the town. Dozgchen Ponlop Rinpoche was in his mid-twenties, dressed in gold and crimson robes, with a crew cut and gold-rimmed spectacles. His address was on the subject of Hearing, Contemplation and Meditation in the Kagyu tradition. He spoke quietly and methodically, peppering his address with Americanisms: he spoke of 'spiritual cash or credit', and using 'a route map to enlightenment'; he spoke of 'audio dharma' and 'visual dharma', playing with the terms as if they were child's toys, beaming with undisguised pleasure whenever a particularly felicitous phrase tripped off his tongue. He wore a digital wristwatch that he would glance at from time to time, before throwing the meeting open to questions.

These were earnest people, grappling conscientiously with difficult problems. How can I work ten hours a day and still get consistency in my studies? How do I reach emptiness? Is emptiness enlightenment?

'Emptiness', said the Rinpoche with a smile, 'is the first step to enlightenment. The question is, how do you attain emptiness without *spacing out*.' He smiled delightedly.

Afterwards people gathered in twos and threes to discuss the talk and their own spiritual progress. 'I get that we have to move from emptiness to enlightenment,' said one woman to her friend. 'But what I want to know is, how do you manage to give up cigarettes *and* coffee?'

There was another song about Woodstock that kept running through my mind – a song Van Morrison had written in 1970, while living in the town, called 'Going Down To Old Woodstock', and which appeared on his album *Tupelo Honey*. Morrison came from Belfast, and the song reflected something of the Irishman's romantic infatuation with Woodstock's arcadian beauty; against a backing of a church piano, appropriate to the cathedral-like splendour of the pine forests, he sang of domestic tranquillity as sweet as the smell of woodsmoke from a log-cabin chimney.

It was a good song to be playing as one drove along the country lanes around Woodstock, the autumn sunlight playing between the trees, igniting the fallen drifts of leaves in glowing pools of red and gold, the sturdy houses dozing peacefully in the quiet afternoon. At one point, a young deer suddenly leapt into the road in front of the car, regarded me with startled eyes, then, deciding I was harmless, wandered nonchalantly into the undergrowth.

Woodstock seemed like a paradise at times such as this, and it was easy to see why so many refugees from the city had made their home here. One day, I met Graham Parker in town. Parker was an English rock singer, who had risen to prominence in the late Seventies playing gritty rhythm and blues on the club and concert circuit, and who had found as great a following in America as in Britain. The last time I had seen him, he was living in a flat in Maida Vale. He still had the flat, but now he and his family lived in a house set in its own land outside Woodstock.

We had lunch in a vegetarian taco restaurant on Tinker Street, as Parker talked enthusiastically about his new life, his 3 acres of land with his own orchard. That autumn he had been pressing apples for juice, raking leaves, and hiking into the hills with his young daughter, looking for snakes. 'In England you've only got three species and you're hardly ever likely to see any of them; here you've got fifteen in the Catskills alone.'

At Halloween, he said, the village green was crowded with everybody's children in costumes; there were stalls, apple dunking – 'It's like It's A Wonderful Life. It gets to you, it really does. In England you'd have lager louts and the whole thing would end in a punch-up.' Woodstock was a friendly town, he felt. Maida Vale had its own share of pop stars; you go shopping in the local supermarket and run into Annie Lennox or Chrissie Hynde, 'but you'd never get together and do anything with them, because the atmosphere doesn't encourage it'. In Woodstock you could bump into Rick Danko or Levon Helm of The Band, John Sebastian, formerly of the

Lovin' Spoonful, Todd Rundgren, or any number of people, and end up playing on their records or sharing the stage at a benefit concert. 'It's benefit heaven round here,' insisted Parker. And he was right. The noticeboard in the Tinker Café advertised benefits for schools, for ecological groups, for a local musician suffering from cancer.

'It's the spirit of Woodstock,' said John Sebastian, when I spoke to him next day. 'Nobody really wants to charge their friends anything when they play, but we're always looking for excuses. The minute somebody's loft burns down or anybody falls ill, you got a benefit on your hands. There's probably a bigger community of musicians here now than there ever was in the Sixties, and I think the mood's better now than it was then. There isn't the fuss, and there's more kindness.'

Sebastian was something of a paterfamilias to the Woodstock musical community. An erstwhile pop idol, he was one of the few musicians still living in Woodstock who had actually performed at the Festival, and had gone on to weather the fickle mood swings of the business and build himself a steady and respectable career as a songwriter and performer.

He lived a couple of miles out of town, past a golf course, down a narrow lane, over a fragile bridge and along an unmade track. His house was set in a clearing in the woods, a rambling ranch-style property in brick and wood, with a large sun-deck, a dog barking in the yard. The downstairs hall was hung with framed photographs of Sebastian and his wife Christine taken during the Sixties, at the height of the Lovin' Spoonful's success. They showed Sebastian with a straw-blond curtain of hair, steel-rimmed glasses and clad head to toe in tie-dye. Sebastian had always been strong on tie-dye. Now, in his white cambray shirt, his grey shoes and tidy haircut he had the appearance of a benign schoolteacher.

Sebastian first arrived in Woodstock in the mid-Sixties, at the invitation of Bob Dylan, who at that time was still living in Albert Grossman's house. A good scene, Sebastian remembered, very creative. 'Bob was writing prolifically, and that was very inspiring from a songwriter's view, because I had never been around somebody who spent the whole time at the typewriter, reams of paper rolling off ... all this wonderful language. It made me think, I like this – sit around and smoke 80 million cigarettes and have things rolling off my typewriter too.'

He had returned intermittently through the Sixties, and watched how things had changed in the wake of Dylan's escalating success. 'You could sense this was becoming a real musical town, but there was also a tremendous amount of elitism in the air, because Dylan's fame was so imposing. It was of Beatle proportions in America, so suddenly you had a lot of people arriving in town trying to find out where he lived, where he was to be found. And that changed things. Two or three years earlier you could announce at the Bear Café that there was a jam session and you would accumulate whoever wanted to play; you wouldn't accumulate anybody who didn't. Well, now you would accumulate people who wanted to *watch* other people play, and that instantly changed the atmosphere. To me, it made them seem odd; I felt self-conscious, and so that scene finished for me.'

By then, the Lovin' Spoonful were in eclipse, and the centre of gravity of the recording industry had moved to the West Coast. Sebastian and his wife settled in California, although his stock as a stage performer remained high on the East Coast and he would stop over in Woodstock from time to time. His friend the songwriter Fred Neil (who wrote 'Everybody's Talkin'' for Nilsson) lived in town. Sebastian and his wife would take a room at the Millstream Motel. 'We'd spend a few days there, bring along our dyes, set up shop and tie-dye Fred Neil's entire wardrobe over a weekend.' Sebastian laughed. Talking of musical associations, did I know that the Millstream was the inspiration for the old barbershop quartet song 'Down By The Old Millstream'? I thought about the broken refrigerator, the TV blitz, the suicide cabins. It seemed unlikely.

By 1975, says Sebastian, it became obvious that his days as a recording artist were numbered. 'I had this feeling when I went into the office of Warner Bros in Burbank and saw all these Alice Cooper posters on the wall. I thought, this could be a difficult time for anybody who's going to be John Sebastian.'

There and then, he decided to move back East, where he still

had a following as a live performer. The money from the Lovin'
Spoonful days had gone. ('Not that we'd seen much of it in the first
place,' he said. Only in 1990 did the group start receiving artists'
royalties that had been owed to them since 1969.) But in 1976 he
wrote the theme tune for a television series called 'Welcome Back
Cotter', about the erstwhile class dunce who goes back to his old
school to teach a class of troublemakers. The royalties from
'Welcome Back' had bought the Sebastians their Woodstock
home.

Now Sebastian made a comfortable living, performing around
the eastern states, making the occasional album or commercial.
And 'Welcome Back Cotter' was still in re-runs, producing the
occasional royalty cheque.

Listening to Sebastian talking enthusiastically about his life and
working routine, a pleasant, steady round of professional engage-
ments and domestic tranquillity, the excesses of the Woodstock
Festival seemed far away. Sebastian's own recollection of the
Festival was hazy. What did he remember of the Woodstock
Festival, I asked.

'Not much,' he said with a smile. He had gone along as a spectator,
with no intention of performing. And like everybody else he had spent
a fair part of the weekend ingesting illegal substances. 'And then I
suddenly found myself on stage playing. It was one of the first times
I'd played on my own for more than a coffee house full of people. I was
relatively unprepared, fairly stoned; I didn't have an instrument; was
not on the bill. I certainly wish I'd had some idea I was going to play,
because whenever I play I don't usually go get stoned.'

What now struck him most forcibly about the Festival, he said,
was the feeling of camaraderie. 'As I said from the stage, everybody
had been sitting around talking about how things *could* be, and it
seemed like everybody who had ever done that was suddenly in
the same place at the same time. It gave us a tremendous feeling of
power. But at the same time it was a real turning point. I came to
understand at that show just how powerful this music was becoming – me, and hundreds and thousands of promoters and businessmen who were more concerned with money than music were also

discovering it. I think it was the moment when money began to topple what had been a really good time.'

From time to time, he said, his family and friends would put on the video of *Woodstock*, the movie. 'It's kind of embarrassing ... It makes me want to point out that I've done twenty-five years worth of playing without the assistance of cannabis, LSD or anything else. It looks like a guy smashed out his brain having a really good time, which in some respects is true.'

There was something touching about this recollection. Woodstock meant something different to everybody you talked to. To Day, stranded on the expressway, it had been the doorway to the promised land. To Sebastian, on stage in front of 400,000 people, it was a hazily pleasant memory, tinged with embarrassment about his lack of professionalism, his irresponsible younger self. The tie-dyes, the drugs – they belonged to another age, another person, which seemed to have little to do with the schoolmasterly figure which John Sebastian now presented. Some other visitors had arrived, and someone asked if they might smoke a cigarette in the house. 'Better not,' said Sebastian. 'The kids'll be home soon.'

The next morning I went to meet the town supervisor, Brian Hollander, outside the town library. I sat on a bench in the sunshine as mothers shepherded children to and fro. They were testing the appliances at the fire station next door, and the sudden shriek of a siren split the air, causing the children to cover their ears and cry delightedly in unison.

Hollander was in his early forties, quietly spoken, but with the efficient manner of someone accustomed to demands on his time and practised in putting a limit on them without causing offence. We had precisely one hour before he picked up his kids, he said. We walked briskly along Tinker Street, Hollander nodding genially and dispensing greetings to passers-by, and into a café, filled with people breakfasting on croissants and fruit and idling over the weekend papers. Several people came by to shake his hand and pass the time of day: he was evidently a popular figure.

Hollander came from Boston, where he played in a rock band

and drove a taxi – 'the quintessential musician's existence', he laughed. He first arrived in Woodstock in the late Sixties, to play in the folk concerts and 'Sound Outs' that preceded the Woodstock Festival, and which had drawn folk performers like Happy and Artie Traum, David Bromberg and Richie Havens to town. Hollander moved to Woodstock for good eighteen years ago. He had worked as a journalist, then for local radio, and been drawn into local politics. In 1982 he ran for the New York State Senate, 'a Don Quixote-type run against a guy who couldn't lose'. And didn't. Hollander worked for Democrat New York State governor Mario Cuomo. In 1987 he ran for the position of town supervisor. Woodstock had always been a Republican town determined by old family politics and interests. 'People suddenly started to realise that the old-boy network didn't work any more; the town needed a more sophisticated sort of government.'

Hollander won the election. Now, four years later, he had been voted out. He did not seem to be sorry to be going. Town supervisor was a thankless task. He was chief administrator, chief fiscal officer in charge of an annual budget of $5 million; he had to lead the legislature, draft local laws, and make sure he said 'hello' to little old ladies in the street – all for a salary of just $33,000 a year, with a staff that consisted of two part-time secretaries.

Part of his problem as town supervisor, he said, had been maintaining the fine balance of power and economics in the town, between the old, land-owning families and the incomers who had been drawn by Woodstock's air of nonconformity, and the tourists who flocked to the town during the summer months. These undercurrents and schisms had shaped Woodstock life more or less since the arrival of Ralph Whitehead's Utopian community at Byrdcliffe, but they had been thrown into sharper relief in recent years.

Since the Sixties, when there had been a spate of housing developments on the fringes of town, building in Woodstock had been rigorously 'zoned' to protect the character of the town. Tourists loomed in the time-honoured guise of both blessing and curse. Because Woodstock was a pretty town, people wanted to visit. But the more people who visited, the less pretty it became. The tourist industry had driven up the rents along Tinker Street, beyond a price which providers of basic services could afford. The town had become as dependent on tourism as an addict to methadone: in summer, it was the only part of the local economy that counted.

For years the town had been hemming and hawing about providing proper accommodation for visitors, but the only proposals that developers deemed economically feasible were for a hotel which would incorporate conference centres, health spas and the inevitable 5-acre car park, and the town certainly didn't want that. Which is why I was staying in a Howard Johnson's.

The old Woodstock families were in the position of old families everywhere, said Hollander – land rich, but cash poor. The temptation to sell off parcels of land for property development was enticing, but development put more strain on existing resources. 'We go in and lay down zoning laws about water supplies, and these rural people resent those restrictions – "It's my land and I'll damn well do what I like with it."'

And this, said Hollander, is where sewerage came in.

Sewerage. It was the unspoken sub-text of Woodstock life, the blot on the Utopian dream. Almost ninety years before, Hervey White and Ralph Whitehead had fallen out over the plumbing arrangements at Byrdcliffe. And here came sewerage again, bubbling up like a fetid, bad-smelling dream to haunt Brian Hollander. The present crisis had first started stirring in the Seventies, as the influx of newcomers began to put intolerable strains on the town's antiquated sewerage system. In high summer, the town stank to high heaven. Sewerage was discharged into neighbouring streams and low-lying land. The situation became so chronic that the county board of health threatened to close down the town. At the end of the decade a plan for a conventional sewerage plant outside Woodstock was voted down in a referendum. In sewerage, as in all else, Woodstock had a reputation for nonconformity to maintain. And in 1980 an engineer from Boston sold the town a revolutionary new system in sewerage treatment – the Aqua-culture plant. Costs quickly spiralled. The system had to be revised. The state had originally agreed to fund it, but because the system was now a revised one, they refused to meet the additional costs.

In 1987, the new system went on line, servicing some 600 properties. It had cost $19 million – 'enough money', Hollander noted wryly, 'to supply a Taj Mahal sewerage system to each property'. The town of Woodstock was left with a debt of $7.5 million. As town supervisor, Brian Hollander inherited the responsibility of raising the money. A Democrat, an idealist, a man who had sat around campfires and played guitar with Richie Havens, Hollander looked at the sewerage situation through idealism-tinted lenses. The new sewerage system had been installed in properties in the centre of town that needed them most. These tended to be owned by people who could least afford to carry the burden of any sort of levy. Hollander argued the case of the common good. If the centre of Woodstock stank to high heaven, he reasoned, the whole town would suffer. Tourists would stop coming; shops and businesses would suffer; the local economy collapse. Everyone benefits from good sewerage, he argued; therefore, everybody should contribute to clearing the town's debt. He proposed a universal levy of $70 a year. 'Trust in government', he said laconically, 'plunged to a new low.' At length the town voted down Hollander's proposals. 'It was a vote against government, because government had once told them they wouldn't have to pay for it, and now I was suggesting they should.'

Power, Hollander quoted the old adage, is the ability to convince damn fools to do what common sense dictates they should have done in the first place. But he had failed. His political life had turned, quite literally, to shit.

'I know more about sewerage, sewerage treatment and municipal finance than I ever wanted to know,' he sighed. And so he was leaving office, disappointed, yet also relieved to be going. His last duty as town supervisor would be to organise a benefit concert, to raise the money to pay off the town debt. It would be a concert, said Hollander, 'not to benefit the sewerage system, but to benefit the people who've been screwed by government.'

It was the one thing that Woodstock was dependably famous

for; its abiding mythology, the memory of people gathered around campfires, brought together by music to celebrate a common purpose. In 1969, that common purpose had been peace, love, revolution, the hope of a better world. Now the common purpose was sewerage. Nobody could say Woodstock hadn't learned a thing or two.

The road from Woodstock to the town of Bethel ran through the lower slopes of the Catskill Mountains. It was one of those glorious autumnal Sunday mornings where the countryside lights up like a firework display, where the world seems perfectly at peace with itself. The road ran through small towns and hamlets – tidy family homes behind picket fences, people raking leaves in front gardens, the aroma of burning leaves hanging in the air – falling away as the rake of the hills grew steeper, the folds more pronounced. These were 'The Jewish Alps', a place of resort hotels, summer camps, made popular by Jews fleeing the suffocating New York summers.

Dishner's Bungalow Colony, Catskill Funland, Stern's Holiday Homes – they looked sad, neglected places, closed for the winter, or boarded up altogether with 'for sale' signs posted by the road. It was hard to imagine all of this coming alive in the summer; it was as if the carnival had moved on for good, enveloping the area in an air of narcolepsy. The road dipped down an incline into the town of South Fallsburg, looking faded and down-at-heel, a stoplight swinging in the wind above a crossroads. On one side of the junction there were kosher restaurants and butchers, Hebrew shop signs; on the other side, a soul food shack, a delicatessen, black people standing on the pavements, shivering in the watery sunlight. The marquee of the Rivoli Cinema read 'Thank you for your patronage. See you next spring'. But the cinema looked as if it had been deserted for years.

Outside Monticello, the road suddenly grew crowded with pick-up trucks, driven by grim-faced men, bandaged in winter jackets and caps: hunters. The radio was broadcasting 'courtesy notices': 'Don't just shoot at the sound of rustling in the undergrowth. Make sure you have your prey properly identified and targeted before shooting. Avoid killing others.'

Feeling the call of nature, I stopped the car along a secluded road and hiked off the road into the bushes, hoping that anyone in the vicinity had been listening to the same radio station I had.

The mythology of Woodstock seemed to evaporate with every mile that I travelled. Bethel was too insignificant to be marked on my road map and I stopped several times to ask directions. The replies were polite, bemused and ultimately pitying. 'You can git there, but I don't know *why* you wanna git there. Ain't nothin' there but a field,' said a lugubrious black man at a filling station.

'State said they were going to do something, but I don't know what, and they didn't do nothing,' said a man behind the counter at a hunting supply shop, pointing me back in the direction I'd come.

The road now ran through rich farmland. White farmhouses dotted the hillsides, and silver grain silos, glinting in the sunshine, looking like missile launchers.

Outside Bethel, I turned off and followed a twisting, tree-lined lane deeper into the countryside. New houses had been planted along the roadsides, in timber and brick, radiating the aura of money. The road curved upwards to a crossroads, with a farmhouse and stables on one corner, and a view across country, neatly divided into fields, dotted with trees. This had been Max Yasgur's farm. But Yasgur had sold out years ago. The land had been redrawn, parcelled into a neat little pattern of usefulness; trees had sprouted along the perimeters of the fields. The topography no longer made sense as the site for a gathering of the nations.

A stone marker had been laid a short distance from the crossroads, shaped in the distinctive Festival logo of a dove of peace on the neck of a guitar. It read:

This is the original site of the Woodstock Music and Arts Festival, held on August 15, 16, 17, 1969. This marker erected and owned by Louis, Nicky and June Gelish 1984.

I wondered who Louis, Nicky and June were and what they were doing now. The weekend of twenty-two years ago had clearly meant a lot to them, but the claim of ownership struck a curiously discordant note, inconsistent with what one imagined the ideals of Woodstock to have been. Did they imagine that anyone would steal it? Had the farmer whose land it was on insisted that Louis, Nicky and June admit to ownership, embarrassed lest any of his friends think he owned it himself? On the base of the marker had been inscribed the name of all the performers who had played at Woodstock. Santana, The Who, Sha Na Na, Jimi Hendrix, Ten Years After. It was a roll call of the dead and the forgotten. And there was John Sebastian's name too, except that Louis, Nicky and June must have been otherwise engaged when Sebastian climbed on stage with his borrowed guitar, stoned, grinning, optimistic, to have his name engraved on history, because they'd managed to spell it incorrectly – Sabastian.

The man from the filling station had been right. There was nothing much to see once you got here, and it was hard to imagine what appropriate use or gesture the State of New York could contrive to make the site seem more notable. I got into the car, and drove back to Bethel. I stopped in town at the Bethel Country Store and post office, an old wooden structure that looked like a backwoods church. A notice on the door said, 'The Lord's Day (Sunday) Closed'.

There was a poster in the window, a picture of the teeming masses of Woodstock, under the caption 'An Aquarian Exposition', which had been bleached almost invisible by sunlight. On a pole outside, two T-shirts flapped in the wind like Tibetan prayer-flags. One said, 'Site of the original Woodstock Festival: Peace and Love'. The other showed a cartoon character, his finger upraised in a gesture of crude dismissal. It read, 'I'm Bart Simpson. Who the hell are you?'

Chattanooga
CHOO CHOO

Pardon me boy, is that the Chattanooga Choo-Choo,
Track 29, boy, you can gimme a shine
I can afford to board a Chattanooga Choo-Choo,
I've got my fare, and just a trifle to spare

Contrary to the song, the Chattanooga Choo-Choo does not leave track 29 of New York's Pennsylvania Station, bound for Chattanooga. Nor, alas, did it ever follow the route the song describes, affording the eager passenger 'dinner in the diner/nothin' could be finer/than to have your ham 'n' eggs in Carolina'. That was poetic licence. The old *Tennessean*, as it was called, skirted the Carolinas altogether, as it rolled through Washington and Bristol, Tennessee, to arrive, at last, at Chattanooga.

It is no longer possible to choo-choo from New York to Chattanooga; the route was scrapped in the Sixties for reasons of economy. Nowadays you must travel to Atlanta, Georgia – a journey of some eighteen hours, shoehorned into a sleeping compartment the size of a wardrobe – and proceed to Chattanooga, 125 miles west, under your own steam.

In the lounge car of the 1.35 *Crescent City* train (New

York-Washington-Atlanta-New Orleans) four voluble black men were playing cards and 'outbadding' each other. 'Brooklyn? Man, you can come out of your house, turn a corner and be hit on 'fore you know what's happenin'.'

'That's nothin', man. The Bronx ... I'm tellin' you, girlfriend of mine got mugged and she had nuthin' on her. They tell her, we comin' back and next time we come by you better have somethin' for us, or we take yo' ass ... Believe that?'

'Everywhere bad now, man.'

'Yeah, everywhere bad.'

It felt good to be leaving the North, to have been catapulted out of the concrete bullpen of Pennsylvania Station, and to have the industrial wastelands of New Jersey and Pennsylvania slipping by outside the window, the rusting gas cylinders and the derelict warehouses, their gaping windows like smashed teeth, all testament to the diminishing importance of the railways; a reminder that the action had moved elsewhere.

I felt I had known the song 'Chattanooga Choo-Choo' almost as long as any other in my life. My father loved two kinds of music: brass bands and dance bands. In the front room of the house we had a radiogram, called, as I recall, a Rigonda. It had been made in Russia – which meant it was affordable – a great beast in a polished wood cabinet, standing on spindly modernist legs, with two speakers the size of small wardrobes, which produced a roar of sound, perfectly tempered to the marches of the band of the Royal Air Force, and the smooth swing of the Glenn Miller Orchestra. Miller's novelty songs struck a particular chord in me as a child, of course. 'Kalamazoo', with its nursery alphabet first line – 'A,B,C,D,E,F,G,H, I gotta gal in Kalamazoo' – and Chattanooga Choo-Choo seemed simultaneously funny and evocative. Were there really places with such peculiar names? It seemed unlikely. But the effect of these songs lay as much in their evocations as in their melodies or words. They were relics of a world before one's own time: a part of my parents' lives. Hearing them I always felt a curious nostalgia for an era which I had never known, an intangible sense of longing and regret, as if I had somehow inherited my parents' memories, or rather the emotional responses which came with their memories, along with the colour of my hair, my eyes, my disposition. Miller's music seemed to have been for ever playing in a world tantalisingly beyond my own experience, but which had irrevocably shaped the one into which I had been born: a world of war, heroic self-sacrifice, the certainties of right or wrong (the world of the gas mask and steel helmet which gathered dust in the shed, the remnants of the Andersen shelter in the back garden). Glenn Miller died when the military plane he was flying in crashed in the English Channel, just as the one in which the uncle I would never meet did.

Harry Warren and Mack Gordon wrote 'Chattanooga Choo-Choo' in 1934, when a Northern city slicker could still patronise shoeshine boys, and the South evinced an aura of genteel, archaic elegance. Now the shoeshine stands outside Pennsylvania Station suggested one man's austerity rather than another's elegance, and addressing any of the imperious black men who worked the stands as 'Boy . . .' would almost certainly guarantee a one-way ticket to the casualty ward. Nor could the South be seen as a destination of arcadian gentility. The South had grown. It was where the action had gone.

The forests of Maryland slipped past the window, the inlets of the Chesapeake Bay, small boats bobbing in the distance in the gathering dusk. In the dining car I fell into conversation with Henry, a Ugandan who had fled Idi Amin's regime fifteen years ago. Henry had settled in Chattanooga, worked as a college lecturer, then moved north to Philadelphia, and a job in electronics. Now he was on his way back, to consult on the computer system of the Tennessee Valley Authority, the state provider of electricity. Henry had mixed feelings about Chattanooga. The weather and the scenery were wonderful, he said, but the town had always been held back by reactionary attitudes. There was a time when the town had been the same size as Atlanta, but Atlanta had grown, become the boom town of the South, its de facto capital. Chattanooga had been held back by the class system, said Henry, particularly by its ruling elite – a nexus of old Southern families who had always held the town in a vice-like grip. This he said, was 'the Lookout Mountain Crowd'. Henry made them sound like a gang of Western desperados, like the Wild Bunch or the Hole in the Wall gang. 'There has been no progress,' said Henry soberly.

Henry said his friend Eustace would be meeting him at Atlanta; Eustace would give me a lift to Chattanooga, no problem. And the next morning, there was Eustace, waiting at the station in his pearl-grey Mercedes. He presented his card with a flourish: Kigongo International Inc. 'Tennis, golf, leisure,' he smiled. 'A bit of everything.'

Like Henry, Eustace had fled from Amin's Uganda and found his way to America. I could see him in my mind's eye, stepping off the plane or boat, a cardboard suitcase in hand – a refugee, cast in the mould of the founding fathers, intoxicated with America's sense of possibilities. I had seldom met anyone who had embraced the American Dream with quite such unquestioning devotion. As the Georgia countryside slipped by, wooded and misty in the early morning, Eustace propounded a view of survival that was positively Darwinian. 'American business works like this,' he said. 'If I want something you have, I will take it unless you're strong enough to stop me taking it from you. Of course, in an ideal world this is not how people behave. But in the real world it is.'

Evolution had left its mark on Chattanooga. Eustace dropped me at the old Terminal Railway Station, long extinct as a working station and now pressed into service as a hotel called, inevitably, the Chattanooga Choo-Choo. The magnificent booking hall with its vaulted glass ceilings and marbled floors was now the hotel lobby; vintage railroad cars stood beside the old platforms. Guests were invited to 'dinner on the diner' – just like the song. It was a monument to America's propensity for transforming myth into kitsch.

'For decades,' a pamphlet in my room told me, 'Terminal Station bustled with activity, with Presidents and porters, soldiers and statesmen – travellers from across the nation who marvelled at the beauty and grandeur of the station.' But Terminal Station closed in 1970. The Presidents, soldiers and statesmen now travelled by plane – although seldom, one imagined, to and from Chattanooga.

I had intended a walk outside, but there was nowhere to walk. The surrounding neighbourhood had fallen into disrepair; a row of shops opposite boasted only a thrift store and two pawn shops, offering an impressive display of knives and small arms. Railroad tracks crisscrossed the road, vanishing behind brick warehouses and industrial detritus. Chattanooga's centre of gravity lay a mile further on, downtown, where many of the older brick hotels and office buildings had been bulldozed to make way for shining glass blocks, parking lots and a spanking new library and civic centre. Chattanooga had the air of a small town pretending to be a big one. Yet walking around, its pavements were all but deserted. Nobody in America shopped in cities; one would learn this. People shopped at malls.

Chattanooga built its fortune on industry. An abundance of coking coal had fostered the growth of iron-smelting and casting, and the arrival of the railroad did the rest, driven down from the north in the 1850s by a combination of slave and Irish labour. Chattanooga flourished. 'Nature favoured the town,' wrote a wide-eyed correspondent of a Georgia newspaper, the *Athens Post*, in 1880, 'and the enterprising populace is making the most of that kiss of divine affection. Everybody is alive and enthusiastic, embracing already the forerunner of wealth and superior advantages. The city is bound ... to spread and prosper, and he who stands idly in the streets watching the gilded pictures on the car of progress without making the effort to enjoy the luxury of a ride may see his opportunity pass and be compelled to walk all the days of his life.'

The car of progress began to grind to a halt in the Sixties. The textile industry, with its stentorian management practices, was racked by strikes; Chattanooga gained a reputation as a 'difficult' (which is to say, well organised) union town. New investment went elsewhere, manufacturing went into decline, and the railway with it. The umbilical cord that had once connected Chattanooga to every corner of America withered away, and was finally severed altogether. The twelve trains a day which ran through town dwindled to two, then none. The last passenger train pulled out in 1968, leaving Chattanooga with its dubious reputation as being the most polluted city in Tennessee. As recently as the early Seventies, anyone standing idly on the streets, wondering what had happened to the car of progress, and who happened to stick out their tongue could have tasted the grit from the foundries hanging in the air.

Like so many American cities, stripped of its original reason for existence, Chattanooga had invested its faith in new, high-tech industries and in tourism. There had been a massive drive against industrial pollution. Once the filthiest, it was now acknowledged as the cleanest city in Tennessee, surrounded by the most beautiful countryside, the Tennessee River, its lakes and tributaries – 'and since they cleaned up the air,' someone said, 'you can actually see it again.'

But the real geography of Chattanooga lay below the surface.

Eustace had elaborated a finely developed sense of Chattanooga's social evolution. 'There are the people at the top – the very top. They're not going anywhere, 'cause they've already arrived. Then, near the top, you got the people who want to be at the top. Maybe they'll get there. Then you got the middle, the lower middle and the bottom. They're staying where they are. Man, the people at the bottom got nothing to talk about with the people at the top. It's different worlds.'

It was obvious where Eustace wished to be, hard to judge how far he had got, but clear that he was working on it. Lately, he had been invited to play at the golf club of Mr Bob Shaw, a carpet mogul. 'He's about the richest man in America. It costs $30,000 initiation to join the club, then $10,000 renewal,' Eustace chuckled. 'You've got to want to play golf real bad to pay that much money.'

Eustace's social analysis was accurate in spirit, but statistically unsound. Chattanooga's industry had made it overwhelmingly blue collar: with a modest middle class, and a tiny elite, which had always wielded a power disproportionate to its size. These were Chattanooga's boosters, its pocket Rockefellers and Mellons; a handful of old families who had traded up entrepreneurial endeavour to its logical apogee of corporate power. There were the McLellans (insurance), the Davenports (fast food), the Probascos (banking), and the richest and most powerful of them all – the Luptons, who had made their fortune from bottling and distributing Coca-Cola.

This was Henry's 'Lookout Mountain Crowd' – an insular, self-protective aristocracy, spoken of with a mixture of wryness, envy and awe – who had ruled over Chattanooga from their homes in the hills above the city, and who now distributed their largesse through philanthropic trusts, and replenished their social cachet through the Cotton Ball, an institution inaugurated in 1933 with the nostalgic theme of 'the old South', and still held each year to launch their daughters on to what remained of the Chattanooga social scene.

The road up to Lookout Mountain was lined with handsome timber houses in the colonial style. Private driveways disappeared into the woods, hinting at yet more opulent, hidden dwellings. The air would never be tainted up here. You could look down on Chattanooga and believe that the laws of natural selection had carried you all the way to the top of the world.

Coming back to earth, I took the freeway towards Knoxville, then turned on to a thickly wooded valley road, following the signs to Dayton. It was a Monday morning, and virtually every radio station on the car stereo seemed to be ringing with gospel music and sermons. The Reverend Jesse Pratt was preaching temperance in a thick Tennessee burr. 'One ounce leads to 12 ounces, radio friends, and 12 ounces leads to the barrel.' The Reverend Pratt gave way to an old-time gospel group, strumming guitars and banjos, and singing in high, plaintive voices – heart-rending enough to bring the devil to his knees – urging the radio friends to wash themselves in the blood of Jesus.

A creaking ferry carried me over the broad sweep of the Tennessee River. The road twisted and turned through woods, then the woods gave way to farmland, and neat clapboard houses beside the road. In the graveyard of a country church, almost every stone was decorated with fresh flowers. It felt like God's own country; wholesome, untainted. A place of implacable certainties, implacable faith.

The Rhea County Courthouse was a handsome stone building, set back from Dayton's Main Street on a lawn, surrounded by elm, oak and poplar trees. Upstairs in the main courtroom a family shifted nervously on the bench seats, awaiting a hearing. The basement of the courthouse had been turned into a museum, commemorating its most famous case. The Scopes Monkey Trial, held in a sweltering July in 1925, was one of the most extraordinary events in American legal history, bringing together two of the most eloquent and charismatic advocates of the day to argue whether or not Americans had the right to learn Darwin's theory of the evolution of the species. It was a trial that tested the polarity of faith and reason; of religious fundamentalism and scientific progress, and its reverberations could still be felt across the American South today.

Clarence Darrow was a political liberal, who had made his reputation as a lawyer fighting cases on behalf of the poor, the disenfranchised, the working man. His adversary William Jennings Bryan was a former leader of the Democratic Party, who three times had run unsuccessfully for President (in 1896, 1900 and 1908). Bryan was a populist, a brilliant orator on the stump, who in his later years turned his rhetorical powers increasingly to the cause of Christian fundamentalism. He argued for prohibition, temperance; his World Fundamental Association promulgated the need to stick to a rigorous and literal interpretation of biblical teachings in the face of the 'heresy' of scientific materialism.

Even before the Scopes Trial, Bryan and Darrow had exchanged blows over the theory of evolution, and the challenge which teaching it in schools posed to traditional biblical beliefs. Bryan had launched his own campaign against 'the evolutionists' in the popular prints, quarrelling with university professors and offering $100 in cash to anyone who would sign an affidavit to the effect that they were personally descended from an ape. After Bryan launched an attack on science in the *Chicago Tribune*, Darrow answered with an open letter posing fifty questions to determine whether Bryan thought the biblical account of the creation of the earth was literally true or poetic allegory. Bryan replied: 'I decline to turn aside to enter into controversy with those who reject the Bible as Mr Darrow does.'

In fact, Darrow was a Christian, albeit one with a healthy streak of irreverence. Visiting the Holy Land he was taken to the Sea of Galilee where Christ was said to have walked on the water. When told that it would cost $15 to take a boat across the lake, Darrow replied, 'No wonder Jesus walked'.

Tennessee in the Twenties was fertile ground for William Jennings Bryan's beliefs, and Bryan's speech 'Is The Bible True?' had been influential in persuading the Tennessee legislature to introduce a bill in 1925, which became the Butler Act, to prohibit the teaching of the theory of evolution in the state's schools. When the American Civil Liberties Union announced that they would finance a suit to test the bill as an infringement of the Bill of Rights, a consortium of Dayton businessmen rallied round to provide a suitable defendant.

Twenty-four-year-old John Scopes actually taught maths and chemistry, but he agreed to stand as the defendant, having taught biology briefly when another teacher fell ill. 'And you can't teach biology', he said, 'without teaching evolution.' Bryan had not practised law for thirty-six years, but he offered his services to lead the prosecution. As soon as he heard of Bryan's involvement, Clarence Darrow immediately volunteered his services free of charge to lead Scopes' defence.

The trial became a national circus. A caravan of newspapermen, tent show evangelists, holy rollers, carnival monkey owners, flimflam men and rubberneckers flocked to Dayton by railroad. One thousand people jammed the courtroom each day, spilling over on to the lawn outside, where they listened to the progress of the trial by loudspeaker.

Schoolchildren were called to testify John Scopes had taught them that man had evolved from a single organism and is a mammal – like a monkey. Darrow split his shirt gesticulating: fundamentalists, he railed, were 'after everybody who thinks': this was a trial about bigotry and ignorance.

The climax came in an epic confrontation when Bryan himself was called to the witness stand and cross-examined by Darrow about the literal truth of the Bible. Darrow hedged his adversary into admitting his belief that Jonah may indeed have been swallowed by a whale, and Eve been made from Adam's rib, but Bryan balked at admitting to a belief that the world had been created, literally, in six days. The debate was expunged from the record as being not germane, and realising that he could not win the case on a point of law, Darrow asked the judge to instruct the jury to find Scopes guilty. Scopes was fined $100; and while the conviction was subsequently overturned on the technicality that the jury, not the judge, should have set the fine, the Butler Act was upheld. It was not repealed until 1967.

Five days after the trial, William Jennings Bryan died, from a combination of diabetes and a heart condition, which had been exacerbated by the rigours of the trial, and his personal ordeal in the courtroom. He spent the days before his death in Dayton, looking for a site for his last bequest – a college where the teaching of fundamentalist Christian principles would be upheld.

Bryan College was set up a winding road in the hills above Dayton: a collection of plain, functional brick buildings, a reception area of clinical tidiness. The students bustled purposefully along the corridors: one had seen these eager expressions and tidy haircuts before, in the congregations of the evangelical prayer meetings on Sunday morning television.

Dr Richard Cornelius, a professor of English, greeted me in his office – a lugubrious man in steel-rimmed spectacles, sucking on the end of a pencil. We talked about the legacy of Bryan and the Scopes Trial. The saddest thing, said Cornelius, was that in a great many Tennessee schools evolution theory was now taught as a fact. 'And that's a terrible thing, because it's a theory, a hypothesis and one should teach it that way. What you have here is a sorry situation where a religion is being attacked.'

Bryan College strived to redress the balance. Students were taught an interpretation of Genesis unfudged by metaphor: that the earth was created in six days of twenty-four hours; that the earth is only 6 to 8,000 years old, not the millions of geologists, biologists and evolutionists. 'We try to present both sides,' said Cornelius, 'although, of course, we tend to be favourable to our side.'

The Scopes Trial, he said, had earned Dayton the nickname of the Buckle on the Bible Belt (the belt of Southern States, Florida, Georgia, Tennessee, Mississippi and Arkansas, where Christian fundamentalism was at its strongest) – and not much had changed since then. 'For most people in these parts witness, belief, is central to their life. Fundamentalism and evangelism are strong and healthy as people see the emptiness of liberalism and all this New Age thing. We are fundamentalists, but we wouldn't, say, handle snakes like some of them way down south do. That's off the deep end as far as we're concerned.'

I wondered how Dr Cornelius reconciled biblical truth with that other great American faith of free enterprise. 'Independence ... Pay your own bills; don't get handouts – you could harmonise that with the scriptures,' he mused. 'But then you get your materialism coming in, so that's a question. It's true that if you just look out for that dollar – the survival of the fittest – then that contradicts what the Bible says.' Cornelius sucked on his pencil and regarded me suspiciously, as if to say, where the hell was all this leading anyway?

'America's going more materialistic – soft on luxury – and we fear for that in Christian circles. We have our problems in Tennessee. We have a lot of drugs. The soil round here is real good for marijuana.'

The Scopes Trial produced many ironies, but the supreme one was this: as far as the town of Dayton was concerned, the motive behind it was not to debate freedom of speech, the conflict of science and religion, or to ask whither educational standards in American schools. It was simply to put Dayton on the map. It was a good, old-fashioned business opportunity. A consortium of businessmen in Chattanooga had actually tried to put up their own culpable evolutionist teacher in order to have the trial staged there, but they had been outflanked by the Dayton boys. And it was Dayton that had reaped the profits. The Scopes Trial had made a great many people rich: local tradesmen, novelty manufacturers, monkey trainers, the writers and publishers of the topical songs which had flourished in the wake of the trial (my favourite was 'Bryan Believed In Heaven – That's Why He's In Heaven Tonight'), and, of course, Hollywood, which had produced the film *Inherit The Wind*. In short, it was a typical story of American enterprise and opportunism. Social Darwinism in practice. Eustace would have loved it, I thought, as I drove back to Chattanooga in a teeming rainstorm.

It was curious, this relationship between enterprise and religion which had dominated Chattanooga, and held its social and economic infrastructure intact. The fittest – well, the richest anyway – had clung on tenaciously to their power and position over the generations, but now another species, lean and hungry, had swum into the pool of Chattanooga life.

It was Lamar Alexander, the former governor of Tennessee, who had initially courted investment in the state by the Japanese. Alexander had wooed the Japanese in their country, and in Tennessee, pointing out not only the economic potential of the state, but also its geographical resemblance – mountains and rivers – to their own country. The Japanese felt right at home. Now there was a Nissan car plant outside Nashville, and in Chattanooga itself there was Komatsu, NA Industries, Sofix – $100 million worth of Japanese investment in the city. The Japanese were shopping in the malls, taking over restaurants and filing applications to local golf clubs.

It was Eustace who had first alerted me to the golf club as a true barometer of social standing. 'You see, it used to be that they didn't want blacks playing on their courses. That wall came down. Now it's the Japanese. They can't stop them legally, of course, so they put up the fees so high that no one can afford them. Then they say, we'll put you on the waiting list and you just stay there for one month, six months, a year, until you get tired and don't want to join the club any more. I know that one,' he added darkly.

There were sixteen golf courses in Chattanooga. It seemed enough for everybody, but then that was hardly the point. It was which golf course that counted. An American working at Komatsu was sanguine. 'The Japanese like to interface and intermingle – that surprised me. They seem to enjoy the independence of being alone, but then again they blend right well. 'Course, there's always some resentment, but we know we've got to compete world-wide. Having the Japanese here means job security, survival. We want success. That's the mind-set.'

I was curious to know whether it was a mind-set shared by the Lookout Mountain Crowd. I telephoned the Davenports. Rodolphus Davenport Jnr had founded Krystal Hamburgers in 1932, in a small corner store in Chattanooga, with the gimmick of selling square-shaped hamburgers for a nickel apiece. Krystal Burgers now straddled the South. I asked to speak to Rody Davenport. 'Do you want Rody the third, or the fourth?' asked the telephonist. I wasn't sure, but the third was en route to Antigua on his yacht, and the fourth was otherwise engaged. She sounded under duress. Outside the Krystal building local environmentalists were demonstrating against the use of Styrofoam containers in Krystal restaurants. Trouble-makers . . .

Jack Lupton, however, said he would be pleased to meet me, in his office at the top of Chattanooga's most commanding tower block. In Chattanooga, Lupton meant Coca-Cola. Jack's grandfather, John T. Lupton, had been the first man to put Coca-Cola in bottles, an idea that had made him one of the richest men in America. He had passed the business to his son Carrter; who, in turn, had passed it to his son, Jack. (Jack's son was named – you guessed it – Carrter.)

No family better embodied the principle of seizing the half chance, exploiting it and growing exceedingly rich than the Luptons. No family better embodied dynastic power in Chattanooga, or the peculiar inbreeding that sustained it. Jack Lupton's wife Alice was the sister of Scott (banking) Probasco; Jack's sister Elizabeth was married to Rody (hamburgers) Davenport, the third.

Jack Lupton was a handsome man in his sixties, radiantly tanned, dressed in slacks, a sports shirt and a windcheater emblazoned with the name of the Honors Club golf course. Jack owned the Honors Club. Jack told me the story of how his grandfather had made his fortune. Until 1899 Coca-Cola had been available only at drug-store soda fountains. Lupton, a lawyer by profession, and his friends were baseball fans. Wouldn't it be neat to be able to drink Coca-Cola at the game, they thought; supposing we put the stuff in bottles? 'And with that marvellous, simple, *beautiful* start was born the Coca-Cola bottling business,' said Jack Lupton with a flourish.

Jack's father had expanded the business across America, and Jack himself had consolidated it. Then, in 1986, he sold the Coca-Cola bottling company to the parent company in Atlanta for $1 billion, and settled back to concentrate on his golf stroke, and philanthropy. Now the Luptons' charitable trust, the Lyndhurst Foundation, extended into almost every facet of Chattanooga life: housing, education, medicine.

'I was always in love with the bottling business,' said Jack, 'but my father put me on the foundation board and he gave me the gift of how to give intelligently, and the agony and the ecstasy and just *superhuman* rewards you get.'

What did it mean to be a Lupton in Chattanooga, I asked.

'Leadership,' said Jack, without missing a beat. 'It really does. But I *love* it.'

He spoke with the authority of one utterly certain of his destiny. Did he, I wondered, believe in evolution – the survival of the fittest?

'That's the darndest question . . . Why do you ask?' I mentioned my visit to Dayton, the Scopes Trial. 'Well,' said Jack. ''Course, I was brought up here in the Bible Belt, but I think with age you mellow. To me, that strenuous worship of the Bible, and literally believing all of it, comes close to destroying your own belief in God through Jesus. It's not a very *progressive* religion; it holds you back. Everything revolves around the good book, but nowhere in it does it say, get up off your butt and go and do something.

'This is an extremely conservative pocket of people here in Eastern Tennessee. The Jews couldn't make a living in Knoxville, just away from here: they got run out years ago. They're the tightest people in the world in Knoxville, and the next tightest are here in Chattanooga. They kick the tyres pretty hard here before they buy anything. It's a conservative, very insular community, and for a long time we didn't do enough. Chattanooga had the opportunity to blow the South away. We were a rail and a river centre. We were on the list of the top ten cities to be bombed during the Second World War – if they could get here. That's how important manufacturing was around here. But Atlanta had the airport first, and that's what counted. They had a very progressive mayor –

Hartsfield was his name – and he took Atlanta and just left everybody else in the dust.

'But I need to tell you, Mike, that Chattanooga is in a renaissance right now.' Jack walked to the window and pointed to a site beyond the low-rise rooftops, by the river's edge – the site of Jack's new project, the Tennessee Aquarium. 'A half a million people pass through this town every year on their way to somewhere else; they don't even unpack their suitcases. This'll make them stop.'

It would, said Jack, be the only freshwater aquarium in America; the pinwheel for myriad new industries, a way of revitalising the river.

'Fishing ...' said Jack, with feeling. 'It's like motherhood and apple pie. There's nothing wrong with fishing.'

What made this better still, he said, was that the whole shooting match was being built with private money – Jack's, and his sister Elizabeth's. 'And that is unique. We answer to ourselves. We're not "hornswaggled" by politics, which has America by the throat right now. Those idiots in Washington need to be killed.'

What about the Japanese, I asked. Surely they too provided a catalyst for revitalisation; they were lean, fit, enterprising; they'd got off their butts and done something; they seemed the very embodiment of the Darwinian principle in action. Jack looked doubtful. 'Well, I'm not too terribly thrilled about that. We've got too many of them here, doing what we should be doing. The reason they're here is because they make the best damned cars – which we used to do. But I'm fearful. When they begin to mess around with your entertainment business, your leisure business, before you know they'll be taking over your newspapers and television stations and then they're going to begin to subtly affect a whole lot of things. It's bound to happen.

'That frightens me, and I'm not just an old Jap-hater. They're a different culture – different as night from day. I'm a golfer, and when I see the Pebble Beach course out in California go to the Japanese, why that hurts my heart. People round here laugh at me and how much money I've got sunk in the Honors Club, and I say, don't laugh too loud, I might just sell it. They say, you wouldn't dare.' Jack chuckled meaningfully.

Would Jack Lupton have the Japanese at his golf course, I wondered. 'We got one Japanese interested in a membership,' said Jack. 'Owner of a restaurant chain in Knoxville. He said he'd move his family to Chattanooga simply to get a membership. That's 120 miles! Can you believe that? Our subscription is not closed. But we're looking at him very closely – for his sake, not ours.' Jack paused. 'To see if he would be comfortable.'

He had walked to the window and now was peering out across the rooftops, down towards the river, and the site of the new Aquarium. Back in primordial time, Darwin tells us, life incubated in the oceans and rivers, then crawled forth, took form, substance and intelligence, moulded and shaped by the laws of natural selection. Survival. That was the Darwinian key. I thought of Eustace, and the Rhea County Courthouse; I thought of all the chances Chattanooga had missed, and the nice houses up on Lookout Mountain. And something told me the Japanese restaurateur would not be joining Jack's club for a while.

Long distance information,
give me Memphis, Tennessee . . .

I had been in Memphis barely two hours before I walked into a fight. I had flown in from Chattanooga; picked up a hire car at the airport, taken a wrong turn off the freeway, and meandered into Memphis through the suburbs. I arrived at my hotel harassed, tired, in need of a drink.

In the hotel bar, a drunk on the next stool grew irritated by my English accent. 'Ah just bet you're a lord.'

A lord? Did he really say *lord*? 'No, just an ordinary guy,' I said.

He breathed closer. 'I jes *know* you're a goddam lord, and I know you're full of shit.'

The conversation, such as it was, had taken a clear turn for the worse. I extricated myself with a shrug. The bartender was sympathetic. 'Asshole thought you were the law . . .'

It took a while to come to terms with Memphis. There were enough courtesies to remind you that, yes, this was very much the South: enough of an edge to remind you that this was the big city. In the middle of the night I was awoken by shouts from the street outside and the sound of music from a passing car, shaking the window frames. The next morning, outside the hotel, a panhandler begged for spare change; a black man in a threadbare overcoat fell into step beside me – 'Yo, slim, what's happenin'? Whatcha need? Whatcha need?' – and vanished as quickly as he had come.

A friendly bartender helpfully sketched in the city's 'no-go' areas on a tourist map. 'Let's see ... I'd stay away from here, here, here ... oh, and here.' All that was left in the immediate vicinity, it seemed, was a small area of intersecting streets, islands in a sea of furious crosshatching. The bartender was white. The unspoken assumption was that the areas of threat were black.

More than half the population of Memphis was black. Thirty years ago a black man would not have been allowed to eat at the same table as me, stay in the same hotel. The Civil Rights Movement had eradicated the evil of segregation, and it was here in Memphis that Martin Luther King, who had had a dream, and spoken of it in the most remarkable and moving oratory in modern times, was murdered in 1968.

The Civil Rights Movement had eradicated the evil of segregation, yet separation remained an unspoken, though universally accepted, fact of life. Blacks lived in the south of the town and its inner suburbs; whites in the north, and in its outer ones. Blacks and whites worked in the same offices, treated each other with equable politeness, then went their separate ways. I had noticed this in Chattanooga: two hamburger restaurants, on opposite corners of a downtown road junction – one filled predominantly with whites, the other predominantly with blacks, as if operating on separate laws of magnetism.

Driving through South Memphis, it slowly dawned on me that I had driven miles without seeing another white motorist, let alone a white pedestrian. This was not the ghetto of scabrous tenement blocks and congested housing projects that one might find in a northern city, but a sprawl of clapboard houses and bungalows, in varying stages of neglect and disrepair. Groups of young men lounged on the verandahs and street corners, smoking, many of them wearing plastic shower caps, to preserve their Jheri-curl hairstyles.

A glance at the street map revealed that there was no need for a middle-class white even to pass through these areas. The construction of the freeways meant that commuters from the outer suburbs could be swept into the city's business district, park their cars in underground car parks, be siphoned up into their air-conditioned offices – and reverse the process at the end of the day – without ever needing to be confronted by the poverty and hopelessness lurking on the fringes of the city. This seemed such a satisfactory prophylactic to any untoward middle-class feelings of unease that I began to wonder if it had not been planned that way.

Chuck Berry's song 'Memphis Tennessee' is a delightfully sly twist on the familiar theme of separated love. The distraught singer pleads with a telephone operator to connect him to 'my Marie'.

'We were pulled apart because her mom did not agree/And tore apart our happy home in Memphis, Tennessee.'

The twist is that Marie is:

'only six years old . . . information please/Try to put me through to her in Memphis, Tennessee.'

Berry recorded the song in 1958, but it was not until 1963 that it became a hit in Britain, when Berry enjoyed a belated surge of popularity through the offices of such groups as the Beatles and the Stones covering his material. Chuck Berry wrote brilliantly about the American landscape. His song 'The Promised Land' was an exhilarating evocation of a journey across America to California – the Promised Land of the title – in the tradition of what is probably the greatest 'road song' of all, Bobby Troup's 'Route 66!'. In 'Sweet Little Sixteen' Berry called up the names of American cities – 'They're really rocking in Boston, Pittsburgh PA . . . All over St Louis, way down in New Orleans/All the cats want to dance with, Sweet Little Sixteen' – in an invocation of the big beat of rock and roll that was sweeping across the nation. While 'Back In The USA' was a sublimely dumb litany of reasons to be patriotic: skyscrapers, freeways, drive-ins, jukeboxes, corner cafés 'where a hamburger sizzles on an open griddle all day'. Who would not have wanted to live in Chuck Berry's America, a teen heaven of fast cars with big fins, bobby-soxed sweethearts, and the endless tug of the big beat? 'Anything you want they got it right here in the USA . . .' he sang. There was no more persuasive salesman for the American Dream.

Berry actually grew up in St Louis, 285 miles up the Mississippi River from Memphis. But it seemed fitting that black music's most eloquent rock and roll poet should have immortalised Memphis in song, for the city had always been an important centre for black life and culture. You might even say it was Memphis' destiny. The city was founded in 1819, a frontier town that had grown quickly on the back of King Cotton, 'white gold', and its favoured position on the river, at a point where three states – Tennessee, Mississippi and Arkansas – converge. But in the late nineteenth century the city was ravaged by a series of cholera and yellow fever epidemics, decimating the population and driving from the city almost everybody who had the strength or wherewithal to leave. But curiously – prophetically – most of the newly emancipated black population of Memphis was unaffected by the epidemics, spared, it is believed, through a natural immunity carried with their ancestors from Africa.

The reconstruction of the city attracted greater numbers of blacks from the outlying countryside of the Mississippi Delta, and the educated, professional classes from the North. The largest and most vibrant black community in the South grew up along the southern edge of the town. Its heartbeat was Beale Street, the black Broadway – a thoroughfare lined with theatres, cheap hotels, bars and the less salubrious juke joints, gambling halls and bordellos. It was here, so the myth has it, that W. C. Handy, a cornet player in a minstrel band, first heard the field chants and refrains that the workers had brought with them from the Delta cotton fields, and formalised them into America's first indigenous music – the blues – memorialising the town in his 1910 composition, 'Memphis Blues'.

In its years as the black Broadway, virtually every black musician of note had played on Beale Street. Riley 'B. B.' King – America's greatest living blues musician – polished his craft along Beale Street; it was while working as a radio disc jockey for WDIA, presenting the 'Sepia Swing Club' that King took the moniker 'Beale Street Blues Boy', later abbreviated to 'Blues Boy King', and then to plain 'B. B.'.

But in the Sixties the smile was wiped off the face of Beale Street and its surrounding neighbourhood. In a massive urban clearance programme, a half-mile strip south of Beale was swept clean of its brick storefront shops and frame houses; grass seed was thrown on the rubble, and then, seemingly, just left. The result looked like a scorched earth policy masquerading as civic planning, creating a grubby *cordon sanitaire* between the centre of town and the border of South Memphis, marked by a handful of decaying housing projects and deserted buildings. What had been the thinking behind it? I asked one long-standing, white, Memphis resident. 'To move the black people out of the city,' he said flatly.

In a belated recognition of its cultural significance, Beale Street itself had experienced an eleventh-hour reprieve. It had undergone a transformation into that most hazardous of American notions – a historic district, its disreputable and licentious face cosmeticised for the tourist trade. The famous Daisy Theatre had been renovated; the former brothels and gambling joints now housed gift boutiques and art galleries, and new clubs were opening up on every corner. Beale had become a kind of Disneyland of the blues.

In the Rum and Boogie Café, the jukebox was loaded with rhythm and blues hits from the Sixties by Otis Redding, Albert King, the Staple Singers – all of whom recorded for the Memphis label, Stax, in the last great epoch of the city's music scene. On stage a group of young white musicians, fronted by an elderly, blind black singer, was playing to an audience made up almost exclusively of white college kids and young professionals. It was a microcosm of the history of the blues, a study of how black culture had influenced, informed and ultimately been co-opted by whites.

No single person more vividly embodied this principle than

Memphis' most famous son, Elvis Presley. Presley was actually born in Tupelo, Mississippi, but the family moved to Memphis when he was thirteen. As a young punk he hung around Beale Street, and bought his clothes at Lansky Brothers – the spiffy sports coats and shirts in neon blues and get-down pinks, which were worn by the bluesmen and street cats. Presley made his first recordings in the early Fifties for the local Sun label, owned by a white man named Sam Phillips, who had specialised in recording blues singers such as Howlin' Wolf and Junior Parker. An enlightened individual, Phillips could recognise the prejudice that hindered his black artists; he once recalled that the jukebox opera-tors who called by each week to collect Sun records would tell him, 'These people [the blacks] are ruining our children.' 'Now these were basically good people,' Phillips recalled, 'but conceptually they did not understand the kinship between the black and white people in the South. So I knew what I had to do to broaden the acceptance.'

What Phillips needed was a white artist with the sound and excitement of a black one, to sell to an audience too hidebound by their prejudices to accept the real thing, or as Phillips himself famously put it, 'If I could find a white man with the Negro sound, the Negro feel, I could make a billion dollars.'

Presley was the missing link. His first release for Sun was 'That's All Right (Mama)', a song written and originally recorded by Arthur Crudup, a black country-blues singer who was one of Presley's formative influences as a singer. At a time when radio stations segregated music by colour of origin as much as style, Presley's record was initially played on black rhythm and blues programmes, not white country ones (there was, of course, no such thing as rock and roll radio in 1954). Most people assumed he was black until they saw him.

It is difficult now to comprehend the fuss that Presley caused. In his first, insurrectionary flush of fame he was the target of gimcrack politicians, baptist ministers, tub-thumping opportunists of every persuasion, railing against the pernicious influence of 'nigger music' on white teenagers. But within a handful of years, all that was forgotten. Presley's manager, Colonel Tom Parker, a carnival barker and flimflam man before he took Presley under his wing, made Elvis whiter-than-white, bleached the last drop of black influence from his music. Elvis went to Hollywood. Arthur Crudup – and, for that matter, Sam Phillips – stayed at home.

Elvis Presley Boulevard was an endless thoroughfare of fast-food restaurants and used-car lots, decked out in plastic bunting. I had expected Graceland, the home where 'the King' lived and died, to be set in fabulous seclusion. But given the choice of whichever piece of prime real estate his fortune would avail, he had chosen to spend his days in a mock-baronial mansion, set on the crest of a hill, offering a commanding view of a four-lane highway. The environs of Graceland had been somewhat enlarged since Presley's death, to accommodate parking space for some 10,000 cars and tour buses, and a sprawling complex including tourist shops, a motor museum, and Presley's private jet and tour bus.

A small bus carried us up the drive to Graceland itself. We entered with the hushed reverence of visitors to the Sistine Chapel, except that here was not symmetry, beauty, and the spirit in flight, but heinous taste, berserk ostentatiousness, the evidence of a soul unhinged. We trooped through its fantasy rooms and corridors, admiring the carpeted walls and ceilings; the nitrous-yellow leather bar fittings and fake animal skin furnishings; the security cameras in every room, linked to a central console so that Elvis could spy on his guests from the privacy of his bedroom – closed to the public 'out of respect for Elvis'.

Graceland felt all wrong. Rather than being depicted as an allegory of the mutating properties of celebrity, Elvis's life had been airbrushed into a pure Horatio Alger story, the poor boy who had come from the backwoods to find fame, fortune and international renown.

The 'walk of fame' was clogged with the gold records, the stage costumes, Elvis' collection of guns (his 'favourite' was a turquoise-handled Colt 45) and his honorary sheriff's badges. 'Elvis had a love and respect for law enforcement,' the guide, a matronly woman, whispered reverentially. She stressed his philanthropy, his strength of character, his love for mother and country, his profound religiosity. 'They called him "the King of rock and roll",' she murmured, 'but he would tell them, there is only one King, and that is Jesus Christ.' Elvis, she said, was a keen student of philosophy – a facet of his character curiously overlooked in most accounts of his activities and enthusiasms.

I looked in vain for the icons of his downfall: the pill bottles, the framed doctors' prescriptions, the symbolic plates heaped with artery-inflating junk food. But they were nowhere to be found. An aura of fraudulent sanctimoniousness hung in the air.

'It's like an anthropological study of how religions get started,' said a man beside me, under his breath, as we stood in the 'meditation garden' gazing blankly at the floral tributes adorning the graves of Elvis, his mother and father. And he was right. It felt like a low-budget Lourdes, but then what was Elvis anyway if not a modern-day saint? Pick up any supermarket newspaper and you could read an account of a new, miraculous apparition. In earlier times, he would have manifested on mountain tops, in grottos or olive groves: now he appeared in Burger Kings, stacking shelves in supermarkets or pumping gas. Elvis was truly a twentieth-century saint.

There were priests in Elvis-ology – academics and anthropologists: you could study Elvis Presley in college cultural studies courses. He had long since ceased to be a person, and become instead a metaphor for America's longings and its sins. But the people around me at the graveside did not look like college professors or experts in deconstruction; rather these were the simple keepers of the faith – people who had danced to Elvis, made out to Elvis, thrilled to Elvis. Women dabbed at their eyes with handkerchiefs, or clutched at their husband's arms for support, and afterwards they thronged the souvenir shops, scrabbling among the T-shirts, key-rings, mugs and ballpoint pens, which were the inevitable detritus of commerce. Behind a counter sat an elderly man wearing a mechanic's cap and a bewildered expression. It was Vester Presley, an authentic, living relative; one of the communion of saints, selling his autograph.

*

Chuck Berry's 'Memphis, Tennessee' had been co-opted as the theme tune for a campaign to sell the city at home and abroad. B. B. King's genial, sweat-dappled face loomed large in tourist posters. Graceland and the Sun studios were already on the tourist map, of course, but in a leap of bureaucratic imagination the original interior of Studio A from probably Memphis' most successful recording company – Stax – was being constructed in the Music Hall of Fame at the city's newest architectural landmark, an office and entertainment complex called the Pyramid.

Stax Records had a personal significance for me. I grew up fatally enamoured of the music of such artists as Otis Redding, Sam and Dave and Carla Thomas, at a time when soul music was a sacred flame, jealously guarded by what seemed to be a small coterie of devotees. For a short while in my mid-teens I edited a fanzine called *Soulbeat*, produced in my bedroom in the hours when I should have been engaged on homework, printed on an ancient duplicating machine, and sold by mail order. I would write to American record companies, wildly inflating the circulation figure, begging for photographs, records, scraps of information. Envelopes from Stax would fall through the letter box like manna from heaven, bearing singles and artist biographies, written in a prose designed to invest the musicians, their every action and gesture, with the significance of myth. I knew next to nothing about chemical formulae and historic dates, but I knew that Rufus Thomas made up his song 'The Dog' the night he played in a small nightclub in Millington, Tennessee, after watching a woman dance, and that Booker T and the MGs cut 'Green Onions' on a summer afternoon in 1962, when a singer they were supposed to be backing failed to show up, and that MGs stood for 'Memphis Group'. From the perspective of South London, South Memphis seemed impossibly romantic.

The Stax label had been founded in 1960 by a white couple, Jim Stewart and Estelle Axton, who opened a record shop and recording studio named Satellite Records in a disused cinema on McLemore Avenue in South Memphis. (The name Stax, a conjunction of Stewart and Axton, would come later.) Stewart's personal preference was for country music, but almost before it had properly begun, Stax had become enmeshed in the curious interplay between young whites and black music in Memphis. Estelle Axton's son, Packy, played with a group called the Mar-Keys, who performed from time to time in the clubs and dance halls of the black neighbourhood of West Memphis, across the Mississippi River in Arkansas.

In 1961 the Mar-Keys released a honking instrumental called 'Last Night' on the Satellite label. The record's success on the rhythm and blues charts opened the floodgates at Satellite. Local rhythm and blues singers began to congregate around the studio. William Bell; Rufus Thomas – who as a disc-jockey and comic performer was something of a local institution around Memphis – and his daughter Carla. The 'house' rhythm section, Booker T and the MGs, was made up equally of black and white musicians.

Stax was not the only place in the South where music provided a rare instance of racial integration. At the Muscle Shoals studios in Alabama, a house rhythm section made up entirely of white musicians, raised in the country music tradition, provided the backing for a series of outstanding black soul singers, including James Carr, Jimmy Hughes and Percy Sledge. But it was Stax that enjoyed the most prolific success.

One of the architects of that success was a local songwriter named Dave Porter, who along with his partner Isaac Hayes, wrote and produced a series of hit singles throughout the 1960s for Sam and Dave, including 'Soul Man', 'Hold On!, I'm Coming' and 'When Something Is Wrong With My Baby'.

Before arriving in Memphis, I had been told that the best way to find Porter was to make enquiries at the chocolate concession stand at Memphis Airport. It seemed an unlikely way to make a connection, but it worked. After the collapse of Stax in the late Seventies, Porter opened his own recording studio in town, but also branched into the sideline of novelty confectionery. The sales assistant at the airport stand rang Porter from behind a counter stacked with chocolate images of Elvis Presley and the Stars and Stripes, and an appointment was made.

Porter was an amiable, quietly spoken man, who greeted me at his studio, in a converted warehouse close to the river, lined with gold records, citations and publicity pictures of Dave himself, shaking hands and posing with sundry music industry dignitaries.

He had grown up in South Memphis, he said, attended the local Booker T. Washington High School, where he had a reputation for cutting wild. He had hardly seen or spoken to white people until he left school and took a job in a grocery store just across the road from the Satellite shop and studios. The store was run by a white man. 'And, man,' said Dave, 'that guy, he'd get mad at me if he didn't think I was working hard enough, sometimes for no reason at all, and he'd kick me like an animal.'

He started drifting into Satellite as a customer. Then he tried his hand at writing songs, and before you knew it he was on the studio payroll, one of the first black people to be on salary in a creative role. 'It was against the grain for me – this chocolate face – to be there,' he said, with a slight smile. Remember, this was the early Sixties: the time of segregation. He would sit in the studio and write songs with the MGs' guitarist Steve Cropper, who was white, but they would never eat in the same restaurant. 'But I never wanted to, you know? I was too busy wanting to write a hit record to worry about that.'

Away from the public eye, the black musicians went out with white girls, he said, and the white musicians with black girls, and nobody paid much heed. 'I think in the music business people have never been quite so hung up on the race thing. But there was that homogenisation there – you began to see a change in the mind-set of people. The climate was ready for black music to be accepted all over, and what made it real *soulful* at Stax was that the white influence was there, but it didn't predominate.

'Blacks were making a lot of money in this town; there was a pride then because of the success we were having, and the whites didn't feel intimidated because we weren't taking their jobs. You had the pride there in the black community and the respect in the white.'

The assassination of Martin Luther King, at the Lorraine Motel in Memphis in 1968, changed all that, said Dave. He could still remember the night it happened, 4 April. He was in the studio working when the news came that King had been shot. A bunch of people drove down to the Lorraine; it was less than a mile away. There were hundreds of people on the streets around, he remembered, nobody knowing what to say or do, simply feeling lost, hurt and confused. Even the sky looked angry, 'like you could *feel* something catastrophic had happened.'

The next day, South Memphis was cordoned off by police, and some of the white musicians had trouble getting to the studios. There was a lot of awkwardness that day, Dave said – nobody wanting to catch anybody's eye – 'a black and white thing', that had never been there before. 'I'd have to say the studio vibe became different, because nobody thought that was necessary, you understand? Before that, every day you went to work it was on the understanding that you didn't bring in any of the crap from the world outside, 'cause at Stax we didn't count numbers, who was black and who was white.

'But that day nobody knew how comfortable to be. When something like that happens, no matter how much you want things to be the same, they can't be. It did something, for sure.'

The Stax label carried on producing music, of course. But for Porter, and those others who had been there from the beginning, the mood had changed. Jim Stewart, the founder, sold out shortly afterwards and the label was taken over by a black man named Al Bell. For a while the label prospered, but then Stax ran into financial problems – the victim, it was darkly rumoured, of a record industry and banking squeeze, to put the label out of business and make its most successful acts available for 'cherry picking'. 'Less said about that the better . . .' said Porter, bringing the subject firmly to a close. Memories are long in the music business.

I liked Dave Porter with his gentle, self-deprecating manner; the obvious pride he took in his achievements. It was a long time since he had written a big hit record, although 'When Something Is Wrong With My Baby' had recently been back in the American charts in a new recording by Linda Ronstadt and Aaron Neville.

'That just broke me up, man,' smiled Porter. 'I guess it's become a classic.' His own studio was used mostly for recording commercials, he said, although he had recently been working with a couple of local singers, cutting tracks in a contemporary groove. Memphis still had a lively little music scene, he said, but not as lively as the old days. 'I don't believe in living in the past,' he told me, 'but those days were good, real good. But some of the fun just went out of it all.'

I wanted to be closer to God, and on Sunday morning I drove out through South Memphis to church. The clapboard shacks gave way to more prosperous bungalows and family houses: suburbia, dozing in Sunday morning sunshine. The Mississippi Boulevard Christian Church occupied a corner position, the size of a football field. New Oldsmobile Cutlasses, Sunbirds and Spirits clogged the parking lot, disgorging people in Sunday finery.

The MBCC ('the church that dares, because it cares') was a modern building, with a two-tiered auditorium, fitted with plush blue velvet seats. It felt like a civic theatre – its size a testament to its position as the wealthiest black church in Memphis. Its foremost patrons were the family who owned Memphis' only black bank. Its congregation was enormous. There were some 1,600 people at the 11 o'clock service; another 1,800 had attended the earlier service, at 8 a.m. The choir filed on to the stage, some seventy people in all, in white robes. A drum kit, bass, electric organ had been set up in front of them. I was the only white person in the congregation.

The senior pastor, the Reverend Alvin Jackson, was a tall, slim and immensely energetic man in his early-thirties. He preached a sermon of fervent intensity on the theme of How Deep Is Your Religion, about the requirement for total immersion in faith, in Jesus. The recitation began at a measured pace, then, almost without one noticing, slipped into a higher gear. 'We've got a whole lot of spiritual midgets and retards walking around here,' said the Reverend Jackson. The congregation hummed approvingly, 'yessir' and 'Amen', waving their upturned palms in the air. 'We gotta stop standing in the same place, telling the same old lies.'

'Uhuuhhuuhhh.'

'Now George Bush ...' The Reverend Jackson paused while the congregation let out a disapproving hiss of air, as if confronting a pantomime villain. 'George Bush – he's only *ankle-deep* in religion. He goes to church every Sunday, but he doesn't do anything for the black people in this country that don't have enough food to eat or jobs to go to, or a roof to put over their head ... I say, Mr Bush! That's ankle-deep religion, I say, that's not enough!'

'Yessir,' said the congregation. And 'AMEN!'

A woman on the stage beside Reverend Jackson – another pastor – had risen from her seat and was now jogging from foot to foot, clapping and shaking her head. There was an organ chord. A drum roll. Now members of the choir too were out of their seats, waving hands, sighing and moaning.

'Then you got your waist-deep religion,' the Reverend's face was wreathed in righteousness, as if he was no longer responsible for the words he was speaking, but was simply a mouthpiece for the spirit. 'With waist-deep you got Jesus residing, but he ain't presiding; Jesus is the resident, but he ain't the president! You got to go all the way in, brothers and sisters, all the way in.'

'AMEN.' Now the organ, drums and bass guitar were talking the same language. Some kind of melody was emerging. Nobody had needed to make an announcement or give a signal; the congregation were out of their seats, spilling into the aisles, fanning the air with prayer sheets, swept up in the fervour being generated from the stage.

'Jesus is the physician,' the Reverend Jackson was singing now. 'He's the witness. Ah've experienced Jesus!'

It was as if the air had been charged with electricity, or as if layers of one's own skin had been suddenly torn back, the raw nerve endings exposed. I felt torn, unaccountably, between grinning like a fool, and bursting into tears; I was ready to crawl to the Promised Land on my knees. And so, it seemed, was everyone around me.

Buoyed on such a tidal wave of faith, it was easy to see how the church had provided the sustenance and support against a largely hostile world through the trials of segregation; how it had sustained the promise for a better life.

After the service, the Reverend Jackson invited me to a lunch for new church members. There were some 200 people in the hall; young couples and families with children, dressed as if for a birthday party. It was a lively, generous spirited occasion, with chicken and corn served on paper plates, a great deal of laughter, but with an underlying edge of seriousness as the Reverend urged them to join prayer groups, Bible workshops, the Teen Ministry – get immersed. The new members listened with alert, committed expressions.

The Reverend told me that the Christian Church (Disciples of Christ) was actually of mixed denomination. 'Lyndon Johnson was a member and – believe it or not – Ronald Reagan,' he chuckled, 'though we don't proclaim that too loudly.'

But blacks and whites don't worship together, I said.

'Well,' the Reverend gave an eloquent shrug, 'let's just say it's different styles.'

The church had been the crucible for the Civil Rights Movement in the Sixties, in Martin Luther King's time, I said; were things different now?

The black church was still involved in civil rights issues, said the Reverend, but less than in the past. The Mississippi Boulevard Christian Church was one of a group of thirty in Memphis that ran an economic development fund, to encourage small black businesses, and support programmes for the young and the elderly. 'But it's hard. The number one problem we face in this city is the problem of race. There are still two Memphises – black and white. We got a black middle class, but the majority of black people are on the poverty line or below. Blacks are just not part of the economic mainstream in America, and there's never been a real attempt on the part of government to make them so. It's one thing to pass laws about equality, but another thing to make the commitment to enforce the spirit of those laws.'

In the South, said the Reverend, the church was still strong, still a force of influence, because the South was conservative. The

MBCC was a prestigious church. Families travelled from miles around to worship there, and the church was vigorous in its recruitment of new members, assiduous in maintaining their commitment, in terms of both faith and money. They were presently engaged in a fund-raising drive to pay off the remaining $400,000 mortgage on the new church premises ('And when that happens,' the Reverend had told the congregation, 'we're gonna have us a mortgage-burning service here!' 'Amen!')

There was no trace of despondency or resignation in the faces of the congregation at the MBCC, but these, it seemed, were largely the middle class, which the Reverend Jackson had been talking about.

Flipping through the TV channels in my hotel room I chanced upon a situation comedy about a black family, the Jeffersons, who, as the theme tune had it, were 'moving on up'. But an article in the Memphis *Commercial Appeal* gave some indication of the uphill nature of the struggle. According to a survey conducted by the National Opinion Research Centre at the University of Chicago, 62.2 per cent of white Americans thought that blacks were 'less hard-working' than whites; 53.2 per cent thought blacks were 'less intelligent'; and 77.7 per cent thought blacks would rather live on welfare than work. Astonishingly, 30 per cent of the blacks surveyed shared the view that whites tended to be of higher intelligence.

Memphis seemed to have been blighted by these attitudes. There were, I was told, a mere 100 black lawyers in Memphis; 100 physicians; 12 black judges – a poor representation for a city of 660,000 people. The black business community was negligible. Blacks accounted for more than half the population, yet wielded insignificant economic or political power.

There was one place in Memphis where the implication of these statistics seemed to come into sharper focus: the Lorraine Motel. It was here that the dream of black advancement was dealt a resounding body-blow when Martin Luther King was shot dead.

Now, some twenty-five years after his death, and after much prevarication, haggling and countless false starts, the Lorraine was in the process of conversion to a museum of the Civil Rights Movement. The Lorraine Motel stood a handful of blocks from Beale Street, in an area of warehouses and brick storefront buildings that had been spared the wrecker's ball, and were now caught in a limbo between dereliction and renovation. A chain-link fence had been erected around the motel; half of it had been demolished, but the two-storeyed wing where King was shot stood precariously among the confusion of building work, and on seeing it, the memories of newsreel footage and newspaper photographs swam back into focus. I walked to the back of the motel, tracing in my mind's eye the trajectory of the bullet, fired from a flophouse on South Main Street, 60 yards from where King stood, on the balcony of room 306.

In the years before desegregation, every important black visitor to Memphis had stayed in the Lorraine; King had come to Memphis to support a strike by city sanitation workers: his decision to stay at the Lorraine was a symbolic one. His murder there carried misfortune in its wake. Three hours after King's death – as riots were breaking out in cities all over America – the owner of the Lorraine, a woman named Loree Bailey, suffered a stroke and died. The motel passed to her husband, Walter, who had been working as a porter at the nearby Holiday Inn.

Walter Bailey resisted the temptation to turn a quick buck on his tragic inheritance. He declined the offer of one entrepreneur to construct a cable car from the flophouse to the motel balcony, call it Bullet's Flight, and sell tickets at a dollar apiece; he ignored the suggestion that he should rent out room 307 (where King actually slept) for $300 a night. Instead, he turned the room into a sorry, makeshift shrine, and it was never occupied by a paying customer again.

But business at the motel was never the same after King's murder. The Lorraine declined into seediness, a reproach to the inability of the city of Memphis to organise a fitting memorial to King's life. Eventually, in 1982, Walter Bailey filed for bankruptcy, and the Lorraine was bought for $240,000 by the nascent Civil Rights Museum Foundation. Bailey was allowed to continue managing the motel, until his death in 1988, when the Lorraine finally closed.

The driving force behind the transformation of the Lorraine was D'Army Bailey, a black Memphis judge. I went to meet Judge Bailey for a drink at a restaurant in the east – which was to say, white – part of town. He arrived in a gold Jaguar, dressed in a mink jacket and wearing a large diamond ring on his finger. He ordered a vodka and Seven with a twist.

Judge Bailey was born in Memphis, the son of a Pullman car porter. In 1962, he went to the Southern University in Baton Rouge, Louisiana, where he had thrown himself into the Civil Rights Movement. 'I felt fortunate to come along at a time of tremendous change,' he said. 'It's the full Hegelian cycle of thesis and antithesis.' The Civil Rights Movement, he went on, was a time of tremendous enthusiasm and optimism, 'the sense that we as young people were able to rise up and exploit our strength.'

For Bailey, exploiting his strength resulted in his expulsion from Southern University for political activities. He moved out to Berkeley, California, where he served on the city council, returning to Memphis to work as an attorney, before becoming a judge.

'Memphis is a city of harsh resistance to advances in Civil Rights,' he said, 'but then what American city is not? But we in Memphis are in as good, if not better, a position to take up the baton and continue the work that remains unfinished, because of our numbers and our willingness to admit the problems.'

Bailey had a way of turning negatives into positives. Because racism had never been disguised in the South, he said, black people were under no illusions about the size of the problems they faced. The attempts by the government to reverse positive discrimination legislation, and cutbacks in government welfare programmes were less demoralising in Memphis because the black people of the city had never properly tasted their benefits in the first place. 'Some parts of our community are so hard hit,' said Bailey, 'that the cutbacks don't make any difference. You can't cut back any further than the poverty line.

'Opportunity is higher in Memphis,' he said, 'because we're not completely demoralised. You can rise so far as a black in this country and then you run into a door that's firmly shut. Since we haven't risen so far, we haven't experienced those knockbacks.'

Memphis, said Bailey, was a town 'where a black man can feel like a man. It takes you back to mother earth; you can regroup and rethink. We've got here a strengthened strain of that raw material of blackness that has always existed in the South.'

No other city in America had demonstrated the energy or commitment to raise $10 million to commemorate the Civil Rights struggle; that in itself was a testament to the efforts of Bailey and his colleagues (and the fact that twelve of the fifteen blacks in the Tennessee state legislature came from Memphis), but also to the way in which attitudes had changed among white legislators and fundraisers. 'That museum means a *lot* in this town,' Dave Porter had told me. 'Memphis should take a big pat on the back for it. It speaks for just how far race relations in this town have come.'

The next day, I joined Judge Bailey for lunch with some members of the museum committee – white, middle-class women who obviously had connections that went straight to the heart of Memphis' ruling caste. The guest of honour was Dave Dennis, one of the Civil Rights freedom riders in the Sixties – 'a warrior of the movement', as Bailey put it. The lunch was in a chic, and rather expensive, restaurant in Overton Square, a collection of colonial-style buildings that had been dinkified for the tourist and business trades. It seemed odd to be sitting in these surroundings, and ponder the deference with which Dennis and Bailey were being treated. Would the reception in the restaurant have been as cordial twenty-five years ago?

Dennis was a sober, serious-faced man with a tightly-wound manner. Clearly, this visit to Memphis was a duty to the cause, not a pleasure. He looked uncomfortable when Judge Bailey started reminiscing about the movement in the Sixties, as if such things should not be spoken of in mixed company. I asked him what progress he thought had been made in the South since desegregation. 'Let's put it this way.' His expression was unsmiling. 'Black people can come in a restaurant like this now. It's just that the vast majority of them will never be able to afford to eat here.'

Drinking with Judge Bailey the previous evening, I had tried to grapple with this recurring question of separation. Why didn't blacks and whites socialise together, worship together? Why were virtually all the players in the televised football and basketball games black, and virtually all the spectators white? The judge smiled indulgently. 'I don't really follow football. It used to be easier to know which team to cheer for when there were just a few black players. Now there's so many. We've taken over the whole game!'

The judge invited me back to his home. He lived in a capacious house on a private estate, beautifully appointed, with tasteful oriental artefacts. The judge poured himself three fingers of vodka and flipped on a jazz station on the Bang and Olufsen. He was quite the *coolest* judge I'd ever met.

'Let me show you something.' He fetched a cardboard box and carefully began to unpack the contents: plates, cups, cutlery, a salt and pepper shaker. 'Dr King ate his last meal off these,' he said. He unfolded a pink bedspread. 'And this is what was wrapped around him after he had been shot.' The bloodstains were still intact. 'Jesse Jackson likened the Lorraine to Calvary,' said the judge. 'The site of the crucifixion. And the site of the crucifixion is the site of the resurrection. Where Dr King fell is where the movement begins. There is no unifying force in black politics in America now. I'm visionary enough to believe that Memphis can step into the vacuum.'

Not everybody saw it that way. The Museum had had a troubled birth. Dr King's widow, Coretta Scott King, had initially opposed the scheme, on the grounds that it would glorify her husband's death rather than his life. She had insisted that her husband's name not be used in connection with the Museum, for fear of confusion with the Martin Luther King Centre For Non-Violent Social Change in Atlanta, where the Civil Rights leader is buried.

Then there was the problem of Jaqueline Smith. A 'grade-A operatic contralto' who had once sung with an opera company in

Chicago, Smith had worked and lived at the Lorraine Motel until its closure, and her eviction, on 2 March 1988. She had been living on the pavement outside ever since, in a solitary protest against its conversion into a Civil Rights Museum.

I found her under a makeshift polythene shelter, bandaged against the rain in coats and blankets, a sou'wester pulled down over her eyes. I'd half-expected a mad woman, but Jaqueline Smith was articulate, obviously intelligent, quietly explaining that her vigil was a stand on principle. She described the Museum as 'an insult to Dr King and his memory': the site should be developed as a medical centre for the poor, the money raised used for housing, free child-care facilities. 'The admission they're going to charge, your average poor person won't be able to afford that. Dr King came to Memphis to solve the problem of the poor people; he didn't come here to socialise.'

There was something unquestionably dignified about her stand. But it was obviously a gesture of futile heroism. The $10 million the Civil Rights Museum was costing wouldn't have put an Elastoplast on Memphis' social problems, let alone provide a cure. But the Museum would draw thousands of visitors to Memphis; a new generation would learn of the Civil Rights struggles, its sacrifices and its gains. And surely something good would come from that. When I put this to Jaqueline she shrugged her shoulders, and gestured towards the skeleton of the motel, on the other side of the wire. 'When Dr King shed blood on that balcony, that sanctified it right then,' she said. 'They're disturbing sacred ground.'

So that was it. A social cause that had become a religious one. I asked if she would accept a donation for food, and pressed a couple of dollars into her hand. She didn't refuse them. I walked back to my car, and climbed in. The rain had begun to fall, and looking back, I could see Jaqueline Smith, staring across the road at the balcony where Martin Luther King had died, waiting patiently for her own Calvary.

meet me in ST LOUIS

Meet me in St Louis, Louis,
meet me at the Fair...

The hotel was full of born-again Christians. Some 500 upright, smiling people, with large blue laminated squares, the size of paperback books, around their necks, printed with their names – Bob, Luther, Miriam – lending them the forlorn and bewildered appearance of wartime evacuees. They formed queues at the reception, and at the coffee shop for breakfast; they greeted each other heartily in the foyer, clapped each other on the back, huddled over programmes and schedules. The notice board in the lobby announced them as the United Church of Christ Executives' Insurance and Advisory Personnel, meeting in the main ballroom. The Aces Long Range Planning meeting was being held in the Boone Room; the Delta Tan Delta were congregating in the Rivergate.

From the window of my room I looked out over the St Louis Arch, on the banks of the Mississippi, soaring 630 feet in the air – monumental, gravity-defying, a symbol which described the whole history and meaning of St Louis in its graceful arc. This was the gateway to the west. The meeting place of two worlds. Facing east, on the far side of the river, the flat lands of Illinois vanished into an industrial haze. Beyond lay Chicago, Philadelphia, New York – the old world. To the west lay the farmlands and prairies of Missouri and Kansas. To the nineteenth-century pioneers who stopped in St Louis to rest and make provision, west was the new world. In Kansas City, 150 miles away, people wore stetsons.

St Louis was where the Mississippi met the Missouri River. It was where the railroads driven from the east met the railroads driven from the west. It was a junction for migration and trade. The song that had brought me here paid homage to the fact. 'Meet Me In St Louis, Louis' was written by Kerry Mills and Andrew Sterling in 1904, one of a host of novelty songs to commemorate the St Louis World's Fair, which had drawn exhibitors and tourists from all over America. The song had been revived forty years later in the MGM musical of the same name starring Judy Garland.

St Louis at the turn of the century was a big, bruising city, puffed up on its own sense of self-importance. It was the archetypal melting pot: Irish, German, Italian, black – with a thriving river port, manufacturing industries and one of the largest breweries in America (Anheuser-Busch, the makers of Budweiser, still brewed 44 per cent of all the beer sold in the country). But something had gone wrong. From my window, the Mississippi River looked grey and sluggish; nothing moved on its surface. Outside the hotel, the streets were almost empty, bereft of life or vitality. What had happened? I picked up a street map, and dodging Bob, Miriam and the crowds of Christians in the lobby, I headed downtown.

Arriving in new cities, one developed a procedure with maps. You collected one with your hire car at airports – usually a crudely drawn affair, designed merely to put you on the right freeway into the city. It never stopped me ending up on the wrong one. You picked up another map in the hotel lobby, more detailed: there's the river, Broadway, Main, Grand, Martin Luther King Boulevard. These were maps with directions, but no meanings; street names, but no atmospheres. They didn't tell you how a city had grown, how it ebbed and flowed. They couldn't show you a city's history, or take its pulse.

In the Fifties, the Situationists – the European 'intellectual terrorist' group which argued that society was held in thrall by the spectacle of culture, and required counter-spectacle to liberate itself – drew their own, alternative maps of European cities, based on the *derive* (literally, drifting). This was a dream-like walk intended to determine the 'psycho-geographical' patterns of a city – its atmospheres and sensibilities – as distinct from its purely physical ones. I began to draw my own maps: the business sections; the residential quarters; the ethnic areas, how they overlapped and changed. Where the Polish had lived, the Irish, the Germans, the Protestants and the Jews. Where they had moved on to. The areas where the blacks had followed; the Hispanics, and the Koreans. The areas the WASPs had kept as their own. The areas that had been abandoned by the working class, but colonised by yuppies, or by gays. You could plot a city's social dynamic this way, its prejudices and points of resistance. These were the maps of thwarted aspiration and hard-won gain, maps which measured the depth of assimilation, and the endurance of cultural identity. There were constants. The Italian communities in every city were always marked by tidy streets, well-swept porches, mom-'n'-pop joints on every corner. The Italians surrendered nothing. Pole might give way to Puerto Rican, Jew to black, but wherever you went, Little Italy was always Little Italy. Martin Luther King Boulevard invariably presaged a neighbourhood of peeling tenement blocks, boarded-up shopfronts, an air of neglect and desperation.

Downtown was the meeting point and melting pot of these disparate elements – the churning, engine heart of the city. Looking at downtown was like examining the condition of a patient: heart-rate, colour, cholesterol level, bowel movements. It was all there. Downtown. The very word had a ring to it, of cosmopolitan sophistication, the savour of a quickened pulse rate, of dazzling enchantments, illicit pleasures. There had even been a song about it – a very bad song, it's true, sung by Petula Clarke, about going downtown to find happy, smiling people, dancing away their blues.

As trite a sentiment as could be imagined, and as bogus a one too. In modern times the word had come to mean something else, something beyond a simple geographical location. It intimated a whole history in two syllables, a pattern that had been repeated in almost every major city in America, with St Louis as no exception.

The pattern went like this. A city was planted by a river, or grew up at a railhead. Industry and commerce flourished; the teeming masses settled hard by the factories; the wealthy built their homes on the hill. The centre of town – downtown – became the hub of commercial enterprise, social activity, entertainment. But time, and the tyranny of the motor car, had rendered the old topography meaningless. The city had been gripped by some irresistible centrifugal force that had flung everything to the outer perimeters. With growing affluence, the middle-class city dwellers had moved to the suburbs, where agricultural land was paved over for housing estates, shopping malls and freeways to carry commuters in and out of the city. The railways had become meaningless, replaced by road and air freight. Manufacturing and industry had relocated in prefabricated sheds out of town, close to the inter-state highways, leaving the redundant warehouses and brick factories crumbling. The population of the city had declined; the old middle-class areas had deteriorated and decayed; the old working-class ones become crime-infested slums.

There was an ugly name for this phenomenon: 'white flight'. The city had been left for dead – downtown, a graveyard, comprising the Greyhound bus station; a formerly venerable hotel, now a flophouse; sundry low-life bars; a porno cinema; perhaps a blood bank. Downtown: the two syllables now carried an air of desperation and menace.

The hitherto great cities of the North, built on manufacturing and heavy industry, had been most afflicted by this disintegration – Pittsburgh, Gary in Indiana and Detroit, which had become almost a euphemism for the urban nightmare. These cities were economic dinosaurs, their decline a symptom of the great population drift South and West, from the 'Rustbelt' of the North to the 'Sunbelt' (a term describing the band of states running from Florida to Arizona, which first surfaced in the late Sixties, but gained common currency after a series of *New York Times* articles describing the trend in 1976). But even the Southern cities were not immune to the degeneration of downtown. The migration to the South had been to the suburbs, or 'greater metropolitan areas' – not to the heart of the cities themselves. I had been struck by the sense of desolation in both Chattanooga and Memphis, the streets of the city centres all but deserted, save at lunch-time when the office workers would emerge from their air-conditioned tower blocks to snatch a sandwich or a hamburger.

David Goldfield, a professor of history at the University of Northern Carolina, and a specialist in urban history, described a resident of Memphis talking of that city's downtown district in 1978. 'You can stand on Main Street now and see to where the city limits were fifty years ago, and it's all vacant land.'

The story was the same everywhere: of decline, degeneration, of places outliving their sense of purpose. 'I wouldn't wander around downtown St Louis after 7 p.m.,' one woman cautioned me, then paused for thought. 'But then again, there's no reason to wander round anyway. There's nothing there.' And she was right. By 6.30 the streets of downtown were all but deserted as the last commuters nosed their cars through the side-streets to the freeway entry for the long haul back to the suburbs. An eerie quiet descended, like an empty Hollywood backlot. But any one of my Christian conventioneers could have walked the street without fear or embarrassment. The low-life seemed to have been vacuum-cleaned from view: police prowl cars cruised under the sodium lights. Walking between the soaring tombstone office blocks, there was not a soul in view, and no human sound: only the barely perceptible electronic sigh of air-conditioning, electric lighting, computers humming, hawing, shifting gears, spewing out data – the living dead, come to claim the night.

In 1900, an Englishman, William Morris, visited St Louis and took note of the 'black stinking slums' where 'women and children are as squalid and dirty as you would find people of the same class in the black slums of an English city.' St Louis was then the fourth largest city in America – after New York, Chicago and Philadelphia – boasting all the attributes and amenities of a major metropolis, and subject to all the customary big-city practices of political corruption, venality and strife. In the same year that William Morris visited the city, a transit workers' strike left three people dead and fourteen wounded after clashes with strike-breakers. Two years later, in an episode known as The Big Cinch, a crusading Democrat attorney, Joseph Folk, popularly known as 'Holy Joe', won twenty-three convictions against city officials for bribery and perjury, and led a purge to clean up St Louis, closing down gambling operations and driving out phoney investment firms. Thus, it was in a spirit of regeneration that the mayor, Rolla Wells, announced St Louis would host a World Fair, to put the city on the map.

St Louis embarked on a programme of wholesale restoration and rebuilding. Hotels, shops, new homes sprouted around the proposed site of the Fair, Forest Park, in the northern part of the city. A new trolley-car system was laid. A matter of days before the Fair opened, clear water suddenly sprang forth from the city's mains supply – it had hitherto been an unsavoury, muddy brown colour.

The centrepiece of the Fair was the 'Ivory City', consisting of twelve gigantic exhibition palaces, the smallest covering 4.1 acres, the largest 18.4 acres – dedicated to such themes as Machinery, Manufacturing, Education and the Liberal Arts. A 47-acre Philippines Reservation, stocked with natives and animals, illustrated the newly discovered glories of empire (America had acquired the Philippines from Spain in 1898, and finally secured the colony after a three-year war against Filipino nationalist resistance). Authentic Boers and Englishmen were shipped across the Atlantic to re-enact the highlights of the Boer War, newspaper accounts of which had excited the American people. An exhibit called The Galveston Flood recreated the tidal wave that had killed 5,000 people in that Texas city four years earlier. And 'The Hereafter' afforded sinners an exclusive preview of 'the shades of Hades, depicted with startling realism by the most advanced mechanical and electrical ingenuity.'

All of this was suffused with a distinctly improving air, born of

the belief that America stood at the pinnacle of civilised achievements and values. The pygmies imported from the Belgian Congo,
the cavalcades of native American Indians – these had not been
assembled to celebrate the innocence and purity of the hunter-
gatherer's way of life, but to illustrate the evolution of man from
'savagery to enlightenment', and the civilising effect of American
culture.

It was all quite a show. Almost 20 million people thronged
through the gates in seven months. To everybody's astonishment,
the Fair reaped a profit of $600,000. Henry Adams, a commentator
of the day, was moved to rhapsody. 'The world has never witnessed
so marvellous a phantasm, by night Arabia's crimson sands had
never returned a glow half so astonishing, as one wanders among
lines of white palaces, exquisitely lighted by thousands on
thousands of electric candles, soft, rich, shadowy, palpable in their
sensuous depths . . . One enjoyed it with iniquitous rapture.'

There was not much iniquitous rapture to be found in St Louis
nowadays, it seemed; but the World's Fair had left its legacy in a
certain elevated cultural tone. It was estimated that at the time of
the Fair, at least one hundred millionaires lived within twenty
blocks of Forest Park. And millionaires lived there still, in rambling,
fin-de-siècle mansions, set in leafy, private streets, hedged with
trespassers-will-be-prosecuted signs. And millionaires, like everybody else in St Louis, could visit the numerous museums in Forest
Park, and the city zoo, free of charge, thanks to the Zoo-Museum
District Tax.

The World's Fair still represented some mythical golden epoch
for St Louis, although the town had grown and prospered for the
following thirty years. It was after the Second World War that the
decline set in, and the exodus from the city began. Twenty miles to
the north of the city, the small town of Clayton was earmarked as
'a suburban growth centre'. It grew homes, shopping malls and its
own business district, decimating the time of the suburban com-
mute. Similar communities grew up around the perimeter of St
Louis, sucking business, and people, out of the city.

By the mid-Sixties, downtown St Louis was in a state of chronic decay. Before the war, the population of the city was 825,000. It was now around 400,000 – although a total of 2.5 million lived in the greater metropolitan area. But now, I was told, St Louis was picking itself up, dusting itself down. New life was being breathed into the city.

Downtown St Louis Inc was an association of businesses and professional firms that had been set up to provide a focal point for selling St Louis to the world. Their offices on Broadway were a model of inner-city regeneration, located in a Twenties office block that had been stripped clean of its dank and gloomy interiors, and refurbished in pristine corporate neutral.

Al Cortopassi, the director of marketing, sketched a graph of downtown St Louis' fortunes: the blossoming industrial years; the post-war decline; the first glimmers of renaissance, beginning in 1965 with the construction of the St Louis Arch. Designed by a Finnish architect, Eero Saarinen, the Arch had 'given people a reason to come back to St Louis', said Al. It was America's tallest national monument, an architectural wonder; something to say you'd seen. And it did look magnificent. You could see it from way off, playing hide and seek among the new skyscrapers, hanging over the skyline like a steel rainbow. The Anheuser-Busch sports stadium was completed in the same year as the Arch, planted next to the old Capitol Building – an act of planning similar to relocating Wembley Stadium beside Westminster Abbey. These had been the catalyst, said Al. And through the Seventies and Eighties, downtown had mushroomed: new office blocks, plazas, the St Louis Centre – trumpeted as 'the largest downtown enclosed shopping mall in the nation' – had been constructed on the back of a raft of tax incentives for property developers.

St Louis had also been the largest recipient of any American city of urban development grants for renovating and gentrifying old housing. 'Rehabbing' had become a buzzword in the city, clawing back from decay areas like Soulard and Lafayette Square, with their handsome brownstones and Victorian frame houses, encouraging young professionals back into the city from the suburbs. These people were called 'urban pioneers' – a euphemism which hinted none too subtly at the view of the inner city as a jungle, fraught with hidden perils.

But now, the expansion had ground to a halt. The tax incentives had dried up. Recession was biting hard. Only one new office block was under construction downtown, and you could take your pick of vacant space. The urban development grants had been abolished; the flood of urban pioneers dried to a trickle. But Al was ever optimistic. From his office on Broadway he continued to issue a steady stream of imprecations and enticements for businesses to forsake suburbia, come back to the city. He handed me a sheaf of promotional material, trumpeting the virtues of a move downtown. Ample office space! Restaurants and cafeterias! 'Increased networking opportunities' (a euphemism for 'bumping into other people on the pavement'). This is what cities had always been. Had people forgotten so soon?

One had the feeling familiar in so many American cities of a place attempting to reverse into the future – and how monumental this task was. How, for example, could you expect to reverse the tyranny of the motor car – with its imperious demands for six-lane freeways through the centre of town, parking lots where once there were houses – without some sort of comprehensive public transport system? The Federal government had earmarked $288 million for a light-railway system in St Louis, but it was years from completion.

Al was reaching for more plans and flow charts. A new indoor stadium, the Kiel Auditorium, would be completed shortly. There were plans for another complex, including a convention centre, a hotel and a football stadium (with a new team to put in it) – all at a cost of $500 million. 'Football is the sizzle, not the steak,' said Al. 'Because football will only use it ten or fifteen times a year. It's the conventioneers we're after. Those 20,000- to 30,000-strong conventions – the Baptist churches, the lawyers, the dentists – the city's got nowhere to put those – yet.'

Conventions and tourism. That was the future, said Al. St Louis was putting its faith in being a meeting place once more. Roll on the United Church of Christ Executives Insurance and Advisory Personnel: the Lions, the Elks, the sundry associations of Lawyers,

Accountants and Chiropractors. Roll on the tourists who wouldn't migrate back to the suburbs each night, but who wanted shops, bars, cinemas, nightclubs – who wanted St Louis' heritage.

God knows, there was enough of that. Like so many towns and cities in America that had grown up intent on obliterating anything with any claim to historicity, St Louis had now, belatedly, recognised that 'heritage' could be profitable. Everywhere one went in the city, there was evidence of heritage-at-work. Photographs from a hundred years ago showed the St Louis waterfront crowded with working steamers: a forest of funnels; people hauling coal and goods; passengers embarking on the three-deck steamers – 'the Mississippi beasts' – which plied the early tourist trade up and down the river. Now the waterfront had been tricked out with wrought-iron street signs, authentic period cobbles and bogus period gift shops. Once upon a time, twenty-two separate railroads converged on St Louis (more than any other American city). But the last train left the Union Station in 1978, and it had now been converted into a hotel and a ritzy shopping mall.

This belated fervour for preservation, for heritage, produced some rather touching, quasi-comical results. Quite ordinary brownstones and warehouses, which had somehow evaded the demolisher's ball, were now regarded as quaint antiquities, architectural landmarks; rows of terraced houses which would go unremarked in an English city were proudly earmarked as 'historical districts'.

'It's private money that's turned this city round,' one man told me. 'Not the city politicians.' The Union Station development, I was told, had been kick-started by a company from New York; without them it would have become just another health hazard. I didn't know how true this was, but the conventional wisdom in neighbour-hood bars was that St Louis was politically hamstrung: Democrats controlled the city; Republicans controlled the county, and they couldn't agree about anything. It was the inability of the two ruling bodies to agree on a site for a new football stadium that had caused the St Louis Cardinals team to desert the city altogether, and move to premises in Phoenix, Arizona – an act of blatant opportunism akin to Arsenal accepting a lucrative offer to decamp to Norwich or Newcastle. 'Well, the money was good and they were greedy, I guess,' one man admitted. 'But that's America. Life looks better somewhere else, so you move on. But,' he added with a chuckle, 'they haven't done shit in Phoenix.'

Ray Hartmann was the founder and editor of *The Riverfront Times*, a weekly news and listing magazine, which you could pick up for nothing in restaurants and bookshops. I liked Ray the moment I walked into his office. It was the untidiest I had seen in America. Most American offices had a preternaturally antiseptic air about them. Hewed to a corporate uniformity, they were zones of strategic self-importance; neat graphs on the wall, no smoking signs, name plates on the desk to remind you to whom you were talking. They seemed designed to repress rather than encourage the personality of whomever inhabited them, to bend them to a preordained role and shape. By comparison, Ray's was an anarchist's playground – a complete tip, with something of the insouciant ambience of a transient flophouse. Newspapers and magazines had been hurled on the floor, to accumulate in dense drifts of newsprint; mountains of papers and documents piled up on his desk, all but burying a battered word-processor. Citations and awards for campaigning journalism hung at precarious angles on the wall, as if they had been thrown there from a distance. One commended Ray for 'speaking up for the little guy'.

Ray was a short man, with a shock of black, unruly hair, and a manner that made it hard for him to settle in one place for long. 'Sit down,' he commanded, sweeping papers off a chair on to the floor. I sat. He stood up. I stood up. He vanished from the office, returned, sat down, stood up again. 'Wanna eat?' We went to 'the Hill', a working-class Italian neighbourhood of fastidious clean streets, freshly painted bungalows and neatly trimmed lawns. Some of them boasted flagpoles, flying the Stars and Stripes. We found a little corner 'mom-'n'-pop' restaurant, with check tablecloths and nostalgic scenes of the Bay of Naples on the walls.

After college Ray had worked as a speechwriter for the Democratic governor of Missouri, Kit Bond. When his parents died, he launched *The Riverfront Times* with his inheritance, as a 'college paper for the real world'. The paper now employed forty-two people. Every major city in America had a newspaper like *The Riverfront Times*. They were the heirs to the legacy of the underground press which had proliferated in the Sixties; alternative newspapers with a haircut, attuned to the preoccupations of the generation that had come of age since the Sixties, with their advertisements for futons, mountain bikes and transcendental meditation courses; their pages of restaurant and rock reviews.

Most were content simply to service the consumer aspirations of their readership. But *The Riverfront Times* had principles, 'to question authority and the assumptions that other media accepted', as Ray put it: 'to question the shape of the table'.

Questioning the shape of the table was not a common preoccupation of mainstream American journalism. America's only national daily, *USA Today* – the journal of hotel breakfast rooms and airport departure lounges – offered no in-depth news or analysis; only easily digestible stories, pie charts of national trends, and the customary glutinous showbusiness gossip. Every city had at least one daily major newspaper, but any kind of rigorous analysis, or criticism, of the status quo was noticeable only by its absence. There were few independent voices, and the parochialism of their news coverage was staggering. Travelling across America, reading newspapers in Memphis and St Louis, it was easy to believe that Europe did not exist at all, so seldom was it mentioned.

St Louis had an honourable newspaper tradition. America's oldest college of journalism was at the University of Missouri in Columbia, and the city's oldest existing newspaper, the *Post-Despatch* (in fact, its only existing newspaper) had been founded, and was still owned by, the Pulitzer family, who inaugurated America's most distinguished journalism and literary prizes. The inability of St Louis to sustain more than one daily newspaper was a microcosm of the history of newspaper publishing in America, an industry which in the last twenty years had been ground down by the process of merger, takeover and closures.

Readership of newspapers in America had declined by two-thirds over the past forty years. The evening newspaper business had been hit hardest, by suburbanisation and the growth of TV news. The migration of the business community to the suburbs, the growth of what were known as 'edge cities', meant a dearth of train-bound commuters into the cities, and there was no margin in shipping evening editions of city news out to the suburbs. In St Louis, the decline of the big city newspapers had been exacerbated by the phenomenon of 'the shoppers' – free-sheets, largely made up of discount soap-powder coupons, given away at shopping malls – and the growth of daily suburban newspapers, concentrating on local news. It was another symptom of how people cared only for what happened on their own doorsteps, another symptom of the atomisation of American life.

The readers of The Riverfront Times, said Ray, were, on average, ten to twelve years younger than readers of the Post-Despatch: it was a paper for the baby-boom generation, people to whom the libertarian concerns of the Sixties perhaps sounded only a distant echo. The Riverfront Times had campaigned on the gamut of liberal concerns: rights to abortion, freedom of speech, drugs use and other civil liberties issues – the issues which the Post-Despatch conspicuously ignored. The revitalisation of downtown had been a matter of contention, the way resources were deployed for boosting commerce at the expense of other needs such as housing and education. But gentrification was one of the things that was saving the city, said Ray – the colonisation of neglected inner-city neighbourhoods by yuppies. The conflicts between the poor, who had always lived in these neighbourhoods, and the wealthier incomers was, Ray admitted, 'one of the hardest issues for us to get a real handle on'. Yuppies, after all, were The Riverfront Times' constituency.

St Louis was a paradoxical city, said Ray, 'a frustrating city in many ways'. Architecturally and culturally, it was a fair mixture of the old and the new. The quality of life was relatively good; the cost of living relatively low. Despite its size, it had retained something of its homely, mid-Western character. The people were friendly. 'Its biggest weakness', said Ray, 'is that like a lot of American cities it hasn't come to grips with its bi-raciality.' The population was approximately 50 per cent white/50 per cent black, but it did not have the political tinderbox tensions of New York, or the apocalyptic gang warfare which afflicted Los Angeles. St Louis had been spared the race riots that had torn apart other American cities in the Sixties and Seventies, but that, said Ray, was due as much to luck as to any accommodation of minorities within the political status quo. 'This city is still in the grip of a white, patriarchal power system. There is no power-sharing here, and it's hurt us. We're about the same size as Atlanta; they've got crime and homelessness too, but they've also got the 1996 Olympics, because they have a strong bi-racial coalition. If you get the white business interests and the black community united you get stuff done. And we can't do that here. There's not that sense of living and working together. It's not just a question of not hating. We've got that in St Louis. It's about working together.'

One day I drove the car out to the outskirts, to plot the geography of the city from the outside in. St Louis unpeeled like a series of skins: the mess of suburbs, built-up agricultural land; then the genteel fringes of Forest Park, and the university campus, with its tarted-up Victorian family dwellings; finally the layer of old warehouses, factories, stockyards and the down-at-heel squalor around Martin Luther King Boulevard, with its meshed and boarded storefronts, its crumbling brownstones, a stingy bar with a crudely etched sign, 'Just Brothers'. Nobody, it seemed, had any plans for gentrification or heritage around here.

I arrived back at Broadway, outside the offices of Downtown St Louis Inc. For all its much-vaunted commercial revival, downtown St Louis still felt curiously bereft of humanity. It was mid-afternoon on a typical working day, yet I counted no more than a dozen people walking in a stretch of two blocks along Broadway. I walked into the St Louis Centre. This was a switch. The geographical imperatives of downtown dictated that shopping malls were usually flung to the furthest reaches of the city. But the St Louis Centre was slap in the middle of downtown, part of the bait to lure people back to the city.

The Centre contained 130 shops, as well as two separate department stores. People milled around listlessly, looking for something to spend their money on. The psychology of shopping malls is different from the psychology of busy streets. The geography implies a moral obligation to buy. Why else would you be there? It's not as if you're passing through on your way somewhere else. Your credit card itches in your pocket like a revolver. The Aqua Tower – a vertical fish tank, 6 feet high, 'perfect for that room corner', suddenly seems a snip at $498. A solitary fish swam in it, like an eccentric piscine Donald Trump. There were eleven shopping malls ringing St Louis and I would have wagered the price of an Aqua Tower that, give or take a few thousand square feet of retail space, they were all pretty much the same; all with a Gap, a Florsheim shoe shop, a Radio Shack, a boutique filled with expensive and useless gifts. I would have bet you couldn't buy a second-hand book, a Swiss Army knife, a dozen screws, or have a kettle or watch repaired in any of them. I went back on to the street and into a small camera shop to buy some film. I was the only customer. 'How's business?' I asked. The girl behind the counter pulled a face. 'Terrible. There's nobody on the sidewalks any more, not since they opened the centre.' The shop, she said, was due to close in a month.

It occurred to me that living here it would be difficult to feel as if you belonged to St Louis, or the city belonged to you. You could call yourself a Londoner, a New Yorker, but a St Louiser? It didn't ring.

I had talked to Al Cortopassi about this feeling of belonging, of civic pride. Some 75 per cent of the population lived in the suburbs: the city itself, its inhabitants, its problems, meant nothing to them. Al agreed that it was a sorry situation. 'People huddle together out in the suburbs; it's real insular. They just drive through places on their way to work. They don't give a thought to the place they're driving through.' I asked Al where he lived. 'Real nice neighbourhood,' he said. 'We've got our own schools authority, our own police force, good neighbours.' And where was this Utopia? Al looked a bit sheepish. 'Out the other side of Clayton,' he said. That was a forty-five minute drive out on the freeway.

I left Al resolving to visit Lecleve's Landing, down by the riverside. I wanted to see something of the new-old St Louis, the city on the rise; the riverfront warehouses and stores that had been converted into restaurants, shops, clubs. A slice of authentic heritage life. It was less than half a mile away, but I took the car. Nobody walked in St Louis. I drove parallel to the river, looking for a right turn under the freeway that would take me to the river's edge: a sign for Lecleve's Landing slipped by. Too late! I took the next right, a slipway on to the freeway; caught up in the rush-hour traffic I was shunted a mile back in the wrong direction, trying to cross lanes, looking for an exit. I hiked right again, doubled back past the baseball stadium, and into a traffic jam. I had read much about Lecleve's Landing in Al's pamphlets. There were plans to link it to the new convention centre with 'walkways', lined with lampposts and trees. It seemed a novel idea: pavements, people walking about. I wondered whether it would ever catch on.

What's made Milwaukee Famous
has made a loser out of me

*It's late
and she is waiting,
And I know I must
go home*

What made Milwaukee famous was beer. But what made Milwaukee nervous was murder. They had caught Jeffrey Dahmer, but they had not yet tried him. But everybody was familiar with the inventory of contents, discovered by the police who searched his apartment on North Twenty-fifth Street, a couple of miles from downtown Milwaukee. There were seven skulls and four heads, three in a free-standing freezer, one in a box in the refrigerator. In the freezer compartment of the fridge, there were assorted body parts. Headless torsos, mutilated pieces of bodies, hands and limbs were found in a 57-gallon barrel, along with a collection of photographs of people in various stages of dismemberment. Dahmer would be charged with thirteen counts of first degree intentional homicide, and two counts of first degree murder; although he would personally confess to having killed seventeen young men.

It was unusual – serial murder is always unusual, of

course, although perhaps not unusual enough – but particularly so for Milwaukee. Things like that didn't happen in places like this. Milwaukee was the eighteenth largest city in America; statistically, it was one of the safest. It made you think twice, knowing about this assemblage of body parts, gruesomely hacked, ghoulishly collated. So close too. You walked the streets half looking over your shoulder, expecting to catch some contamination of madness on the air, to be offered some signifier, some explanation. But, naturally, there was none.

Milwaukee was cold. The winds off Lake Michigan blew down the skyscraper canyons of Wisconsin Avenue and Broadway, sending the litter dancing skittishly along the sidewalks, pinching the faces of passers-by, bandaged in scarfs, hats and winterproof jackets. A band of black boys, teenagers, moved down Grand, shouting and rolling their shoulders, and people moved aside, eyes cast down. Milwaukee was far from being the biggest city in America; it was not the richest, the most industrious, nor the most picturesque. But there were times as I drove around it that it seemed, curiously, the most American. Milwaukee's skyline was a pocket Chicago, a mini-Houston. Driving in at dusk along the south shore, one could see the skyline etched against the cold, red northern sky, see the lights sparkling like diamonds in the skyscraper windows, and one could feel one's spirits lift in anticipation. But the skyline was only a shadow play, a façade. Once you had slipped behind the screen, inside its folds and shadows, the play was only humdrum and mundane after all; the streets all but deserted. Milwaukee's ordinariness was laid bare – a mid-Western city where people worked hard, shopped in malls, went quietly into the night to their surburban homes, and only sometimes thought of murder.

Don Dooley, a former newspaper journalist, took me for a drive. Journalists never retire, and Don now filled his days preparing a newsletter for the Milwaukee Chamber of Commerce, spiced with local news and titbits gleaned from the national wires: 'State Governor Tommy Thompson has signed a bill making it illegal to operate a car whose radio/stereo can be heard 75 or more feet away. We thank the legislature for its mercy and now await enforcement.'

Don was proud of Milwaukee. He steered his car along North Lake Drive, on to Shorewood and White Fish Bay – lyrical names that evoked perfectly the atmospheres of the neighbourhoods to which they belonged: dignified and capacious houses on quiet, wide streets, with their views across the lake, cold and flat in the morning light. It was the view of the city that anybody would have wished to show a visitor: prosperous, orderly, safe.

We circled around and drove in from the north, through the inner city: the familiar landscape of project housing; the food stores with steel-grilles over the window, making them look less like shops than supply depots in a war zone; the litter-strewn scraps of wasteland; the worn faces of the people standing patiently, interminably, at bus-stops. Only the very poor in America did not travel by car, and politicians didn't care about the very poor. They were the least important constituency. In most American cities public transport provision seemed to be somewhere below Third World levels.

Don said nothing as we drove through the slums; one could sense anger and embarrassment in his silence. This was not the Milwaukee he wanted his visitor to see. But every American city had its festering inner core, and Milwaukee's was no worse than most. Such places were a point of national, not local, shame; the permanent reminder – like a grinding toothache – of the failures of capitalist democracy, as surely as the gleaming towers of downtown, a mile away, were the triumphalist symbols of its successes. Driving through such places I always found myself astonished that such abject poverty and such obvious wealth could coexist, astonished that the ghettos did not rise up in anger and unleash a carnage that would make the achievements of Jeffrey Dahmer seem modest by comparison.

'Schlitz – The Beer that Made Milwaukee Famous'. Branco Radicevic brandished the brown beer bottle and read aloud the legend printed on its side, in a typographical script that had passed from commercial currency many years ago. 'Not a bad beer', said Branco, 'for a good city.'

He put the bottle carefully back on the shelf. It came with the building. In an earlier incarnation, the Three Brothers restaurant – proprietor Branco Radicevic – had been a neighbourhood tavern, owned and operated by the Schlitz brewery. A globe advertising Schlitz beer still stood on the roof of the restaurant. It was a listed monument. Beer was Milwaukee's heritage.

Beer, of course, had fuelled countless country songs – drinking it, crying in it, blaming it for your troubles, then slugging back more to drown them out. The 'drinking song' was a country genre all its own, but there was no better example of it than the song which had brought me here, 'What's Made Milwaukee Famous (Has Made A Loser Out Of Me)', which had been a hit for both Jerry Lee Lewis and Rod Stewart.

There was an amusing story behind the song, which its composer Glenn Sutton told me when I spoke to him in Nashville. In 1968, Sutton was working as a staff producer at Columbia Records, but was already enjoying a growing reputation as a songwriter. 'My music publisher, Al Gallico, asked if I could provide a couple of songs for a Jerry Lee Lewis session. I'd put it off and put it off, he was pestering me, and then finally I had a call saying they needed a song for the next day. I said, sure thing. Al said, what's it called? I didn't even have a song at all, let alone a title. I was sitting on a stool in my office, and somebody had left a newspaper on the table; I happened to glance at it, and it was open on a full-page advertisement for Schlitz – The Beer that Made Milwaukee Famous, and so I just said to Al, it's a drinking song called "What's Made Milwaukee Famous". I'd written a lot of drinking songs before then, but I'd never thought of that. So I just went home, wrote it that night and the next day we cut it.'

Jerry Lee Lewis – no slouch himself when it came to drinking – took the song to number two on the American country charts. Rod Stewart made it a hit in the British charts four years later, and the song had become a country music standard, with versions by some twenty different artists. It had even prompted the accolade of an answer version, 'What Made Milwaukee Famous (Has Made A Poor Man Out Of Me)', by George Jones and Sandy Sands.

Sutton's song was a neat summary of the conflict between the bar room and hearth and home.

It's late and she is waiting/And I know I must go home/But every time I start to leave/They play another song/Then someone buys another round/ And whatever drinks are free/What's made Milwaukee famous, has made a loser out of me.

But despite occupying a small niche of country music history, 'What's Made Milwaukee Famous' was not a popular song in Milwaukee itself. Whenever I mentioned it, people either expressed total ignorance (which I found hard to believe), or looked vaguely disapproving, cleared their throats and changed the subject. I hadn't realised a song could cut so deeply to the quick, but the Wisconsin sensibility evidently did not take easily to mockery, reproach, or cheap gags at their expense. They had known too much of it.

Chicago was a mere 70 miles to the south. Milwaukee had suffered from such close proximity to its more urbane and sophisticated neighbour. Chicago had Frank Lloyd Wright architecture, Chagall mosaics, the Chicago Bears, the blues. It had all the vim and zip of a world city. About all that Milwaukee could say for itself was that it was the biggest city in Wisconsin. Wisconsin was the largest cheese-producing state in America; and it was the veal centre of the nation. It was true, people spoke highly of Milwaukee's sausages, but they weren't Frank Lloyd Wright or Chagall. You could see why Milwaukee felt tetchy, defensive, hard done by. The city had an air of dour, plodding industriousness; its people a heavy, literalist manner, devoid of irony. They didn't mock their city, and themselves, in the way New Yorkers (or people from Chicago, come to that) did; it betrayed a lack of confidence, a feeling of inferiority. The only thing Milwaukee people laughed at in themselves was their reputation for stinginess. But even this seemed simply a way to make themselves seem more interesting, more colourful, than they actually were. Everybody I met in Milwaukee was unfailingly hospitable and generous.

Don invited me to join him and a friend for dinner, at the Three Brothers. It was the oldest restaurant in Milwaukee, in the South Shore district of the city. The South Shore had originally been an Italian neighbourhood, and still bore the signs: the tidy streets of row houses, immaculately maintained; the bars and delicatessens with Italian names stencilled over them; above all, the feeling that you could walk there at night without trouble.

The Three Brothers was a Serbian enclave. We ate goulash and drank strong Yugoslav beer, and talked about Milwaukee. And as we were finishing our meal, Branco joined us and ordered a bottle of wine on the house. He was a man of indeterminate age, with a drooping moustache, which lent him a mournful Balkan demeanour, and he wore a beret – one imagined for the benefit of the customers rather than himself.

Branco described himself as a refugee from communism. During the Second World War, he said, his family had been involved in the resistance movement against the Germans. 'What the Nazis did to me and my family did not bother me so much,' he said. 'That was war. As a soldier you accept that more readily than what your own people did. The communists wounded me more, because they were my own people.'

He fled from Yugoslavia in 1956, and travelled to London. In Yugoslavia he had studied law; in London he worked as a tiler – 'You know the Guildhall?', he said proudly. 'I laid those tiles.'

His father had already come to America, settled in Milwaukee. He had bought the restaurant where we now sat when it was a tavern, and renamed it the Three Brothers, as a legacy for his sons. In 1959 Branco came to join him. 'To arrive in a new country,' he said, 'there is always the feeling of the unknown, but for me it was a good feeling – the anticipation of a new life, a better life. Now I feel as if I was always here.

'For me, the experience of living in America has always been beautiful. When I first went to Florida, I was intrigued by Cape Canaveral. I didn't see the signs saying "No entry" and I drove right up to a rocket. I take pictures! And when I came back on the road I realised what I'd done, and I was scared. I saw a soldier and tried to explain to him what I'd done. And do you know what he said to me? 'I hope you liked the rocket, sir. Have a good day, sir!"' Branco smacked his hand delightedly on the table, making the glasses jump and rattle. 'Do you know how different that is from a communist country? Living here nobody has stopped me and asked "where are you going, what are you doing?" Living here I've never feared anything.'

This area, the South Shore, was a good area, he said; one of the best in Milwaukee. 'Do you know?' He poured the last of the wine. 'There has not been one murder in this neighbourhood for as long as I have been here. Not one! If something happen to you on the street, if you yell for help, you would have six guys out helping you. The only neighbourhoods that are good are neighbourhoods where people care for each other. You go anywhere else, you realise this is paradise.'

The German immigrants who arrived in Milwaukee in their thousands in the mid-nineteenth century thought Milwaukee was paradise too. They came among friends. In 1850, two out of three immigrants arriving in the city were from Germany or Austria; Milwaukee had six German-language newspapers, and agents waiting at the harbourside in New York, warning newcomers not to make the fatal mistake of settling in Chicago, where the Irish were.

After the Germans came the Polish, the Czechs, the Slovaks, the Serbs, the Croatians, the Italians, the Ukrainians, some Irish too, and a whole slew of Scandinavians. It was as if the whole of northern Europe had resettled here, jostling for their own piece of turf, carving up Milwaukee into national territory: Poles, Irish, Italian and Serbian on the south side, the Germans on the north. The legacy of these settlements was everywhere. The area of north Milwaukee was still called Germantown, and there was New Berlin to the west. Serb Hall — a working-man's club-cum-community centre, and the hub of the Serbian community — was a mandatory stop for any politician on the stump, somewhere to be photographed slapping backs, guzzling sausages and beer. There were festivals for all of them – all dirndls, polka music and drinking songs. The name of the Mayor of Milwaukee was John Norquist.

These immigrants were hard-working and enterprising. They made farm equipment, heavy goods, machinery. As recently as twenty years ago, Milwaukee had as high a proportion of its working population in manufacturing as any other American city. They thought their homes were their castles. At the turn of the century, it was said that in no other city of its size in the world did so many workers own their own homes. You could see them still in the old working-class neighbourhoods – mile upon mile of neat little wooden bungalows and cottages with gable roofs and clapboard covering.

And they drank like fish. Milwaukee owed its beer industry to the Civil War. At the outbreak of the war, in 1861, there was one tavern for every ninety-three of the town's residents, but the most popular drink was whiskey. The war brought two things: a tax on liquor, driving up the price of whiskey, and an epidemic of hop louse in the Eastern states. Wisconsin was spared, and new markets suddenly opened up for the German brewers of Milwaukee.

The Germans had the expertise, the technique and the names, which sounded as if they were minted to be put on beer bottles: Schlitz, Pabst, Blatz, Gettelman, Miller, and more. The breweries expanded their empires into real estate – hotels, restaurants and taverns. They slugged it out in sponsored beer gardens, and on Milwaukee's street corners: a different brewers' tavern stood at each corner on every crossroads in the working-class districts, squaring off against his rivals. (The practice was stopped at the turn of the century with a ruling that taverns could sell whatever beer they liked; but at crossroads in the older parts of town you can still find a tavern at each corner.)

Pabst opened what was claimed to be the biggest restaurant in the world, Pabst's Harlem, on 8th Avenue in New York, and, allegedly, hired actors to walk in off the street, order a beer and sing out in carrying tones, 'I am drinking the health of Milwaukee's greatest beer brewer, Captain Fred Pabst.'

Pabst might have had the most absurd promotional techniques, but Schlitz remained the biggest and richest of all the Milwaukee brewers. The story goes that when fire ravaged Chicago in the late nineteenth century it was Schlitz that rushed in emergency supplies to the parched Windy City hordes. From then on, the Schlitz bottle carried the tag, 'The Beer that Made Milwaukee Famous'. Schlitz was owned by the Uhlein family, good benefactors to Milwaukee. They inaugurated an annual circus parade (which continues to be held each year, and is the biggest in America) and built the Uhlein Hall, the city's main performance centre. For a while Schlitz was the best-selling beer in America, until it was overtaken by Budweiser in the late Fifties. Schlitz eventually sold out to the Stroh Brewing Company, in Detroit. Stroh still produced a beer called Old Milwaukee.

The biggest brewer in Milwaukee was Miller. One of the smallest was Sprecher. I'd never heard of Sprecher beer before arriving in Milwaukee, but local people said it was the best brewed in the city – a proper ale, brewed not for the mass market, but for the beer connoisseur.

Sprecher had been founded by Randy Sprecher, a tall man in his early forties with unruly hair and a walrus moustache that gave him the weatherbeaten look of a California surfer. Sprecher came from Oregon. He had studied as an oceanographer, then, on a trip to Europe, discovered a taste for German beer. He had returned to college, in California, and graduated in something called 'fermentation studies' with the idea of founding his own brewery. For four years he worked for Pabst in Milwaukee, saving and biding his time. Then he set up shop, in an old warehouse down by the railyards, and built his own business from scratch. Now he employed eighteen people, and brewed nine different kinds of beer.

'People knew me as a real maverick,' said Randy. 'They called me California Dreamer, but I had enough withal to set it up on my own money. I did everything 100 per cent: built it, did all the engineering, brewed the beer to my own recipes, sold it myself out of a truck. It's just a little bootstrap operation, but I put the whole thing together on sweat equity.' *Sweat equity.* It was not a phrase I had heard before, and it conjured up a peculiar whiff of the late Eighties, combining the language of the aerobics work-out and the go-go glamour of Wall Street before the crash.

Randy Sprecher was a traditionalist. He brewed his beer to time-honoured German malt recipes. Mention of America's premium brands – Bud, Miller, Coors – brought a wrinkle of contempt to his face. These were hardly beers at all, he said: they were advertising campaigns, sold with a lot of meaningless pictures of fast cars and scantily clad women. Before Prohibition America had made good, strong beer. But during the Second World War it was watered down, to be shipped to the troops in Europe. Thus the public had been weaned on to the weaker stuff, to 'get them to drink more of less'. Randy spoke of this as though it were a microcosm of the American condition.

'People take beer seriously in Milwaukee,' he said. 'You don't talk unless you've got a bottle of beer in your hand, at the ball game, bowling. If you go fishing you always go with a six-pack or a little schnapps. That's the way it is in Milwaukee. That's why this brewery is successful.'

He walked me around the brewery, tapping the stainless steel cylinders, inviting me to admire his handiwork, pausing to sample a brew, taken with a chew of beef jerky – strips of meat cured to the toughness of shoe leather. The basic techniques of brewing have not changed much in 150 years, and I could see him cast in the mould of a Joseph Schlitz or a Captain Fred Pabst. Randy's forthright, confident and capable manner, the plaques and awards on his wall for brewing competitions and Milwaukee 'Entrepreneur of the Year' reminded me of Ray in St Louis, and the dreams of Eustace back in Chattanooga. Budweiser would produce 90 million barrels of beer that year. Miller around 45 million barrels. Randy Sprecher would produce just 7,000, brewed on sweat equity, and tasting all the better for it.

The Holiday Inn in Milwaukee was like a ghost town. The bar was deserted; the restaurant bereft of custom. If you wanted a cup of coffee after 11 at night you had to cross the street to the Dunkin' Donuts stand, where a bum stood shivering outside the door, begging enough spare change for a coffee and bite from whomever walked through.

I sat in my hotel room, watching the news, taking seismic readings of a nation eroding at the edges, the old certainties called into question, the future confused. A local high school dance had been cancelled, on the grounds that slow-dancing could lead to students being prosecuted under the laws of sexual harassment. The news item rounded up the stock dramatis personae: the students waving banners and chanting in protest; the school principal who had enforced the ban – a clear victim of media, if not sexual, harassment – attempting simultaneously to emphasise the gravity of his decision and show that he was a man who could recognise a ridiculous situation when he was in the middle of one; and the judge who had said the dance could go on, ruling with judicial severity, 'I expect the kids will dance close, but there's nothing wrong with that.'

Something was clearly wrong in a country where even as noble an institution as the high school dance had become a minefield of legal wrangling over what constituted sexual propriety.

Ever since visiting Woodstock I'd been looking for other signs of the legacy of the Sixties, and I supposed this was one of them. The college students who had grown up on campus politics in the Sixties, with its disparate strands of radicalism – embracing feminism, black pride, gay pride and so on – were now members of faculty, leading the assault on the most fundamental cultural assumptions. This was not simply a question of cultural relativism versus cultural absolutism – the Dead White Male argument; not simply a question of whether to teach Shakespeare or Andrea Dworkin in literary class. The consensus of American life had fractured into a myriad of single-issue claims.

The Clarence Thomas case, in which the candidate for the Supreme Court stood accused of sexually harassing a former secretary, had galvanised America, suddenly bringing every aspect of sexual behaviour and representation under renewed scrutiny. To feminists, Thomas' vindication was widely seen as a triumph for the forces of the old chauvinist order, but it was also a symptom of how that order was changing. A television news item reported threats of further legal action against a TV commercial for Old Milwaukee Beer, on the grounds that it challenged sexual discrimination laws by featuring a girl in a bikini. 'America's changed,' said a lawyer. 'These kind of ads won't be seen on television any more. The Clarence Thomas case has changed all that.' You could hear the sound of beer-swilling slobs all over America, scratching their heads and guffawing in disbelief.

These changes were clearly confusing to Americans. One middle-aged businessman told me that he had recently lost his secretary of some ten years' standing, and confessed that he had no idea how to address her replacement. The cosy paternalism which had always sufficed was no longer deemed correct and appropriate. He evinced the wistfulness of a plantation owner lamenting the passing of slavery.

The terminology was confusing. Black people were no longer black at all; instead they had become 'Afro-Americans', or the arch 'men and women of colour'. A similar problem arose with the question of America's original inhabitants. The favoured term was 'native American'. But was the term 'Indian' really so pejorative? As a white middle-class male I could see nothing wrong with it, divine no colonial or imperialist associations. But the debate about nomenclature was first and foremost about a group exercising the right to choose what they would be called, rather than accepting the choice made by others. It was easy to mock these apparently trivial distinctions and stipulations; harder to understand the sensitivities which lay behind them, impossible to pretend that the consequences could not sometimes be quite absurd. In Michigan, a college football team that had been known as the Hurons, after a local Indian tribe, had changed their name to the Eagles so as not to offend Indian people. A member of the Huron tribe had promptly filed a civil liberties suit to have the name changed back.

Milwaukee had taken its name from the Potawatomi Indians; *Manh-a-wauk-ee seepe*, means 'gathering place by the river'. And, like most American cities, given absolutely nothing back to them. There were some 8,000 Indians living in the city itself, but many thousands more scattered on reservations around Wisconsin. They had always been a silent, almost invisible presence. Until, that is, they started running bingo games.

When I first heard of Indian bingo, I assumed it was some kind of joke – a cockamamy way of native Americans keeping themselves amused. But if it was a joke, it was the Indian people who were laughing, all the way to the bank. Indian bingo was among the biggest growth industries in Milwaukee – indeed, throughout America.

The Potawatomi bingo hall did not look like the most valuable piece of real estate in Milwaukee. A huge prefabricated shed, it was set in an area of industrial dereliction, hedged by railway stockyards and the elevated ramp of a six-lane expressway. The shed was dressed up like a Christmas tree in blaring neon and fairy lights. An enormous Stars and Stripes fluttered from a pole. It was 4 in the afternoon – dead time – but the car park was almost full.

Inside, the hall was the size of a football pitch, lined with tables where people sat, watching the numbers flashing up on an electronic scoreboard and frantically scratching at their cards with felt-tip pens. Signs on the tables hinted at their devotion, suggested planning, preparation, the thrill of the outing: the Bingo Buddies; Crazy Thelma; the New Lucky Elephant. Perhaps three-quarters of the congregation were women, of all ages; most looked broad in the beam, dressed in polyester stretch pants, with teased hair, spectacles, sucking on king-sized menthol cigarettes. (This question of weight was a delicate one, but the fact remained: America is a country of overweight people, walking metaphors of its ferocious consumerism, and I saw more fat people in Milwaukee than in any other town or city I visited.)

American Indians, sprucely dressed in white shirts and red waistcoats, strolled up and down the aisles selling lottery cards or jabbering into walkie-talkies ordering food for the customers so they would not have to leave their tables – king-size hot dogs, paper plates heaped with steaming bratwurst, jumbo cartons foaming with diet-Coke.

In an area off to one side, more people were feeding coins into pull-tab machines. A display of clocks artfully suggested membership of an exclusive clique of gaming clubs around the world: Caesar's Palace, Las Vegas; the Taj Mahal, Atlantic City; Loew's

Hotel, Monte Carlo; Potawatomi Bingo, Milwaukee. There were long queues at the smoke-shop. Regarded elsewhere with the same suspicion and disdain as wife-battering or child molestation, here smoking was a vice regarded with a piteous indulgence, if not to say actively encouraged.

The roots of Indian bingo lay in a general move by Indian tribes, after generations of apathy and indifference, to invoke treaty rights, sometimes going back centuries, which were made in return for Indian territory. There were some 800 separate treaties negotiated between the American government and various Indian tribes. It was estimated that as many as 400 had never been honoured.

In Wisconsin, this had led to Indian tribes invoking traditional spear-fishing rights that had been ignored for years, after two Indians were arrested for spear-fishing on a lake in Northern Wisconsin in 1983. The Indians contested the case in court under the old treaties, and the charges were dropped. Suddenly, it was open season. This had caused some resentment among other fisher-men, limited to fishing at certain times, and used to having the best of the catch to themselves. The traditional Indian method of spear-fishing, it was argued, was to use a rowing boat and a flaming torch to attract the fish: nowadays, the Indians used high-powered electric torches; they fished over the statutory bag limits, taking more than they needed and selling the rest. Sour grapes turned to violence. Indians had been attacked on the lakes by other fishermen; and high-powered boats had been used to scare the fish away.

Fishing was one thing. But bingo quite another. The Indian gaming industry owed its existence to the peculiar status that Indian tribes have traditionally held under American law. This views them as 'dependant sovereigns', effectively giving tribes equal status with State government. This meant that while states had complete criminal jurisdiction over the tribes, only Federal law had civil jurisdiction.

The Seminole tribe in Florida became the first to test the implica-tions of 'sovereign status' on gambling in 1979 when, with the aid of a shrewd lawyer, they won the right to open a high-stakes bingo hall on their reservation, free of any controls by the State of Florida.

The Supreme Court ruling laid down that if a game is permissible in a state, no matter what the restrictions laid down by State law, the Indians had the right to carry on the same game unrestricted. Under the Indian Gaming Regulatory Act, tribes could operate bingo games without any state interference. In an attempt to mollify state authorities, however (and in acknowledgement of their theoretical equal status with the tribes), the law stipulated that permission to run 'high-risk' gambling operations – casinos offering roulette, black jack and so on – was reliant on tribes negotiating an agreement, or compact, with the state.

Once the floodgates opened, there was hardly an Indian tribe in America that hadn't found itself a fancy lawyer and a syndicate of local businessmen willing to foot the start-up costs in return for a cut of the profits, and turned the reservation into a bingo hall or gambling casino. Indian gaming was still in its infancy – a poker game of local laws and regulations played out by judges, commissioners, governors, members of tribal councils and lawyers (lots of lawyers) – but already some economists were describing it as the fastest-growing industry in the world: from point zero to billions of dollars of wagers per year in just twelve years.

The success of the industry inflamed old arguments about gambling and the agonising dilemma it had always presented between two fundamental and apparently contradictory traits in the American character: moral probity and the search for the big buck. Outlawed at the turn of the century, gambling had slowly come back into American life during the Depression, with the introduction of racetracks and the legalisation of casinos in Nevada. This piecemeal legalisation in certain states had always seemed sufficient to assuage the American enthusiasm for gambling. Las Vegas, Lake Tahoe and, on the East Coast, Atlantic City had been places of pilgrimage for those with a hunger for throwing away good money after bad: Las Vegas, in particular, in its combination of specious glamour, glitter and greed, was as much a symbol of the American experience as the Statue of Liberty, the Hollywood sign or the Mount Rushmore carvings.

It was the introduction of state lotteries, as a way of raising funds to subsidise state programmes – a morally justifiable excuse for a flutter – which finally broke the back of puritan resistance to gambling. New Hampshire was the first state to introduce a lottery, in 1964. By 1991, state lotteries were selling more than $20 billion worth of tickets, more than the combined receipts of all the cinemas and record stores in America.

Gambling was not illegal in Wisconsin, but it was strictly controlled. The state ran its own lottery, and allowed dog-racing. Bingo had always been legal, but only on a non-profit basis, and with a maximum payout of $1,000. Until Indian bingo came along, the main bingo players in Wisconsin were the Catholic church. Games played in draughty church halls were an invaluable source of church income, particularly for inner-city parishes with declining congregations. But these were strictly nickle-and-dime affairs. Indian bingo, with its no-limit games, had blown the church hall game apart. In Wisconsin all eleven tribal governments operated high-stake bingo halls, or had negotiated pacts with the state to run slot-machine and casino operations.

There was some glorious poetic justice at work here. After years of being downtrodden, deceived, driven from their homelands, consigned to the most lowly and menial station in American life – their old hunting grounds now paved over with shopping malls, freeways and Exxon service stations – the Indians had finally taken their revenge in the way America understood best. They were getting rich. And the motherlode was bingo. The badlands of the reservations had turned out to be gold mines after all. The Seminole Indians of Florida, who had started the ball rolling in the first place, had gone from the welfare line to building up stock portfolios in cattle ranches and hotels.

'What you're looking at here', said John Burke, 'is the new buffalo.' Burke was the director of Omni Bingo, joint partners with the Potawatomi tribe in the Milwaukee bingo hall. Seated in his upstairs office, with a view down on to the floor, crowded with fat ladies in polyester suits scratching away at score cards, Burke seemed an improbable spokesman for the Indian cause: a dry-mannered, well-manicured man in his early fifties, dressed in a cashmere sports jacket, gold-rimmed spectacles dangling from a chain around his neck.

Burke had been in the real estate business – 'I didn't even know what a bingo card *was* three years ago' – until he was approached to lead a consortium to set up and manage the business on behalf of the Potawatomi tribe. Omni had provided $3 million to build the hall, the expertise and the management, in return for 40 per cent of the profits. The remaining 60 per cent was divided between the Potawatomi reservation, upstate in Forest Hills, and an Indian community school in the city of Milwaukee.

This, he said, was 'one of the largest, most technologically advanced, high-stakes bingo halls in the world', playing thirty-five different in-house games, with payouts of up to $30,000 each. Every night, the hall was linked by satellite with fifty other bingo halls on reservations across America, to play Megabingo, with a $1 million pay-out.

'Gambling is the best thing to happen to the Indian people in the last hundred years,' said Burke. It had given the Indians the first opportunity they'd ever had for economic self-sufficiency; it had attracted capital to the reservations, so that Indians could start their own businesses. And it had benefited the community at large, taking Indians off the unemployment and welfare lines. About 80 per cent of the jobs in the bingo hall had gone to unemployed Indians either from Milwaukee, or living on remote reservations where work was scarce.

Another tribal reservation in northern Wisconsin, the Menominee Nation, had become virtually self-sufficient on the proceeds of gambling, Burke said. It had funded health programmes and a sheriff's department. The Potawatomi casino, on a reservation at Carter, 180 miles from Milwaukee, had subsidised housing and education programmes. 'And we're sitting on a gold mine here,' he said. 'There's 1.6 million people in Milwaukee, and they're all potential bingo players.' And then there were the coach parties from out-of-town. On weekends there were so many people coming up from Chicago for all-day bingo marathons that the hall had to reserve spaces for locals.

'It's like some beautiful cosmic joke,' said Burke. 'One American city has even approached a local tribe to take over their civic auditorium, and give it reservation status, so that part of it can be turned into a casino to raise money. Suddenly everybody wants to be friends with the Indians.'

Talking to Burke – the cashmere jacket, the gold-rimmed spectacles, the air of cultured affluence – it occurred to me that the Indians weren't the only people profiting from exploiting their sovereign status. The leader columns of the *Milwaukee Journal* asked querulous questions about the gambling 'sickness' afflicting Wisconsin, and particularly about the involvement of outside interests in Indian gaming – the old argument, as one local columnist had it, of it taking white men getting rich for Indians to get by.

The Catholic church too were unsure whether to regard Indian bingo as a blessing or a curse. Church hall bingo was virtually all that kept the poorer parishes alive, Father Ralph Gross, of the Archdiocese of Milwaukee, told me. Since the arrival of Potawatomi bingo, the parishes had experienced a drop in bingo revenues of up to 40 per cent. Potawatomi bingo had negotiated with the city to put up a fund of $100,000 a year over twenty years, to defray the losses of charitable games. But Father Gross estimated that Indian bingo could be costing the Catholic community up to $250,000 a year. 'The parishes are going to have to face losing income,' he sighed. 'The choice is either to close the schools, or build up the idea of tithing among parishioners.

'It's a vexed question. We weren't happy to see Indian bingo move into our area in one way, but we didn't oppose it because we felt the Indian people needed it. They still say that after the novelty wears off, people will return to the parishes, but that hasn't happened so far.' And nor, his tone suggested, did he ever think it would. The revenge for hundreds of years of missionary work was hard to swallow.

The next day I drove up to the Indian Community School, to meet its chairwoman, Loretta Ford. The school was situated in a down-at-heel neighbourhood in the north of the city, on a street of old wooden framehouses, that had clearly once aspired to respectability but had long since fallen into neglect. A sign on the school fence read: Indian Community School; Siggenauk Interfaith Spiritual Centre; Great Spirit Parish; Indian Council of the Elderly – and, below, in big letters, Drug Free Zone. A group of young blacks, lounging on the street corner, scrutinised me carefully as I parked the car and walked through the gates.

The school offices were in a former Lutheran college, a sprawling collection of gloomy, brownstone Victorian buildings, many with their windows boarded, and steel shutters on the doors. The classrooms were housed in a more modern extension on the other side of the street. I was shown upstairs to Loretta Ford's office, a draughty room with old metal office furniture which looked as if it had been purchased third or fourth hand.

Loretta Ford was a middle-aged woman, dressed in jeans, sweatshirt, an old jacket. I imagined she would once have been very beautiful, but you could read hard times in her face. Beneath her apparently quiet, self-effacing manner, one sensed both suspicion and toughness: Ford was a survivor.

The history of the Indian Community School, she said, was one of constant struggle against financial hardship and the indifference of federal and local government. Despite the number of Indians living in Milwaukee, the local education system had always ignored Indian culture and history. 'Traditionally, native Americans are not aggressive; they take what comes along, move with the flow. If they don't like something in the city they go back to the reservation. So parents, instead of trying to fight the system to change it, decided to teach their children themselves.'

The first school, which opened in 1971, was in an old coastguard station on the harbour. (Under the old treaties, any Federal property that is abandoned by the government can be claimed by its original owners – in this case, the Indians.) It had then been relocated in an abandoned city school, but closed down in 1983 after the Reagan government cut Federal funding for Indian programmes. Ironically, given the bingo wars, it was a Catholic foundation, which had originally helped them to move to their present site, enabling them to open the school once again.

'The native American people in Milwaukee have been almost one of the most invisible people in all history,' said Loretta. 'Until we started this school, nobody knew there were even Indians in the city. When we first started talking to them they didn't know what committee to put us under; they'd never dealt with Indians officially before. They had no knowledge of tribal law or treaties, so they had to get a lawyer to come from Boston to deal with our attorneys. This was the first time that a major battle was won by us being aggressive and demanding our rights.'

Loretta was an Ojibwe Indian. She had been born on the Bad River reservation in Northern Wisconsin. 'It's called that because every year the river would overflow and flood the reservation.' It was one of the largest reservations in the state, perhaps 5,000 people living there in all. 'And very poor,' Loretta said. 'There were no jobs, no economic development. Like I say, the Indian people aren't aggressive. They take what's handed out to them, and that's not much.' Loretta's mother and father had never married. Her mother was the breadwinner, and it was hard for her to find work on the reservation, so she moved the family to Milwaukee in search of work when Loretta was twelve.

'Oh, the city!' Loretta remembered with a laugh. 'I didn't like coming to the city after the reservation. As young as I was I remember feeling different, that we were not as good as other people. We used to go into a big department store, called Shuster's – never to buy, just to look around – and I used always to feel real dirty because I was brown-skinned. I'd think, how come all these people look so clean and white!

'At junior high school I was very quiet, introverted; I never had friends. I remember one time I didn't do my homework and the teacher asked why, and I said I'd been to dance practice, because we'd do Indian dancing at home, and she made a big, loud thing about "what is dance practice?" And when I explained it was Indian dance she made fun of me in front of all my classmates. I'll never forget that. I was fourteen.

'Another thing I remember, one of our social studies teachers told us that there was no rice growing in the United States. I raised my hand. For a long time she didn't call on me, because I was so quiet usually. And eventually I said, we have rice on the reservation, wild rice. And she called me a liar. There is no rice, she said. But I knew.

'So those little things . . . Terms that were always used. "Why are you running down the hall like a herd of wild Indians?" Why I remember these things is that they really hurt me deeply when I was young.'

She had no expectations growing up, she said. No dreams. 'I was always like a shadow. I was just there.' She had graduated from high school behind the rest of the class, then taken factory work, on an assembly line putting screws in boxes, in a shoe factory – low-paying work. Then, at the age of twenty-nine, her life changed. Her partner of twelve years walked out, leaving her with three children to look after. She went back to college, and in going back was reawakened to her 'Native American-ness'. She had gone back to the reservation, become involved in the American Indian Movement, attended the pow-wows (the social gatherings) of her mother, and relearned the traditional Indian dances she had forgotten as a child. She had worked with the Indian elderly for two years, and in a day-care centre for another five.

She had never graduated from college, so had none of the professional or academic qualifications you might have expected of the chairman of a school board. But she had something more useful. She was an Indian, and she was committed. The school had been built on that, she said. The education system did not produce teachers of Native American cultural studies, nor of the old Indian ways. So the Indians had to learn themselves how to become teachers of their own people.

I couldn't help but admire Loretta Ford with her quiet, shy dignity and the way she had reached into her past to make some sense of her life and find the stamina and commitment to go on. I kept being reminded of this across America: the power of self-motivation, but also of the motivation that comes through a community struggling to assert itself.

That morning I had watched another item on the television

news, about how the recession was biting into the hitherto protected areas of corporate life. How could white-collar workers cope with the new uncertainties of office life? A psychologist, pressed for an expert opinion, invoked the law of the jungle: look after number one.

Loretta smiled ruefully when I told her about this. There weren't a whole bunch of Indians in corporate life, she said. 'But there are Indian people who have that attitude. That's been the greatest loss, but I have seen a resurgence of Native American people going back to their own tradition. Once they go through this hard line and make something of themselves, they go back, be it to the reservations or the pow-wows. They feel more comfortable there. But it's also a question that as a lot of true Indian history is coming to light, so you take more pride in being Indian, so you tend to expose yourself to being Indian. You've got people in professional occupations coming out now and saying, "I'm Indian, and I'm proud of it".

'People's views are changing. All these groups fighting for ecology, they want to go back to the Indian ways using Mother Earth for their daily needs, but not abusing it. People are starting to realise the old Indian ways aren't so bad.'

And now, I said, the new Indian ways were running gambling casinos and bingo halls. What did she think of that? It had saved the school, she said flatly. In eight months they had been able to clear debts of $2.5 million.

But did she have moral qualms about taking money from gambling? Or fears that it would rob the Indian people of a dignity they had only recently rediscovered? It was a white man's question, and she answered indulgently.

'I have no qualms. The school was struggling to survive. So many times we've been close to closing because we didn't have any financial support. During those years, no one came and offered us help, or premises. During that time the children had to do without books, furniture, teachers.

'With gaming, Indian people now have the opportunity to use it in their best interests while it lasts, because it will not last for ever. So Indians should take from it, build up something for the time when it's not there.'

Loretta walked me over to the school, out past the shuttered buildings and the watchful black boys on the corner. Children were playing on a grassy area outside the school building, watched by a security guard. The guard was necessary, said Loretta: this was an area of high crime, prostitution and drug-dealing, and the children had been approached and threatened.

The school had a hundred pupils, aged between six and eleven, and from a number of different tribes. They were taught the standard curriculum, but also Indian history and culture and traditional Indian skills – bead-work and braiding, making shawls, moccasins, headdresses and dancing costumes – and the importance of spirituality, the concept of the creator and the use of tobacco, sage and cedar in ceremonies. A sweat lodge had been set up in the grounds for those old enough to do 'sweats', communing with ancestors. 'That ground is sacred,' said Loretta; 'and the spirits gave Mr Walking Elk the authority to run the sweats.'

The Indian languages were taught by elders, fitfully because it was hard to find people who could still speak them. Loretta was learning her native language, Ojibwe, for the first time: not only new words, but new concepts. The Ojibwe word for Saturday has thirty letters and translates literally as 'scrub day'. The word for earth translates as 'grandmother'.

There was an informal, but purposeful air about the school. The classrooms were brightly decorated with posters urging a sense of native pride and identity. Loretta introduced me to Mitch Walking Elk – 'our cultural studies teacher' – a tall, powerfully built man of forty, dressed in jeans, with his hair braided in a pony tail. He had an awkward, serious manner, a man who weighed his words carefully before speaking.

The school was closing for the day, but Mitch invited me back to his home for dinner. He lived in the south side of Milwaukee, in an area that had once been predominantly Polish, but in recent years had become progressively Latino. He shared an apartment with his girlfriend, her sister and the sister's nine-year-old son, Daryl. We spooned out chilli from a huge pot on the kitchen table, while Daryl sprawled on the floor playing a video game hooked up to an old black and white TV set.

Mitch was a Cheyenne on his father's side, Arapaho and Hopi on his mother's. His grandmother was born in 1892. 'She knew about Indian things,' he said, 'but she was a nurse. She believed in the Bible.'

He was born on a reservation in Oklahoma. He never knew his father, and his mother lived on welfare. At the age of seven Mitch was sent to an Indian boarding school – 'a place', he said, 'where children would be taken from the Indian reservations to be made like Americans.' Many children stayed in these schools a long time, he said, and that was one of the reasons for the major breakdown in Indian family life.

A place then that discouraged Indian ways? 'There was nothing. No one ever said to me what I say to the kids at school – this is your history, this is your heritage, these are your ways and a lot of people died for them.

'They taught us to a lower standard than a public school, I believe that. The way I look at it, it was like a government plot to keep us from becoming doctors and lawyers and all those successes the other world enjoys.

'From my perspective it wasn't that much different from prison, where I wound up later. The difference was this; in prison, they kill you; in boarding school they make you wish you were dead.'

These were bitter words, but said without bitterness, rather in a matter-of-fact way as if Mitch had learned to put a lid on his emotions. At the age of nine, he said, he started running away from school. He was expelled; put in an orphanage in an attempt to control him; he ran away again; was put in a state training school for burglary and drinking, then state reformatory for violating a suspended sentence and stealing a car. By the time he was twenty-seven, he was in a state penitentiary serving time for four armed robberies.

In 1970, he and three other inmates broke out of jail. On the run, in Arizona he was sheltered by a radical organisation called the John Brown Party, which had links with the Black Panthers and another militant group, Prairie Fire. 'There was a woman there who was hiding us out and she said, "You're in a lot of trouble and maybe part of it is your fault but part of it is this government and its treatment of your people." I never forgot that.'

He was recaptured after six months, but the experience had changed him. In prison he started studying, talking, 'remembering some of the things that Grandma said.'

He was released from prison in 1975, and started rediscovering his Indian heritage. This took a long time, he said. He was drinking and taking drugs; but reconnecting with his Indian ways, taking part in the sun dance rituals – this began to change him. 'The way I look at it, the spirits finally started showing me what I was messing with.' The spirits, his ancestors, brought him back home, he believed.

'When you start out on a spiritual life you acquire spiritual tools, but you've got to respect those tools. You acquire those through different people; you have an older person takes an interest, likes what you're trying to do, and teaches you what they know. They might give you information, or a physical object that contains power, like a feather or something like that. That's a symbol of not just power, but purity.'

He had been given an object like that, but it didn't do to talk too much about these things, he said. They were sacred, and only Indians properly understood them. There was nothing reproachful in his tone as he said this, but it was emphatic in its distance.

Now there was more respect for Indian ways among white people – some white people. But they were Indian ways. There was the new men's movement, with white people running sweat lodges and talking about things they didn't properly understand. This was not good. Indian ways were for Indians.

In reformatory, Mitch said, he had learned two useful things: how to type and how to play the guitar. Released from prison, he started writing songs, performing. He was a modest success playing in coffee houses and at festivals; he had even recorded a couple of albums on small, local labels. I asked if I could hear his songs, and we went upstairs to the room he shared with his girlfriend. A poster on the wall marked the 500th anniversary of Christopher

Columbus' discovery of America. '1492–1992: Five Hundred Years of Occupation. No Cause For Celebration.'

Mitch fished in his wardrobe for the tapes and played me a couple of songs. It was laid-back rock in a southern style; powerful songs about drug abuse, urban violence, Indian life. Heard in isolation they would have struck one as naive agitprop; in the context of Mitch's life story they seemed uncommonly touching.

All of this – his story, his songs, his manner – combined to give the impression of someone who had been reborn. I was struck by the similarity of his story and Loretta's, how two lives had been given meaning by the rediscovery of their 'Indian-ness'. Mitch said the first part of his story was not uncommon and that there were plenty of Indians lost in alcohol, drugs and crime. But perhaps the second part was.

'By rights I should be a dead man, or certainly still in prison. The Oklahoma prison system had me filed as a habitual criminal; they never thought I'd change. But fortunately for me they are not the big boss. They have some control and power, but not the final word. The decision-maker wasn't ready to write me off. The important thing I have to keep doing is to use my mind.

'In some respects there's still a lot of the old me in there. But we all got a purpose in life, and we've got to find that. I know that all of the things I've been through – the ceremonies, the blood, sweat and tears – have been not just for myself but so I can do work for the school and the community.'

These words, which might have smacked of piety, were said with a quiet, almost bashful intensity and one was struck again by Mitch Walking Elk's dignity.

He never expected to become a teacher, he said. He had no academic qualifications; he had been working in a drug and alcohol treatment centre, involved with the Indian movement, when the opportunity to teach presented itself. 'It's the most important thing for me. We're losing a lot of our young people. When you're young, your five senses are really intense, and the world that appeals to those senses is very strong. So a lot of our young people would rather pay attention to that than what is theirs. We've got the real young kids at school, before those other things come into their lives; we have the opportunity to put all the significant, traditional Indian things into their minds first. They're wide open. You can take them in there before the door slams shut.'

That was what he wanted to teach them, he said: to be proud of what they were. The old ways were some immunity to the corrosion of the spirit which modern life carried with it.

'I hate it here, hate the city,' said Mitch. 'Every night you hear fighting in the alley around here. You wake up in the morning and the first thing you hear on the news is that somebody's been raped, somebody's been murdered. It's a sickness.'

When it was time to leave, Mitch said he would walk me to my car, just to be sure. I said there was no need. No problem, he insisted; he was going out anyway, to collect a video. We walked outside and down the street to where I was parked. I got in the car and fumbled with my ignition, and when I looked up, expecting to see Mitch climbing into his car, he was turning back into his apartment, his custodial duties discharged.

The American Bowling Congress was in Milwaukee. The Bowling Hall of Fame used to be in the city, but had been relocated to St Louis, where they figured they'd get more visitors. This said a lot about Milwaukee. After beer drinking, ten-pin bowling was the most popular participatory sport in the city. Milwaukee had the boring paperwork, but all the glamour and the profits had gone somewhere else.

'The Bowling Game' was one of the most popular television programmes in the city. For seventeen years it had been broadcast three times a week on a local station, TV–58, from a purpose-built studio in the Red Carpet Regency Lanes, in the northern suburbs of Milwaukee. This was serious bowling country. I drove 5 miles up the freeway, then took a left turn, which took me through mile after mile of suburb: flat, featureless, identical – a yawning, interminable strip of filling stations, car dealers, fast-food outlets, neat little bungalows and clapboard houses set off from the road. I passed three other bowling alleys before finding the Red Carpet

Regency, set on a fourway junction, opposite a 76 service station and a Dunkin' Donuts. The Red Carpet Regency was a Taj Mahal of ten-pin bowling; fifty-eight separate lanes with a further four partitioned off from the public for use as the TV studio.

The programme's host was Lee Rothman, a man in his early sixties – a TV face, freshly shaved and toned; a good head of silvery hair, gentle eyes, blinking from behind steel-rimmed spectacles, a nicotine burr of a voice. He wore a light brown presenter's blazer. He shook my hand firmly and introduced me to his co-presenter, Tom Kohl, who wore an identical brown blazer. In an earlier life, Lee had been a newspaper reporter, and the wake-up DJ on a top-forty station, WRIT, in which capacity he had introduced the Rolling Stones on stage in the Milwaukee Arena when they first played the town in 1965. He had been presenting 'The Bowling Game' since it started, and enjoyed a thriving sideline doing voice-overs for television commercials. He had also worked in movies, he said – narrating a film for the State Department, advising embassy staff throughout the world on the correct procedure for handling deceased Americans.

'The Bowling Game' was utterly artless. A knock-out competition in which local teams bowled for spot prizes and a chance in the play-offs. 'It's like Andy Warhol said,' Lee smiled. 'Everybody gets their fifteen minutes, and for the people who come on here, this is it.'

Tonight, fame was knocking for the team from Bagley's Menswear; the Schrubbe Carpet Gals; FM Builders and the guys from A–Z Tool Rental. The winner of each game won $25, and there were supplementary prizes provided by sponsors – gift vouchers for Ritter's Inn; a ten-movie video rental; a haircut at the Lion's Den, and a dip in the 'Barrel O' Fun', filled with party packs of potato chips and pretzels. 'Bowling Buddies' out in TV land sent in cards to be paired with the competitors'.

The mood was self-consciously gladiatorial. After each ball the player would walk along the line of their own team, and the opposition, slapping palms like football players who had just scored a touchdown. After a while you could see that this ritual grew tiresome even to the player concerned, but everyone kept doing it. It would have seemed churlish not to.

The spectators sat on raised tiers at the back; the familiar fat women, straining in blue jeans or stretch pants; their menfolk, curiously, thinner, some of them almost emaciated by comparison – working men with weary expressions and a machine-room pallor. One elderly man wore a baseball cap saying 'Best Grandpa in the World'. They shouted encouragement as the players readied themselves to bowl, and applauded dutifully after each frame.

It was a TV show, but it had something of the intimacy and sense of community of a church social, with its prizes that were hardly prizes at all, Lee and Tom's good-neighbour hamming, its mood of cosy conviviality. For bowling was, above all, a social event and – deliberately or not – the producers of 'The Bowling Game' had struck exactly the tone of modest community endeavour which would appeal in the homes of Milwaukee.

The names of the bowlers seemed so particular to Milwaukee, so redolent of the history and the cadences of the city, that I wrote them down. Trina Schrubbe; Ed Filor; Janie Klinky; Dottie Glatz; Lorelei Miller; Gordy and Donna Custer. Gordy Custer had a presence – the bowling shirt, the wrist straps, a certain way of carrying himself as he weighed the ball in his hand, sought an angle of trajectory and delivered it down the lane – which distinguished him from the other competitors. He had been rewarded with a $20 haircut from the Lion's Den, a Henry's Salad Dressing variety pack and a bag of gourmet popcorn from the Barrel O' Fun.

Gordy told me he came from 'a big bowling family'; his mother, his brother and four sisters all bowled. Gordy bowled four or five nights a week in open tournaments and local leagues. 'In this city, if you don't live within 2 or 3 miles of a bowling lane, there's something wrong with you.'

I asked how he and Donna had met. 'It was at the Red Carpet Lanes, Silver Spring,' Gordy said. 'I was just practising and she came over and asked if she could mark score for me, so she did. That was eleven and a half years ago.' Calling up the memory, they smiled at each other, and I could imagine the scene. The young gladiator, stoically working on his craft: Donna, off to one side, watching and summonsing the courage to talk to him.

Their daughter Kandace, who was four, bowled in 'Bumper Bowl' – on a special cushioned lane for kids, 'to teach the basics of the game and to have courtesy for the other bowler', said Gordy – and two-year-old Wayne would do the same as soon as he was old enough to pick up a ball.

I arranged to go bowling with Gordy and his Wednesday night team, Gary's Glass Services, and the following evening I again took the freeway north into the suburbs. The Custers lived in a small, rented house, the sort of jerry-built property you would find on an estate in Birmingham or Coventry. Not old, but already tired.

Donna answered the door in her housecoat and a pair of fluffy slippers. The house was small, and chaotic. The furniture had a hand-me-down look. Clothes and children's toys were scattered on the floor. A country music tape was playing. Gordy was upstairs shaving, showering, putting on a fresh shirt. Donna and I talked while the two children ran around upturning toys. She told me about her family and friends – a catalogue of hardship, unhappiness and trouble; an eighteen-year-old cousin who was in and out of jail and wouldn't work; a supporting cast of young children who were nothing but trouble. All this gave her resolve, she said, to make her own family life safe and secure.

Donna worked in wholesale distribution for a local department store. Normally she was at work at 8 o'clock each morning. But now, with the holiday season coming up, she was expected to be there at 6 a.m. Gordy worked a ten-hour day, driving a truck for an auto-parts firm. They were keeping things together, Donna said.

I asked her about the neighbourhood. It wasn't good, she admitted, but it wasn't that bad. There were a lot of kids running wild, and gangs that controlled the blocks. 'I used to go with a biker, he was a member of the Outlaw gang, but he always kept me separate from that, thank God. It used to be with bikers that raping someone was an initiation. But now it's killing someone.' She said this in a flat, matter-of-fact sort of way, so there was nothing to say in reply, but to shake my head and make the murmurs of horror and sympathy that seemed to have become my lot in the conversation. And anyway, now Gordy was coming down the stairs, spruced up in a clean bowling shirt, with that 'okay, we're set, let's go' kind of air.

We stopped at a filling station for Gordy to buy his evening's supply of smokes – three packs of Merits. On the way, he told me about his life. He was born and grew up in Milwaukee, in a working-class neighbourhood – 'behind the Silver Spring Lanes' – his father of French descent, his mother German-Irish: an unremarkable upbringing, he said. 'What did I want to be? I wanted to be a policeman or fireman. I never looked at being a doctor or lawyer; where I grew up, that never seemed to fit.' His job was a job, that's all. Between him driving a truck and Donna working they were doing okay, but it was a struggle. 'And now you've got this damn recession. If they hadn't opened their mouths to begin with we wouldn't even have a recession. As soon as Bush mentioned the word it gives everybody a reason to put their prices up.'

The main things in his life, he said, were his family and bowling. Gordy had it figured. He might spend $50 on playing – lane fees, playing 'pot' games, where each player put money on the table and the winner took all – but he made $80 a week easy, sometimes $100.

Gordy knew he was good; good enough to go professional. That was what he dreamed about. Winning just one big pro tournament a season could net you $30,000; sponsorship was worth an extra $20 to $30,000. There were fifty or sixty 'pro tourers' pulling down more than $100,000 a year. And Gordy wanted to be one of them. What was needed to qualify was a 190 or better average on two different lanes. Gordy was better than that. Last year he had averaged 225 at the Red Carpet Bolero, and 215 at Dempsters. On his right hand, he wore two rings, American Bowling Congress Awards – ersatz ruby for a 300 (the highest possible score), midnight blue for a 299.

As Gordy spoke about this, you could see him measuring his future in his mind's eye, like a new suit, and liking the fit. And when we arrived at the All Star Lanes he walked in with a strut that suggested he was walking into a national tournee, not a Wednesday night, nickle-and-dime local leaguer – Gary's Glass Services against Hoffman Printers.

The guys were gathered round the table at the top of the lane, glugging beer and slinging down practice shots. Gary, who owned Gary's Glass Services; Al, a retired printer, eighty years of age, and still bowling; Jerry, a high-school teacher; and Dick, who ran an animal crematorium. Wise guys.

Above the lanes were TV screens, tuned to CSN – the cable sports channel: giants moved silently around a baseball court, leaping for a basket, while the ten pins scattered noisily below. On the neighbouring lane, the team from Hoffman Printers were greeted with cursory nods, and the game started without fanfare. As the balls rattled down the lanes it became apparent that the match was actually almost incidental; all the effort and attention seemed to be concentrated on a series of smaller, private games going on within the larger one – side-bets for dollar bills, or who should buy the next round of beers. These games had their own language – 'in the hole', and 'sticking him one'. 'Call that a bowl?' someone hooted when Jerry shot a seven. 'We should stick 'im; you lighten his wallet, he'd get serious. You can't bowl, you gotta buy, right?'

Whenever someone got 'in the hole', the others would strike up a song: 'Hooray for Dick/Hooray at last/Hooray for Dick/He's a horse's arse.' Catching the spirit, other people on the neighbouring lanes joined in, waving their beer glasses as if they were auditioning for *The Student Prince*. And all the while, the bantering, the wisecracking, the put-downs. 'You strike out? You're luckier than a two-peckered billy goat.'

'Are you trying to see how close you can bowl to the gutter out there, or are you just testing my pacemaker?'

'I thought you were gonna move to Montana, where the men are men and the sheep are nervous.'

Everybody had their part to play in this, a series of character roles polished over weeks of Wednesday nights. Gary, the sponsor – 'they only let me play because I provide the shirts'; Al, the veteran, and butt of ageist gags. Jerry, quietly scooping the dollar bills into his top shirt pocket. Nobody talked about work, but between frames I asked Dick about his animal crematorium. 'Pet Lawn Inc,' he said. 'The largest in Milwaukee. We got about 8 to 9,000 pets buried there. Cremations go into millions. That's between 500 and 1,500 pounds a day in weight – your average animal weighs maybe 35 pounds … It's a good business.' He glugged down another beer.

The silent basketball players on the television screens had now given way to film of racing car crashes. The air was thick with cigarette smoke, the clack of bowling balls, shouts and groans; the hermetically sealed world of sports, beer, male talk.

Gordy held himself slightly apart; more earnest, as if what for the others was merely Wednesday night recreation, was for him serious preparation for some future main event. 'See, every lane is different,' he said. 'The run and the texture of the wood; the way they apply the varnish.'

'Naw,' said Dick. 'The only thing different is the barmaids.'

Hoffman Printers had taken the lead. 'It's that damn Al. We're gonna leave him in the nursing home next time.'

'Okay,' said Al, feigning umbrage. 'I quit.' He was a skeletal man with parchment skin drawn tightly over his skull, but arms that were all sinew and muscle. He had lived in Milwaukee all his life. When I asked him what it had been like in the old days he said, 'They used to roll the pavements up at 9.30 each night.'

The larger game was slipping away, but no one much seemed to care; the dollar bills on the table, the beer, the jokes – these were the main attraction. Gordy had taken a cloth from his bag and was now carefully wiping it over his bowling balls, smoothing away the last traces of fingerprints, the traces of varnish from the lane, until they glistened and shone in the lights. He was thinking that tomorrow night he would do better.

24 hours from Tulsa

Dearest darling,
I had to call to say that I won't be
home any more,
'cos something happened to me ...

In Tulsa, I rented a car and found my way to Interstate 44, heading west, through the Oklahoma countryside. It was a peaceful Saturday afternoon, and my Pontiac Sunbird purred past pick-up trucks, thundering semis, family sedans groaning with children. Past Oklahoma City, the road ran as straight as an arrow, the woods giving way to farmland, fanning out on either side, as far as the eye could see. Outside Chickasaw, the road suddenly dipped, revealing a view for miles across the plains. The setting sun lit up the sky in a riot of gold and orange tracers, the Wichita Mountains a smudge of purple on the horizon. You had to hold your breath at the beauty of it all.

I had driven through this part of America before. Almost twenty years before, needing to get from New York to San Francisco as cheaply as possible, I answered an advertisement in the *Village Voice* for something called the People's Bus. The People's Bus was essentially a hippie enterprise, an old National Harvester yellow school bus, which had been 'converted' for sleeping accommodation by removing all the seats and constructing a sleeping 'platform' that effectively divided the bus in half. It was impossible to sit upright in any part of the bus other than the driver's seat; some twenty people were obliged to travel 3,000 miles in a semi-recumbent position. The fare from New York to San Francisco was $30 – absurdly, *ridiculously* and, given the condition of the bus, possibly suicidally – cheap; a fare which only the flat broke, the desperate and the demented – those with absolutely nothing to lose – could afford to pay.

Before leaving New York we were given a briefing. If the bus was stopped by police anywhere on the journey, we were to say we were members of the Church of Community Consciousness, on a pilgrimage to shrines in Oregon. I'd supposed this was because the bus had no licence to carry paying passengers, possibly no proper insurance. But as we chugged across America it became clear that our driver, a wild-haired, bearded man named Ed, actually saw the journey as one of messianic deliverance. At periodic intervals, he would pull the bus over into a lay-by and ask us to stand in a circle, join hands and invoke a spirit of communion for the journey to continue safely – not a requirement on the scheduled Greyhound service. It was excruciatingly embarrassing.

Somewhere outside Salt Lake City, it became clear that the bus not only had no licence, no insurance, but also no brakes. There was a mutiny on board. Ed protested: he had plenty of drugs left; all he needed was sufficient faith from his passengers and he could drive us the remaining 1,000 miles *without* brakes. Several people decided to walk. Eventually, a collection was made, and the bus taken to a workshop for repairs. We arrived in San Francisco after three nights and four days, our spines bent, our nerves jangling, thankful to be alive.

My Pontiac Sunbird was infinitely more comfortable – wrapround seating, automatic transmission, cruise control. Driving on these roads, virtually all that was required was to keep a steadying hand on the steering wheel, while I drank in the view and toyed with the radio. The country music station out of Altus was playing a song celebrating the contribution of the common man – the farmers of Kansas, the auto-workers of Detroit, 'the spokes in America's wheel'; people who didn't care for fame or fortune, but worked hard for their family, their country. Songs were the heartbeat of America: the coded messages of the nation's psyche. You realised this when you were driving, the distances so vast, the entire nation seemingly on the move. That's why so many songs were about the very fact of movement itself – road songs.

Gene Pitney's recording of 'Twenty-four Hours From Tulsa', written by Burt Bacharach and Hal David, was a hit in Britain in 1964, yet it had retained an eerily timeless quality.

'Dearest darling, I had to call to say that I won't be home any more/'Cos something happened to me while I was driving home and I'm not the same any more . . .'

Pitney's tremulous voice echoing against a background of highly wrought, almost neurasthenic melodrama, the song recounts the tale of a traveller who has pulled into an overnight stop and lost his heart to a stranger. The road is where your life can change, where anything is possible. 'Twenty-four Hours From Tulsa' is a romantic song for a romantic idea.

Hal David, who wrote the lyrics for Burt Bacharach's melody, had never been to Tulsa, or anywhere near it, when he wrote the song. David was born in Brooklyn; he had lived on both American coasts, and travelled extensively in Europe. 'But when Burt played me the melody it had that urgency about it,' he told me when I spoke to him in New York, 'a feeling of imminent happening – a kind of *High Noon* feeling, and for some reason Tulsa came to mind.

'Tulsa was a mythical place to me. It spoke of many, many places I had never been that somewhere along the line I always hoped I'd go to. All the dream places.'

I was looking for Hal David's dream place – the place where the traveller in 'Twenty-fours From Tulsa' might have stopped, lost his heart. In my mind's eye I saw it as a roadside motel – a collection of wooden cabins around an office with a screen-door and a sign winking *vacancies*, and next door a cocktail bar and diner, tricked out in neon, with a dance band which had known better days playing 'The More I See You'. The plains of Oklahoma rolled out on either side of the road like a brown carpet, so vast, so empty that your eyes swam looking for the horizon. The town of Cache was a collection of trailer homes and pick-up trucks; Duke, a single crossroads, with a stoplight, a store, a filling station and wooden shacks, trailing away from the road in ragged formation.

I arrived in Hollis for lunch, at the Hollis Inn motel and diner. It was Sunday, and the diner was crowded with people stopping by after church; the men in suits and stetsons, the women in cotton dresses. It was a homely place, with big, old brown Naugahyde booths, laminated tables, a large refrigerator cabinet stocked with pies and drinks, a bustle in the kitchen. It felt like the very heart of America.

The diner was run by a middle-aged couple. The husband stood at an old-fashioned cash till, joshing with customers. His wife took my order. A few minutes later she returned to my table with a cup of steaming black coffee and a small jug of hot milk. This was a novelty. In diners all the way across America, milk comes in little plastic tubs, powdered in sachets, in jugs if you're lucky – but never, ever, hot. 'You're English, aren't you?', she said. 'I know you English always take hot milk with your coffee.' I didn't have the heart to say I preferred cold. I decided to stay in Hollis.

Every morning at breakfast time, there was a traffic jam of pick-up trucks outside the Hollis Inn, as the boys took their places in the diner. Linton, the owner, pushed all the tables in the centre row together, to seat ten on each side. And there they sat, in their bib-and-tucker overalls and battered windcheaters. Everybody wore a mechanic's cap, which nobody took off to eat. They drank scalding hot coffee and devoured plates of eggs and steaming bowls of oats. One would leave, two more arrive, another leave . . . in the space of two hours every farmer in the vicinity must have passed through.

Hollis had a population of 2,600. It was the seat of Harmon County, population 3,600. It had a town hall; a courthouse; a high-school basketball team – the Hollis Tigers – on a 14–0 winning streak; Rip's Auto Body Shop; a livestock commission; a gin where cotton was cleaned and bailed; two filling stations, and a Western wear store. There was a reason for everything in the town, and just about everyone you met had the same attitude: there's no fuss here; this is how it is; take it or leave it; come back anytime.

Hollis was a farming town, and that's about all there was to it. Seventy to eighty years ago the population of Harmon County was around 14,000. There were hundreds of farmers, each working their own small piece of land of, say, 400 to 500 acres. Cotton was the predominant crop. In those days Hollis was just one of a number of flourishing communities in the county – Gould, McKnight, Vinson. But in the Thirties, a combination of severe drought and soil erosion through over-cultivation turned the area of West Oklahoma and the Texas panhandle, Texoma, into a Dust Bowl. Thousands headed West, for California. The coming of automation after the Second World War reduced the need for farm labour still further. The smaller farms were absorbed by larger ones. The old people sold up, the young people left the county. The smallest towns simply died. In the last ten years alone, the population of Harmon County had declined by 25 per cent. Now, there were only a hundred farm-owners around Hollis. Typically, a farmer owned 1,500 acres, and grew a mixture of cotton, wheat and peanuts, and grazed cattle. He might have several hundred acres in one place, several hundred somewhere else. He lived in town, and he commuted to his various fields in his pick-up.

Diversification was the only way. 'You borrow $50,000 to put in a crop, and it gets hailed out, you've still got to pay that note. Or say a tornado. Now you go with a bit of this, a bit of that – you got three or four avenues to make money and surely one of them will pull through.'

Although you'd never have guessed it – everything looked so unrelentingly flat – Hollis was set in a valley. There was only a 25-foot difference in elevation at its furthest reaches, but it was enough to draw water into an underground seam, maybe 40 miles across, which a farmer could tap into for irrigation. Imagine a line drawn along the edge of this valley; on one side of the line, irrigated land could cost $1,200 an acre; on the other side, dry land cost as little as $300 an acre. That's how much difference irrigation made.

Dub Nell was a big, heavy-jowled man in his mid-sixties, with bright, darting eyes, like a bird's. Dub had 1,000 acres in Hollis, part irrigated, part dry, and another 800 acres in Dimmitt, Texas, growing corn, cotton and wheat. He was on the board at the local bank. His family had been in Hollis for three generations, which was as long as anybody. Dub carried a certain gravitas. When he sat down for breakfast in the diner everybody listened. Dub talked slow. Everybody talked slow, but Dub talked slower. People said you could wait all day for him to finish a sentence, but that was all right. It was like watching somebody working on an oil painting. Dub could talk knowledgeably about almost everything that mattered. He was an agriculturalist, meteorologist, economist, mechanic, engineer, all-purpose handyman. The skills and practices of the city seemed paltry and mean-spirited by comparison. 'How much is a bushel of wheat in England?' Dub would ask. Or 'what's the average yield on a dairy herd?' And I, feeling pitifully inadequate, would reply that I had no idea.

Dub spoke of farming with a mixture of love and weary fatalism. Nowadays, it was hard to make a living; the economics just didn't make sense. In 1950, wheat sold for $2.50 a bushel; its price now was only $2.25 a bushel. But in 1950 a new tractor could be bought for $3,000. Today it cost $60,000. Under the government subsidy programme, the 'target price' for wheat was $4 a bushel, which meant that the government made up the difference between that and the market price. But the subsidies were being cut back. The government had the farmer by the balls. To encourage farmers to cut back on production, avoid a surplus, the Conservation Reserve Programme would pay $45 an acre for ten years to grow grass. Now 46,000 acres in Harmon County were under the CRP. The fortunes of Hollis were tied irrevocably to the whim of the seasons. When the wheat held out, or the cotton didn't make, the whole community suffered. There wasn't a business in Hollis that didn't depend on the farmer.

The early Fifties were bad for crops and cattle, and Hollis suffered. The late Fifties were good. The Sixties not so good. Farming required shrewd judgement, knowing when to cash in if you were on a roll. 'Now, old Randy, back in '75, he made good cotton and had a chance to pay off his note on the farm. But he didn't do that. He bought 480 acres more, and in '77 he lost the whole shebang.'

The later part of the Eighties had been lean years. But right now, times were good. The cattle yield had been high, and the cotton fields had produced three bales per acre, rather than the usual one-and-a-half to two. And the price was higher – 70 cents a pound, rather than 40 to 45 cents. People were phlegmatic about this. 'It's not anything the farmer did. It's the Lord. He's kept us humble for quite a while and I guess He thought it was time to bless us.'

Still, some people said they were hurting. Others just shrugged. People always thought farmers were richer than they were, perhaps because it was so hard to tell. 'Holding on to the green' was seen as a virtue: 'Now Doug,' people would say, 'Doug *really* holds on to the green'. This was not a reproach, but a compliment. 'There's some *real* rich people in Hollis, but you'd never know it,' it was said. Nobody put on airs and graces. You didn't suddenly stop meeting the boys for breakfast at the Hollis Inn because the crop was good. Perhaps the old pick-up was traded in for a new one; the children were put through college. Life went on.

'People are conservative around here,' said Dub. 'They know where their money's come from. We all don't luck in on these big deals on the stockmarket. This here's honest money.'

The front page of the *Hollis News* was full of the week's goings-on. The Harmon Memorial Hospital Ladies Auxiliary were holding a benefit Potato Bar to raise money for new hospital equipment. A local boy, Dale Robbins, had been honoured as an Outstanding Young Range Professional at a ceremony in Washington; a gooseneck trailer, diesel pump and four rolls of barbed wire had been stolen from a farm in Harmon County.

I found Judy Webb, the newspaper's editor and chief reporter (in fact, *only* reporter) in her office on Main Street. I asked her, what's it like living in Hollis? 'It's a comfortable, secure feeling,' she said. 'We don't lock our doors. But then again, it's a fast-pace town because you're involved with everything. If you're community-minded, which the majority are, and involved with your children, you can go to something every night of the week. She sketched out her diary: the Chamber of Commerce meeting; the Civic Ladies Organisation meeting; church (two nights); the high school ball game or band recital. 'You know who your neighbours are in Hollis,' said Judy. 'I could write a story on nearly everyone in town, Ron Zimmerman, the sheriff, he lets me know what's happening. About three years ago we had a drug bust up north. After they'd got the gunfire finished with, they called me up.'

Late at night I sat in my room at the Hollis Inn and watched television. There were two advertisements on where to go for help about depression; another for advice about colo-rectal cancer, and a local news item about sleeplessness. I had been noticing these advertisements all the way across America. They constituted an alternative diagnosis of the American body and psyche. There was the offer of psychological counselling in Chattanooga – 'When Life Gets Too Confusing, Call Bright Outlook!' There were constipation remedies in Milwaukee; cures for hair loss in Memphis. Panaceas for sundry, vague, unspecified aches, ailments and afflictions just about everywhere else. These exhortations to wellbeing eventually came to seem like a kind of tyranny, an insidious tool of conformity. You simply weren't allowed to be bald, worried, have bad teeth or stomach cramps. Even one's bowel movements were subject to rigorous scrutiny and judgement. 'Irregularity' was a social stigma, ostracising one from fulfilment in sports, business and social activities. Not even cats could escape this vigilance over their wellbeing. In St Louis I saw an advertisement for 'Mature Cat' – a special low-fat meal for cats over seven, 'because their needs change'. America was a nation racked by anxiety and pain.

The Hollis Inn had been built in 1958, and run out of steam a few years later. Linton Deskins and his wife Bobbie took it over in

1975, fitted up the rooms with wood panelling and Naugahyde armchairs. Few people passed through; the commercial traveller or cowboy, sometimes a tourist straying off the beaten track. Linton also owned some properties along Main, houses that he rented out, and he ran the food concession at the livestock commission. Bobbie ran a fabric shop in town. They lived in a house at the back of the motel, with some chickens in the yard, a basketball net and a big old Chevy, which they never drove. The house had been built in 1900, in Dodson, Texas. That's where Linton and Bobbie had found it. They'd moved it to Jones Street, over on the other side of Hollis, then moved it again when they bought the motel. 'A big truck came along,' said Bobbie. 'They took out the supports, put the house on wheels and moved it over here. They had to take the back roads because of the powerlines.'

At night the only sound was the wheeze of the radiator in my room, the far-off barking of a dog, the occasional pick-up passing through. I thought about Linton and Bobbie's house stealing noiselessly across the prairie. Moving house. Bobbie had made it sound as easy as baking a cake.

Until 1890, the whole of Oklahoma was designated as Indian territory. But nothing was allowed to stand in the way of the inexorable drive westwards of the settlers and ranchers. The treaties were torn up, the Indians pushed out, and the cattlemen descended on the plains. One ranch to the east of what is now Harmon County carried between 60 and 70 million head of cattle. It took a year to round them up and drive them north, to the stockyards of Kansas City. In 1897, Congress passed an act providing for homestead entries on the land, giving preference rights for bona fide residents to file for 160 acres each, and purchase an additional 160 acres at $1 an acre. It was the beginning of the land rush. On the Oklahoma Run, homesteaders lined up in their wagons and at the crack of the starter's pistol dashed to stake their claim. There was plenty to spare.

One night Dub took me to meet his mother. Crystal Nell was ninety-two years old, Hollis' oldest resident, a spry woman who snapped to her feet when I came into the room, pointed me to a comfortable sofa, and settled herself in a hard-backed rocking chair. She had come to Hollis in 1901, or thereabouts, from Hico, Texas, 300 miles away, with her parents, eleven brothers and sisters and her grandmother, in three covered wagons. 'Dad heard there was good land here. He and Mom drove one wagon each, and my uncle drove some heifers.'

Her father, James R. McCarty, staked out his 160 acres, put his home on the line, and staked out another 160 acres in Grandmother's name. He built a half dug-out – a hole 5 feet deep, with earth thrown over a tarpaulin for the roof – until they could build a cabin.

James McCarty was a Baptist preacher. 'Primitive Baptist that is – real old time; the oldest Baptists there ever was. They still did the footwashing, and we didn't have no instrumental music in church. See, what happened was, an old man died up yonder, so two of the boys got on horses and came across the river and asked Daddy to come across and preach a funeral up there, and they built a church right there, on that spot. And it was the only church in the county.

'We went to school, and we worked. Seems like Dad always had corn just the right size for us to pick. Blacks would come in to hoe the cotton. The people in Arkansas, boll-weevil ruined their crop, so they come over here in harvesting. We had a couple of little cabins, and some of them lived in tents.

'Oh yes, we had parties then, and sing-ins and box suppers. That's when they wanted to make up money for the school, to buy some books, and the girls would all get a box and tie it real pretty, fill them up with cakes, and an auctioneer, he'd bid, and the boys would buy it. And if you were sweet on a girl you'd buy her box.'

I asked Crystal if she could remember the Dust Bowl. She rocked on her chair a while, thinking back. 'It was bad. We'd go to bed with wet cloths over our face to keep the dust out. You couldn't even see the sun. A lot of people, that drove them out. Micheline and Alvin Carter, they moved out to California. That's where they got their start. But they came back. Otis Brookman and Ruby – they came back. But the settlers that had been here a long time, we toughed it out. We're used to hardships.

'See, Hollis was a big place then. Saturday night, all the families came into town and you couldn't move in the street, even on the sidewalk. There were two movie houses, the La Vista and the Watt Theatre, and the older people would park their cars and the children would just walk around and around.'

Crystal and her husband, William Bryan Nell, had been together for sixty-eight years, until his death in 1988. Her father was a farmer, and her husband, and so was Dub. She'd raised seven children, and sent five of them to college. She had been to California once, in 1949, and to Louisiana, 'to see the boys off, 'fore Korea.

'You'd call it a hard life. I worked all the time. I never did sit down, 'cept when I was a little girl, I'd sit down by the creek and play there for two or three hours in my playhouse. My children, my husband, that's what made me glad to be alive. I just lived for them. We lived for each other. My husband, he was a good Christian man – he didn't drink or anything.' ('Daddy,' Dub told me, 'he never met anybody that was a stranger' – one of those wonderful turns of rural phrase. 'It was nice to visit with you,' he said one evening as I left his house, a phrase that implied a hospitality of spirit on my part, rather than his; a generous figure of speech.)

'I never hankered for another life,' said Crystal. 'I was satisfied. My dad used to say this was the finest place in the world to raise a family, and I think so too.' She tipped her chair into motion, back and forth, back and forth.

On Sunday night, Linton, Bobbie and I went to church in Childress, 30 miles away over the Texas border, because Bobbie had heard they had a good preacher there. We drove the same flat road. Telegraph wires sang in the wind; tumbleweed was stacked up against the roadside fences. The cotton had been brought in, and the fields lay fallow, brown smudged with white. It was eerily, melancholically beautiful in the fading evening light.

The Church of Christ was a new building, very plain. It was half-full, farmers pressed uncomfortably into suits, bull necks bulging over shirt collars; young men and women with scrubbed faces and devout expressions. The elders sought out strangers and pumped their hands. 'London, England? Well, is that right?' There were no clergy in vestments; no music (I thought of Crystal's father. The Bible, said Bobbie, doesn't say anything about using instruments for worship). We raised reedy voices in a cappella song, and two boys read the prayers – 'thank you, Lord, for this rain we've been having lately'.

The sermon was on the theme of 'the rational sinner', delivered by a pinched-looking man in a dark suit. The rational sinner, he said, believes the world was created by a big bang! As if that makes more sense than what's written in the Lord's book! Evolution was a sin; so were 'unnatural sexual practices'. Members of the congregation followed the sermon, referring to the text in the Bibles on their laps.

Afterwards we went to J-Bob's Steak House, and ate a steak which spilled off the sides of the plate. The waitress frowned when I asked for a beer. This is a dry county, she said; you can't drink alcohol around here. Once again I was reminded with a jolt of how innately conservative this part of America remained. There was an old steam radio in a brown wooden cabinet by the door. The waitress said it had belonged to J-Bob's father. 'I thought it must have,' said Linton. 'We've come over from Hollis, to the Church of Christ. They've got one helluva firebrand preacher there.'

'I heard that,' replied the waitress. 'Well, you mind how you go now.'

We drove the 30 miles back to Hollis without passing another car. The night was as black as pitch, and you couldn't have begun to count the stars in the sky, as the wind hummed in the telegraph wires.

There was a bank robbery up in Gould, in 1974, where a cashier had been killed. Two men from Hollis were arrested, and later one of them was stabbed to death in prison. Then there was Bonnie and Clyde; they robbed a store up in Wellington, north of here.

Dub took a certain pleasure in telling me this, a wry smile on his face. It was as if his stories lent Hollis a faintly roguish air, a savour of disrepute; as if to say, just in case you were thinking nothing happens here, we've had our ne'er-do-wells too.

I went to see the Sheriff. Ron Zimmerman was a tall man with cropped hair and a slow, watchful manner, a gun riding on his hip. You could imagine him turning up at the scene of a crime, climbing out of his grey Buick, his eyes narrowing, and saying what's all the fuss here? Ron said he was holding two boys in the cells right now, from out of state, on possession of stolen property and marijuana. There were twelve cells, 'but it's not very often we run it plumb full'. Most of the criminals he dealt with, he said, were passing through town. 'I know most everybody in Hollis. But we get people coming over from Texas, to drink here. It's dry over there, in Texas. We used to have trouble out at Fuzzy's, out on the edge of town, but we got riding shotgun on 'em and that quietened 'em down.' Ron yawned, as if to say that's all there was to it.

Every shop in town carried a poster in its window announcing its support for a Hollis High School Tiger. The school was the centre of Hollis; its activities and achievements a source of all-consuming interest and conversation. There was no cinema in Hollis, no discotheque, not much of anything. Even people who didn't have children came to cheer at the ball games and hear the band concerts, and spoke of both with proprietorial pride.

Sport, the high-school principal, Larry Palmore, told me, was a vital part of the educational process, because 'with sport the kids learn a lot of things about life.

'Competition is a good thing. No one gains without going out and selling themselves as the person for the job.' Everybody wanted to be on the team, and the school used it as an incentive to do better in the classroom; students had to maintain grades above 69 per cent to be considered for selection.

One evening I went to see the Tigers play basketball against neighbouring Tipton. It was as much a social occasion as a sporting one. There were some 500 people in the gymnasium, banked up on terraces on either side of the court. During time-outs, the Hollis cheerleaders dashed on from the sidelines, formed a pyramid and kicked their legs in the air, while people gulped down popcorn and swallowed Coca-Cola and said hello to their neighbours. Then the cheerleaders from Tipton did the same thing, and people applauded politely.

The boys chivvied up and down the court with screams ringing in their ears – 'Hustle, Chad, hustle.' – and drew admiring glances from the cheerleaders. Hollis maintained their unbeaten run, 80–56.

Judy Boothe, who taught English, asked me if I would come by the school next day, take a class, tell them what I was doing here. They were fifteen- and sixteen-year-olds, the basketball team and cheerleaders. They laughed at my accent, and asked me why the English drove on the wrong side of the road, what I thought about the Royal Family, and how old you had to be to drink in England. 'Eighteen! Ah'm movin' to England, man!' In Hollis you had to be twenty-one.

I asked what was there to do in Hollis, and they chorused 'nothing'. How many wanted to be farmers? Only a couple of hands went up. Most of them wanted to leave town as soon as they were able. We ended up talking about football hooliganism and Acid House. I felt like Mephistopheles. They looked at me as if I was describing life on Mars.

One day I decided to drive out of town, north towards Erick, just to see what the country looked like. It was a glorious day; the fields unrolled on either side of the single strip of Tarmac, neatly tilled in varying shades of brown. The sky was vast, cold and bird's-egg blue. A pick-up passed by; the driver waved, and I waved back. I passed a sign that said Erick, 40 miles, and pulled over to stretch my legs. It seemed too far to drive to see pretty much the same thing I'd left behind. The air had never smelled so fresh. Flat brown fields and a yawning sky had never looked so beautiful. There was a perfect stillness, as if it had always been, and would always be, like this. Back at the Hollis Inn, the boys would be gathering round over steaming cups of coffee and smokes, talking about crop yields and interest rates. I got back in the car and turned back, to Hollis. I passed another pick-up, and waved. The driver waved back. I followed the truck in my rear-view mirror, a mile or more, until it became a dot, and vanished on the blue horizon.

El Paso

Out in the West Texas town of El Paso,
I fell in love with a Mexican girl

Carlsbad, New Mexico, was a dusty, ugly town on the edge of the desert. I stopped at a motel in the centre of the town, left my bag in my room and went to the bar in search of a drink. It was full of men who looked like cowboys or construction workers, with dusty clothes and bad-tempered expressions. Rednecks. The women looked weatherbeaten, hard, tired of life. A sign on the wall said, no weapons. But that was all right – I wasn't carrying one.

When I asked for a beer the waitress asked for my ID. 'But I'm forty years old,' I protested.

She pointed to another sign behind the bar. 'ID Must Be Produced On Request.'

Two men at the bar smirked and swallowed their beers, and I wondered if they'd had to produce IDs too. I went back to my room, collected my passport, returned to the bar, showed my passport and ordered a beer. The waitress served it without a smile.

The tops of the Guadalupe Mountains were lost in cloud, and winding down on to the flat roads of the high desert you could travel for miles without seeing another car. I was driving with God at my side. Well, not God exactly, but certainly his self-elected representatives. Across the panhandle of Texas and all through New Mexico I had been tuned to the evangelical radio stations, hypnotised by the rhythmic warnings of eternal damnation, the need for repentance, the pleas for money. These programmes had a horribly compelling fascination. The picture they gave was of an America in millennial crisis, teetering on the verge of moral dissolution and physical annihilation. The forces of Satan were everywhere in the land. But at last, nearing El Paso, came news of deliverance.

Yesterday, Rick had telephoned Bob on the Evangelical Compassion Line to say that he was a devil-worshipper who played in a heavy-metal band called Hell and sacrificed live animals. Today Rick was calling to say that after intensive prayer and perusing some free literature which had been sent round by the Compassion Line, he had found the Lord. 'I can't tell you how much better I feel, Bob. I won't be sacrificing live animals no more.'

'That's great, Rick,' purred Bob. 'We're praying for you. And if anybody out there wants to make a donation to help continue the Lord's work, here's the credit-card hotline number.'

From animal sacrifices and eternal damnation, to deliverance and a plug on God's own credit-card hotline in less than twenty-four hours ... seldom can El Paso's problems have been solved so easily. It had the reputation of a town impervious to prayer.

Marty Robbins' song 'El Paso' neatly incorporated the two central aspects of the town's mythology: its proximity to the Mexican border, and sudden violent death. A lonesome traveller falls in love with a Mexican girl called Felina, whom he meets in Rosina's cantina. A rival cowboy muscles in on her affections. There is a gunfight, and our hero meets his end 'cradled by two loving arms that I'll die for'.

It seemed a lot of dying had been done in El Paso. A display case in the El Paso History Museum contained the alleged Colt 45 that Constable John Selman Jnr had used to kill John Wesley Hardin, the West's most notorious gunfighter, in a saloon-bar shoot-out in 1895. An explanatory plaque broached the town's bloody reputation with commendable delicacy: 'Indian raids, revolution in Mexico, the proximity of the border as a refuge for outlaws, all contributed to El Paso's reputation as a place where violence was the acceptable way of settling a disagreement.' It was a tradition that had been maintained by the town's principal employer – the military. The Patriot missile, which had been used against the Iraqi Scuds in the Gulf War, came from El Paso.

One day, walking by the courthouse, I was startled to see eight convicts, their hands and ankles manacled together with chains, being led along the busy pavements from the federal detention centre, staring balefully at passers-by. If looks could kill.

El Paso stood at the westernmost tip of Texas, in a fold where the Rio Grande passes between the Chihuahua mountains of Mexico, and the Franklin Mountains of America. The Spanish, who were the first Europeans to reach the pass, in 1598, while following the route of the Rio Grande from the south, called it El Paso del Rio del Norte, meaning the pass of the great river of the north. They founded a settlement on the southern bank of the river; by 1881, the Mexican town of Paso del Norte had a population of 5,000, while the American settlement on the north side of the river numbered only 500. In 1888, Paso del Norte was renamed Juárez, leaving the American town as El Paso. Now, the population of El Paso was around 75,000, the population of Juárez closer to 1.5 million – slightly larger than Birmingham.

The political fact of these being two cities, two countries, had always been confounded by geography. Early travellers described the Rio Grande as too thick to drink and too thin to plough, and it had proved an unsatisfactory border, frequently changing channels and periodically bursting its banks in a manner blithely indifferent to the political requirements of the two countries it was supposed to divide. In 1963, after almost a hundred years of wrangling over land around the river, the United States and Mexican governments signed the Chamizal Agreement, and the Rio Grande was corralled into a concrete channel, a finite border between the two countries.

Its name flattered to deceive. My first reaction coming upon the Rio Grande was one of disbelief and disappointment. Is *that* it? The Rio Grande is no Great River at all. Damming and diverting upstream, for agricultural irrigation, has shrunk the river to the point that where Juárez shoulders up against El Paso the Rio Grande is no wider than Oxford Street, a sluggish brown soup sluicing down a concrete trough. By night, the border vanished altogether. Looking down from the hills above El Paso, the Rio Grande was lost altogether among the lights of the two cities, seemingly merging into one.

Mexico had seeped inexorably across the river, colouring El Paso with its people, its language, its vitality. Some 70 per cent of El Paso's population was Hispanic. The official border between the two countries might have been the river, but the true border was half a mile from the river's edge, at the San Jacinto Plaza. This was where the modern hotels, government buildings and scattered office blocks surrendered to older, narrower streets, thronging with people, and lined with shops so crammed with cheap clothing, electrical goods and knick-knacks they seemed to be bursting at the seams, spilling their contents on to the sidewalks. The old quarter was alive with street-peddlars, jaywalkers zig-zagging between the honking traffic, the blare of mariachi music from shop doorways. There were no English language signs here. Everything was Spanish. The Jewish and Lebanese businessmen who once dominated south El Paso, had long since abandoned the turf to the Hispanics; and now they, in turn, were increasingly relinquishing it to more newcomers. 'Those Koreans . . . man, they're real smart,' one heard it said. 'They get down in that neighbourhood, pay high money for short-term leases, stock those shops with stuff they can move fast, they know people want. Within six months they're speaking Spanish fluently. They're like chameleons.' The people of the developing world, it was said, were bringing life back into the cities. They were its hope. And it was true. These were the busiest, most vibrant streets I had seen since leaving New York, 2,500 miles away. Today 17 per cent of the American population is Hispanic. It is the fastest growing ethnic group in America. By the end of the century it will be larger than the country's black population.

Each day the queue of cars and trucks coming over from Juárez stretched almost the full length of the Bridge of the Americas. On an adjacent footbridge, an endless stream of humanity passed to and fro between the two countries. The economic and social interdependence of Juárez and El Paso could be measured in a string of statistics. There were some 15,000 people living in Juárez with 'legal permanent resident' status in America, who commuted across the bridges each day to work, returning to Mexico each evening. Thousands more crossed over bearing temporary visas, or Border Crossing Cards, to shop or visit relatives. (In order to qualify for a BCC a Mexican citizen had to prove he or she was financially solvent and had a regular job and a permanent residence in Mexico that they had no intention of abandoning.) The border guards in El Paso conducted 100,000 inspections at the bridge crossings each day.

But these figures obscured another, more poignant truth. Each day, hundreds – possibly thousands – of people crossed the Rio Grande illegally. They waded, rowed or floated across on ferries improvised from inflated inner tubes; they gouged holes in the high wire-mesh fence which lined the river's edge; slipped over the steel barriers at the railway stockyards; dodged, ducked, sprinted and dived, to be swallowed up in the teeming mass of downtown El Paso.

Of course, there was a simple reason for this. By day, the view from the hills above El Paso changed. The river, which seemed so elusive, so arbitrary, by night, could now be seen snaking between the two cities, rendering the two worlds it divided with depressing clarity. What night had suggested as twinkling lights in the hills around Juárez, daylight revealed as crumbling slums and shanty towns of stucco and wooden shacks. I imagined myself on those hills, looking back across the Rio Grande, towards the point where I now stood. I imagined myself poor, uneducated, with a family to feed, and thought how seductive the view from that hill must seem.

The welcome afforded to Mexicans coming across America's southern border has always owed as much to pragmatism as to law, varying according to the numbers clamouring for admission, and America's requirement for a cheap and willing labour force. In the early part of the century, controlled migration of Mexicans was tolerated, to work on the railroads. During the years of the Second World War, Mexicans were again welcomed as a cheap and willing labour force, under the *Bracero* programme, to work in farming and manufacturing jobs left vacant by soldiers fighting abroad. But the numbers of immigrants allowed under the *Bracero* programme never quite matched either the demand for cheap labour, or the numbers of Mexicans desperate to fill it. Farmers and fruit growers in New Mexico, Texas and California could increase their profits immeasurably by hiring 'illegals', and there were always immigrants willing to take their chances regardless of the law.

Periodically, the government would undertake a purge. In 1954, during 'Operation Wetback', the border between America and Mexico was sealed and over 1 million people deported back to Mexico. But the *Bracero* programme continued until a public outcry about the legalised exploitation of Mexican workers resulted in it being scrapped in 1964. That same year, the American government expelled a further 104,500 'illegals'. By 1970, the figure of deportations had risen to 400,000. The legal *bracero* simply went back to being the illegal 'wetback', and the exploitation continued.

In 1986, the government tried another tack. The Immigration Reform Act introduced the threat of a prison fine of up to $1 million for anyone employing illegal immigrants. Furthermore, it offered 'illegals' who had been in America since before 1982 the chance to take up citizenship. About 3.2 million people paid $185 a head to become Americans. The nation's official population increased by 2 per cent overnight. But there was no way of estimating the number of 'illegals' who had entered since 1982, and were thus ineligible for citizenship, nor the number of those who had entered since 1986. Nor was there any sign that the flow of illegal immigrants had diminished.

There was a joke in El Paso. 'We don't have wetbacks here. The Rio Grande is hardly deep enough to get your knees wet.' The official term for the impoverished and wretched hordes who came across the Rio Grande each day was 'illegal aliens'. It was a term that effectively cauterised any hint of human need or desperation from the statistics: the term preferred by the Border Patrol, whose job it is to guard the border.

I made an appointment to see Dale Musegades, the Chief Patrol Agent for the El Paso sector, at the Border Patrol headquarters, next to the town airport. Dale had the clipped moustache and brisk, purposeful air of a military man. He wore cowboy boots with his brown uniform, and a tie-clip in the shape of a pistol. An enormous Stars and Stripes stood behind his desk. The pile of the office carpet was so deep that walking across it felt like negotiating a trampoline.

Dale sketched out the parameters of the Border Patrol's problem. The border between Mexico and America was some 2,000 miles long, most of it unfenced. The El Paso section alone included 181 miles of land border, and 161 miles of river, which was patrolled by some 665 officers. 'You know, 20 to 25 per cent of the nation's alien apprehension business is done around here,' said Dale. (San Diego, on the border between Mexico and California, took care of a further 40 per cent.) About 97 per cent of those apprehended were Mexicans, but there were also Guatemalans, El Salvadoreans, Nicaraguans, Hondurans (officially classified as OTM – Other Than Mexican) – an ant trail of migrants, working its way up the Americas towards the honey pot of the USA.

A slide projector had been set up in the office. Dale pulled down the blinds and the show began. It looked like a presentation normally given either to schoolchildren or to government officials with their hands on the drawstring of the public purse. There were slides of the sector headquarters; of the border crossing points at the bridge; the seven checkpoints on the roads leading out of El Paso, and at the airport. Then came the arsenal at the force's disposal: motorbikes, sand buggies, spotter aircraft, helicopters, 'canine units' (a euphemism for dogs) for sniffing out drugs and smuggled currency. 'This is a pursuit sedan,' said Dale in a bored monotone, as the slides flickered to life. 'And this is one of a range of vehicles for transporting aliens.'

Horses had been phased out in 1956, but reinstated in 1980. 'A man riding a horse is quiet. The horse has keen eyesight, a keen sense of hearing. They can see, hear and smell an alien much sooner than a man. The close proximity of a uniform usually elicits a response from these guys,' Dale said drily. 'They sweat . . .' There were pictures of sorry-looking Mexicans, of 'OTMs' being loaded into paddy wagons or 'pursuit sedans', which Dale flicked by without a word.

We moved on to drugs. Dale shuffled slides showing the different smuggling methods: cocaine packed into fake propane tanks, door panels and spare tyres; oil drums that are used to float drugs across the river. In 1990, he said, sniffer dogs at checkpoints had been responsible for the seizure of $46 million worth of narcotics and $5 million in illegal currency.

Drug-running was a palpable evil, and talking about it seemed to make Dale feel easier, as if this was a job manifestly worth doing. But for every drug-runner, there were a hundred, five hundred, a thousand people whose motive for coming to America was born not of greed, but of desperation.

'When we pick these people up, they usually have a bewildered look on their face,' said Dale. 'Many have never been more than 5 miles from their home before. Most of them aren't comfortable about the fact that they're breaking the law; most are law-abiding, church-going, family people who are coming here because that's the only way they believe they can survive.'

It was a traffic in humanity replete with its own demonology, its own litany of misfortune. Crime had elbowed in on the despair. There were toughs who stood at the holes in the fence by the riverbank, charging a dollar or two for every 'illegal' to pass through, and the self-styled entrepreneurs who floated people across on inner tubes. 'Fall in,' said Dale drily, 'and if you don't drown you'll get hepatitis at best.' There were sophisticated cartels, who smuggled over people hidden in the backs of trucks, or in railway boxcars. In 1987, twenty-five people who had been smuggled across the border in a boxcar died of dehydration after the train had been shunted into a siding and left in the high summer heat.

The El Paso Border Patrol made some 600 'alien apprehensions' each day. This, said Dale, was actually a reduction in the numbers of five years ago, when the daily average was running closer to 1,800. But it was anybody's guess whether this reflected a true decline in the numbers crossing, or a quantum leap in their ability to avoid detection. Dale estimated that 50 per cent of those seized in the El Paso sector were on their way north, hoping to make a permanent home for themselves in America. The remainder – and the vast majority of these seized down at the river's edge – were simply 'day-trippers', people with no intention of staying in the country, but who crossed the Rio Grande each day to work illegally as manual labourers, to buy cheap goods which they would sell in Mexico, or to sell fruit (an avocado, which cost $1 in a supermarket, could be bought on the street for 25 cents).

'You walk him back across the bridge, and tomorrow he's there again,' Dale sounded weary just thinking about it. 'Of course, the names change every day we catch them – he's Reyas one day, Moreno the next.'

Dale had a new scheme to target the repeat offenders. Anybody caught five times would be locked up while papers were served for official deportation. At the back of the Border Patrol facility, out on the airport perimeter, was a grim collection of cell blocks behind a barbed-wire fence, where up to 450 'habituals' could be held at any one time.

Pity the poor immigrant. To earn enough to feed his family, a man would have to navigate the Rio Grande, make peace with the tough guarding the hole torn in the fence, evade all the manpower and resources which the Border Patrol could throw at him, all in order to wash dishes, dig somebody's garden or stand at a traffic light, brandishing an avocado at passing motorists.

One local businessman estimated that as much as 25 per cent of the labour force in El Paso was 'illegal', with many carrying forged social security papers and driving licences. It seemed that almost everybody had a cook, a babysitter, a gardener who came in each morning, was paid in cash with no questions asked. It was the law of supply and demand, and it would take more than the Border Patrol to prevent it.

'What you've got to realise is that Mexico is a Third World

country,' Al Velarde, the director of CLINIC (the Catholic Legal Immigration Network Inc), told me. 'I've had friends come from the Lebanon, take one look across the river at Juárez and say they feel right at home.'

Everybody acknowledged that the present immigration laws were unworkable, said Al; that 'the Tortilla Curtain' – a euphemism for the border's fences and ditches – was no deterrent. 'Even while immigration were designing it, the Mexicans were designing ways to get over, under and round it,' he chuckled. 'Sanctions against employers have not been effective, because the government don't have the enforcement muscle. This will only stop when the Mexican government are able to run an economy at the same level as the US; then people won't want to come here. You don't have thousands of people sneaking over the border from Canada.'

In recent years, the American and Mexican governments had attempted to devise a scheme to satisfy the requirements of both countries. Big American companies such as General Electric and RCA opened manufacturing plants in Mexico, close to the border – the maquillardos. The advantages to the companies were considerable. Workers at a maquillardo were paid an average wage of $8 a day, including benefits, compared to the statutory minimum of $3.80 an hour in the US. And there was no troublesome union organisation at the Mexican plants. But now, said Al, people were reluctant to work at the maquillardos. 'When they first opened up you could put up a sign advertising 50 vacancies and 1,000 people would show up. Now you'd have trouble filling the job. People know when they're being exploited.'

The problem, he said, was one of a peasant economy rubbing up against the monolithic bureaucracy of the corporate state. 'Even though things are rough across the river, people aren't doing nothing. They're industrious. People will cross over into America to buy used clothing by the pound in El Paso, then take it back and sell it in Mexico. That's big business for many. So the fellow has to cross illegally to get his stock. He's not going to work in the US, but if he went to immigration and explained what he was doing he wouldn't get a visa because he doesn't have the paperwork.

'Mexico never took foreign aid from America, but what happens is better than foreign aid. Let's say there are 5,000 illegal maids in El Paso, all getting just $60 a week. That's $300,000 going into Mexico – just from maids. If that money was going in foreign aid there would be graft, kickbacks and it would never get to the people that actually need it.'

Sinking into the deep pile carpet in the office of Chief Patrol Agent Dale Musegades, the contradictions of the immigration laws, the apparent futility of enforcement – like trying to grasp a handful of sand – the duties and responsibilities of a rich country bordering an infinitely poorer one ... all of this seemed vast and imponderable.

'People ask me how I keep from being completely frustrated,' said Dale. 'But we do the best job we can. We could use more men. We could use more hi-tech equipment. But you could never stop it 100 per cent. It's a balloon effect; you put your foot on it one place and it just squirts somewhere else. But what would it be like if we weren't here? We'd be absorbing all of Mexico and every other South American country. At least we're a lid; we've got some pressure on it.'

Dale swung out from behind his desk, and paced around the office. 'You know, we used to be a bunch of unsung heroes. You'd say "Border Patrol" and people'd think you were the guys who inspected the fruit or some damn thing.' Dale shook his head. 'You're always the guy taking away someone's labour, or somebody's relative. But the awareness of drugs has changed that a lot. People see we do a good job.

'Here, take a look at these.' Dale had walked over to a display case, hanging on the wall, containing a collection of antique sheriff's badges; mementos of a time of bad deeds and instant justice, when the moral imperatives of law enforcement weren't clouded by complicated questions of politics and human rights. 'Aren't they something?' said Dale. 'You interested in cowboys?' Dale settled back in his chair, as if he had all the time in the world. 'My father was a cowboy ...'

*

'Most of them come in between seven and ten – in order to get a day's work done.' Border Patrol Agent Elaine Moody gave an ironic shrug, and edged her truck off the highway on to a dirt sliproad, running adjacent to the high-wire fence, beside the concrete gutter that is the Rio Grande. Elaine was a tall, heavy-set woman in her early thirties, with horn-rimmed spectacles. She was getting a day's work done too, gunning her truck along the dusty track, looking for aliens.

On the far side of the river, a group of men stood at the water's edge, manhandling an inflated inner tube. They waved at us cheerfully. 'The richest men in Mexico,' said Elaine with a mocking tone. 'Those guys probably make $100 a day at least, charging a dollar a head to carry someone over.' Further along the riverbank, a man wearing waders lounged in the sunshine beside a makeshift raft, waiting for customers. A boy and girl strolled hand in hand, laughing and kissing, indifferent to anything but each other.

The river was perhaps 30 yards across. The fence to our left had been gashed at regular intervals, repaired, and gashed again. It had the consistency of a leaking sieve. 'We used to repair the fences every day,' said Elaine, 'but it just got to be pointless, so now we watch the holes instead. See, what we do is look for people who are down on the river, then we lay back for two or three blocks until they've crossed, then pick them up. You can get in trouble if you try to apprehend them on the river; it's dangerous for them, because maybe they can't swim, and it's dangerous for you because if they've got narcotics or someone they want to protect they can get violent.'

We passed a couple of men, on the American side of the river, but not yet through the fence. They pressed their faces against the mesh, watching us impassively. 'Now these guys are probably drug smugglers,' said Elaine. 'You see the same people every day. Maybe they're waiting for a car, or someone to come by to pass drugs to.' She stopped the truck, glared in a caricature of official disapproval, and then drove on, making no attempt to apprehend them.

We had reached the busiest illegal crossing point in El Paso, under a railway bridge, barely 100 yards from the Border Patrol's riverside holding-pen. 'This is a *real* popular place,' said Elaine. 'If they can get across this run here, and on to the side-streets over there they can just melt in the crowd and we'll never catch 'em.' A group of people were loitering by a large gash in the fence; young men, women and children, all shabbily dressed. They stared back at us with sullen expressions. 'That one there's a prostitute. I know her. And that one's a transvestite,' said Elaine flatly. 'No one's idea of glamour girls are they?' Another Border Patrol vehicle was parked up 25 yards away, the two guards simply sitting there, watching. Technically speaking, the Mexicans were already in America – already illegal – but they made no attempt either to move back or run forward, simply sprawled in the dust. There was something defiant and reproachful in their inertia.

I asked Elaine if she didn't find the whole business just too pitiful. 'I don't like to see mothers bringing their babies over, and the babies are sick. I think that's real pathetic,' she said. 'I used to describe this as a game of hide-and-seek with adults, because I guess that's what it is.' She shrugged, then brightened somewhat. 'But sometimes it can be a real challenge, you know, when you're chasing someone down, they're trying to outwit you and you catch them. If you let yourself get down about the people you didn't catch you'd get really frustrated.'

And what proportion did she think we're caught? 'Fifty per cent? Who knows? I don't think there's really a solution to this. You'd have to do like they had in Germany – put up a wall with machine guns. And we're not going to do that.'

Suddenly, three people ahead of us were making a run for it, kicking up puffs of dust on the path, hurdling the railway track and sprinting across the road, dodging the oncoming traffic. Elaine accelerated and swung the truck after them. We snaked down a side-street, doubled back and jerked abruptly to a halt outside a supermarket. A man stood in our path, panting heavily, a dull look of terror in his eyes. Elaine was out of the truck almost before it had stopped, grabbing his arm, steering him into the back of the truck. He offered no resistance.

We drove back to the holding-pen, and the man was marched

inside. The room was gloomy and there was an overpowering smell of sweat and stale cigarettes. I asked the man, do you speak English? He stared at me and said nothing. Elaine spoke to him in Spanish and translated his answers. He said his name was Aurelio Armanda. He was twenty-six – but looked much, much older. Why had he come across the border? 'I came to wait for my woman,' he said. 'We were going to buy clothes to sell in Juárez.' He said he might make 200,000 pesos – $70 – in one month doing that, to support his wife and two children. He looked shaken, anxious to do or say anything that might alleviate his troubles. He said he had been caught twice before. 'But I won't do it again,' he said, striving to strike the appropriate note of contrition.

'Not today, anyway,' Elaine added with a small laugh.

He was led away to a steel cage, where twenty or thirty people sat silently, waiting to be taken to the bridge and walked back across into Mexico. More officers arrived with more captives, to be processed in a mechanical acquiescence to bureaucracy. An oppressive, stultifying air hung over the room. There were no remarks, no wisecracks, just clipped, bored asides about names and numbers. It was 1.30 in the afternoon, and they had already caught 175 people that day.

Elaine drove me back to the headquarters, to collect my car. She said she had been doing this job for eleven years, and now she was being promoted – a desk job up north. Are you looking forward to it, I asked?

She looked at me as if I was mad. 'Is the sky blue?' she said. It always was in El Paso.

The next morning I paid the 25 cents' pedestrian toll and walked over the bridge to Juárez. Looking down, I could see a group some fifteen-strong loitering against the fence on the American side of the river, waiting for the moment to sprint the last 20 yards, cross another fence and be swallowed up among the early morning shoppers on the sidewalk. A Border Patrol truck swung into view, and the group edged backwards, towards Mexico. Today's game of hide-and-seek was under way.

The official on the Mexican side of the bridge hardly bothered to examine my passport before nodding me through into a grimier, more impoverished world.

The Avenue Juárez was lined with gimcrack souvenir stalls, shops displaying noticeably shoddier goods than their counterparts on the American side of the river, down-at-heel bars, hustlers angling a pitch with weary persistence. 'You want taxi? You want to see old market? No? You want girl then? You want to see donkey show?' At 10 o'clock in the morning? 'Twenty-four-hour donkey show . . .' replied the hustler smartly.

There was some irony of commerce at work here. On the American side of the bridge there were shops crammed with trainers, glitzy beatboxes, food-mixers, Bart Simpson and Ninja Turtle sweatshirts – gaudy merchandise to lure in the Mexican day-trippers. On the Mexican side there were earthenware pots, blankets, stuffed donkeys to lure in the American day-trippers. Mexicans sold junk to Americans; and Americans sold junk to Mexicans.

I stopped in a church and bought a laminated plastic prayer card (manufactured, I later noticed, in Hong Kong). Outside, a line of beggars sat along the wall, striking up a sad chorus of coins jangling in tins. America seemed a lifetime away from here. Walking back across the bridge, I paused again. The Border Patrol were evidently occupied elsewhere. Two figures ran out from the shadows by the fence, dodged the traffic and vanished into the side-streets. Then another one. Two more. A group of four. Just a typical day.

Marty Robbins' song kept passing through my mind. Everywhere I went in El Paso the ghosts of the town's mythic past hovered tantalisingly in view – a street named after a stagecoach company, a row of old adobe buildings that had been spared demolition – but its modern-day counterparts were harder to place. Try as I might, I could not see Chief Patrol Agent Musegades as Wyatt Earp. And today's outlaws seemed a sorry breed, desperate rather than *desperados*; the hustlers who floated the inner tubes across the river and guarded the makeshift 'gateways' in the fence; the penny-ante drug dealers, thieves and pickpockets who worked the streets of El Paso and Juárez. The pedestrian bridge linking the two cities was, apparently, still a place where – in the genteel circumlocution of the Museum of History – violence was the acceptable way of settling a disagreement: Border Patrol Agent Moody told me hair-raising stories about unwary travellers being waylaid with iron bars and switchblades.

The worse the economy became in Mexico, it was said, the higher the crime rate became in El Paso. The popular crime of the moment was stripping cars in order to sell the parts across the river. A map in the local newspaper helpfully pointed out the high-risk parking areas – all close to the river. Fords and Chevrolets were said to be particularly vulnerable, because the parts could be sold on more easily. They did not drive Toyotas in Mexico. People had taken to removing, or welding, the tailgates on their pick-ups to avoid theft. Today's outlaw, it seemed, was an emaciated, nineteen-year-old Mexican in a pair of cheap sneakers, rustling a Ford bumper.

I went to see Leon Metz, a resident of El Paso, and one of America's foremost authorities on frontier and gunfighter lore. Leon was actually born and grew up in West Virginia, and first came to El Paso as a seventeen-year-old airman, in transit to the Biggs Air Force base. Later, he settled in the town, writing a series of books on gunfighters such as John Selman, Dallas Stoudenmire and Pat Garrett. Leon knew Marty Robbins' song, of course, and had studied it for historical authenticity. Complete fiction, he'd decided. There was indeed a Rosina's cantina, over the river in Juárez, out near the racetrack, but that came after the song. But there was no denying, Leon said, that El Paso was a gunfighter's town. Pat Garrett, Dallas Stoudenmire and Wyatt Earp had all spent time there. But the town's most infamous resident had undoubtedly been John Wesley Hardin.

Hardin was born in 1853, the son of a Methodist minister, in Bonham, Texas, named by his father in honour of the founder of Methodism. His life as a killer started at the age of fifteen, when a black man refused to move off a public road so Hardin could take it all. Hardin shot him three times. He later wrote in his memoirs, *The Autobiography of John Wesley Hardin, According to Himself,* that all the white folks thought he did a good thing. He allegedly went on to kill some thirty-nine more people, including one 'for snoring'.

After serving fourteen years in prison for the murder of a deputy sheriff, Hardin settled in El Paso, intending – with no apparent sense of irony – to practise as a lawyer. But drink and his reputation caught up with him. He was rolling dice in the Acme Saloon when John Selman pushed open the batwing doors and shot Hardin three times, in the arm, chest and head. He lay on the ground for two hours, brains oozing through the cracks in the wooden floorboards, while the whole town came and looked at him (a fact Leon disclosed with a certain degree of relish). A newspaper reported that except for being dead, Hardin looked to be in fine shape.

He was buried in the town's Concordia Cemetery, a sprawling, dusty graveyard that the years, and the spread of urban development, had hedged behind bungalow estates and a six-lane expressway. The Concordia was a united nations of the dead. There was a Chinese section, a Jewish section, a Spanish section – evidence of the ebb and flow of the town's population over the preceding hundred years. I had been told that Hardin was buried near the Chinese quarter. I walked around, but could see no sign of it. The cemetery was enormous, and utterly deserted; the stillness broken only by the faint rush of traffic on the expressway. At some gravesides, flowers had been placed in small coffee jars or evaporated milk tins, and fading photographs of the deceased had been laid. But most of the plots were untended, the headstones weathered into indistinction, toppled and broken.

At length, a man came into view. I asked if he knew where Hardin was buried. 'I'm looking for him myself,' he said. Jack Jackson was a relative. His great-grandmother had been the sister of Hardin's father; Jack himself had grown up in Livingstone, Texas – 15 miles from Hardin's birthplace. Jack was in El Paso attending a convention, and had come by to pay his respects. A balding, bespectacled man in a brown suit, Jack did not look like the heir to a gunfighter's legacy. We scuffed around a little, and eventually found the grave, an undistinguished plot of dusty earth. Hardin was buried without a headstone, but in a spirit of historical recognition, the city had lately provided a simple marble plaque, recording his name and dates: 1853–1895. Somebody had laid a child's toy gun on the grave.

'My grandfather was kind of ashamed of him, but he'd always speak up for him because he was family,' said Jack. 'But John Wesley's kind of a hero round Livingstone now. We always say he never killed anybody that didn't need killing.' Jack gave a thin smile. Perhaps he was a chip off the old block after all.

Leon Metz told me that John Wesley Hardin notwithstanding, El Paso's reputation as a violent town was somewhat exaggerated. In 1881, El Paso's most violent year, eight people were killed in shoot-outs, five in one particularly eventful week. But otherwise, in the first twenty-five years of the town's life (from 1873 to 1898), only thirty people died of gunshot wounds. The most frequent offences on the court records in those days were drunkenness, theft, vagrancy and gambling. Adultery and fornication cases also jammed the court. Prostitutes paid a fine of $10 a month, which amounted to a form of licensing, and in some years these fees were the largest source of municipal income.

Leon took me on a historical tour of the town. The building which housed the Acme saloon, where John Wesley Hardin stained the floorboards, still stood, but was now a dress shop. The site where Francisco 'Pancho' Villa, the Mexican guerrilla fighter and revolutionary, once lived was now a parking lot, next door to the Ramada Inn.

We drove north for a couple of miles, on the highway that runs alongside the Rio Grande, then turned off towards the river. The road led down to a small rickety bridge. There was no fence, no checkpoint, no Border Patrol. We bumped over to the Mexican side of the river, and parked next to an obelisk, officially marking the border. A dirt track led into a fold in the hill and, beyond, the beginnings of the shanty town which fringed Juárez.

In 1911, Pancho Villa and another guerrilla leader, Pascual Orozco, assembled their troops here for the assault on Juárez – the battle that began the Mexican Civil War. On the American side of the river, sightseers would gather daily, to take photographs, give money and food.

It was late afternoon, and people strolled across the bridge from the American side, as if returning home after a day's work. You could have moved a revolutionary army across without interference; yet, astonishingly, remarked Leon, few 'illegals' chose to cross here. It was too far to walk into town. 'Crazy, isn't it?' said Leon. 'The average Mexican only wants to come over to visit their relatives, do a bit of shopping or earn a day's pay if they can. The big money can go 3 miles either side of town and walk across the border without a murmur; meantime we've got Border Patrol guards down there holding back people who've come over to wash dishes or buy a T-shirt.'

We walked back to the car, and bumped back across the rickety bridge, stopping to let a man pass, wheeling his bicycle back into Mexico. He froze for a moment, and glanced anxiously into the car. Reassured that we were not officialdom, he waved and walked on, a silent prayer on his lips.

PHOENIX

By the time I get to Phoenix, she'll be rising
She'll find my note I left hanging on the door . . .

The week before I arrived in Phoenix it was named the Best Managed City in America, and driving in from the airport it was easy to see why. Everything looked fresh, clean and new. The streets were lined with palms that looked as if they been planted yesterday. I negotiated a flyover in a blasted sandstone that was so beautifully sculpted that, momentarily enraptured, I almost came up the ramp the wrong way, into incoming traffic. It seemed almost as if any building that had the temerity to be more than twenty years old had been swept away, an affront to municipal aesthetics. I felt sure there was poverty and squalor somewhere – there always was – but the city planners had been thoughtful enough to sweep it out of the view of the casual visitor. Phoenix looked less like a city than an artist's impression of a city: one of those little models with balsawood buildings and pieces of sponge, and no pedestrians to spoil the effect. And it took a day or two to find out that it didn't work.

Downtown, the skyscrapers soared into a yawning blue sky. But at ground level it was a desert. I spent a morning driving around the office blocks, looking for somewhere to buy a small tape recorder, until I gave up in despair. When I told someone of my predicament they laughed. The way to buy a tape recorder was to look up Radio Shack in the Yellow Pages, find which mall they were in, and drive there. It was a day's work. But presumably the easy purchase of a tape recorder didn't figure in the criteria for Best Managed City.

Coming in from the air, you passed over miles and miles of desert and mountains, thinking it would never end, and suddenly there was Phoenix; huge squares of agricultural land, reclaimed from the desert, then an urban sprawl, spilling down a wide valley, like an ink stain, as far as the eye could see.

Phoenix was a natural oasis. The first people to settle there, the Hohokam Indians (it means 'those who have gone') built an elaborate system of canals, between 1,400 and 1,800 years ago, to channel water down from the mountains, and irrigate the land – the basis for the system which was still in use.

In 1950, the population of Phoenix was 300,000, and the principal industry in the city was farming: cattle, citrus fruit and cotton. Now, the population was 2 million. Phoenix was a city that had grown on new industries – electronics, computers, semi-conductors, defence industry contracts – and on the cheap and plentiful availability of land. The city had spilled outwards along the valley, like toy buildings thrown out a box, spawning satellite suburbs and townships, like Scottsdale, Tempe, Youngtown, Mesa.

Only 50 per cent of registered voters had lived in Phoenix for more than ten years. This was a staggering statistic. It was a place that people came to, not from – a symptom of America's mobility, and its restless search for home. This was the history of America, of course. Movement was part of the nation's genetic imprint. America had been built on a series of migrations: the drift of the original settlers from East to West, colonising the new frontier; the drift in the years before the Second World War of southern (principally black) labour to man the factories of the North. In recent years there had been another migration, people giving up on the crime, the decay and the declining industries of the North – the 'Rustbelt' – and heading South and West to the new industries, the new possibilities, of the 'Sunbelt'. By 1981, the geographic centre of the American population had crossed the Mississippi River for the first time in the nation's history, and by the middle of the decade it was estimated to be moving West by 58 feet, and South by 29 feet, each day.

'By The Time I Get To Phoenix' was written by Jimmy Webb, who in the Sixties and Seventies made something of a small industry writing songs about places. Like Hal David, Webb was an American enamoured of the romanticism of his own landscape. He was a fine singer himself, but it was Glen Campbell who made these songs hits: 'Galveston' and 'Wichita Lineman', as well as 'By The Time I Get To Phoenix'.

'By The Time I Get To Phoenix' was not about arriving in the city at all, but about passing through. The singer has walked out on his girlfriend, somewhere further West, and is heading across country:

By the time I get to Phoenix she'll be rising ... By the time I get to Albuquerque she'll be working ... By the time I make Oklahoma she'll be sleeping ...

Jimmy Webb himself came from Oklahoma, but, of course, settled in California when he became a successful songwriter: he would probably have made exactly the trip he describes more than once.

So many American songs echoed this sense of momentum. Going somewhere where the life was better. These songs were like route maps, but true to the stories you heard. 'I came from Alabama, then I worked in Wisconsin, then this job came vacant and I moved here.' One heard this all the time. People had a sister in the North, a brother in the West, parents in the South. Home was where you came from, not necessarily where you lived, because where you lived was provisional, subject to the uncertainties of the job market, personal whim. This momentum engendered a curious sense of dislocation in people, and the further West you moved, the more pronounced it became. 'Back home in Chicago, in the old neighbour-hood.' I heard it said – this from someone who had lived in Phoenix for more than twenty years. There were hardly any old neighbour-hoods in Phoenix to come from. It was a city in which everything seemed random, dispersed, in a state of perpetual improvisation.

'Dislocation is normalcy here.' It sounded a curious phrase when Earl de Berge said it, but it rang true. 'We don't know any different. Our normalcy is change. But that's why a lot of people like coming out here. If you've got an idea, you've got a chance of selling it. You don't have to fight the old structures like you do in other places.'

We were drinking in Durants bar and grill. It was a surprising place to find in Phoenix – dark and plush, with deep-red leather banquettes, bartenders in white jackets and waitresses in red skirts. Durants was a hang-out for local journalists, small-time politicians, public officials, cynics and wiseacres. It was a tableau of loud, beery men and middle-aged women of a certain cracked and precari-ous glamour, laughing raucously, smoking furiously and telling Eddie to set up the same again. Outside was the dry desert air, palm trees lining the broad avenues, and you squinted in the unrelenting sun. In here, your eyes watered in the nicotine fug and the air was blue with expletives. Like so much in Phoenix it felt as if it belonged somewhere else.

Earl de Berge ran a polling company, and he was the only person I met in the entire time I was in Phoenix who had actually been born there. When he was growing up, he told me, Phoenix was just a dusty farm town; two blocks north of where Durants now stood had been agricultural land. Today it was office blocks and shopping malls and housing developments, stretching interminably to the desert's edge. For years, the biggest growth industry in Phoenix had been growth itself. The city spilled outwards, gobbling up land in the maw of new development, encour-aged by rampant 'speculative zoning' of land. Phoenix became a haven for speculators, persuading banks to lend money for land on the basis of its estimated future value. There were plenty of people, delirious on the scent of quick profits, prepared to lend $2 million or $5 million in expectation of a 100 per cent return five years on.

A speculator would buy a strip of worthless desert land, get it rezoned for housing or a shopping mall, then sell it on the promise of profits to come. Of course, the promise was usually bogus. It was a pyramid operation. 'Fast-shoe operators', Earl called them – people juggling 'magic money', who could tap-dance, smiling, out of any sticky situation. Then came the recession. Suddenly money was scarcer; growth slowed down. Phoenix woke up to find itself with new houses that nobody wanted to buy (the town was overbuilt by 18-20 per cent in residential properties); shops that nobody wanted to let; land that was plumeting in value. The banks were caught with their shirts out.

The most infamous fast-shoe operator of all was an Arizona builder named Charles Keating. Keating worked hand in hand with other developers on the practice of 'land flips', buying and selling land in order to inflate its true value, with money from his federally insured savings and loans company. In effect, the government gave him the licence, and the money, to practise speculative building. But Keating couldn't tap-dance fast enough. The pyramid collapsed. Keating's parent company, American Continental Corp, went bankrupt owing investors some $250 million, and Keating himself faced federal indictments for fraud, and a racketeering lawsuit from the government. He was subsequently found guilty on seventeen counts of state securities fraud.

They enjoyed telling this story in Durants. 'Magic money,' they said, laughing and reaching for their drinks. They were happy cynics, inured to the follies of the world, keeping out of the sun.

Everything about Phoenix seemed provisional. It was a place that had set its sights on the future, with no apparent thought for the present.

Each year, between the months of October and June, the population of the valley swelled by some 100,000 with the arrival of a tribe of semi-permanent dwellers from the North – retired people, or people whose business allowed them the luxury of a few months in the sunshine. They were known as 'snowbirds'. The richest snowbirds lived beyond the city limits, towards the desert, in small and exclusive towns like Cave Creek and Carefree. The less rich snowbirds took winter lets in town. There was no such thing as a poor snowbird.

Some 23 per cent of the population of Phoenix was retired. Elderly people came for the sunshine, the dry desert air. It was a place where mortality was kept at arm's length. The affluent suburb of Scottsdale was the headquarters of the Flame Foundation, a group of people who claimed to have found the key to immortality by simply willing themselves to stay alive.

Phoenix was also the birthplace of the 'active adult community' – a euphemism for towns built specifically for, and inhabited solely by, the elderly. In fact, the word 'community' seemed meagre and inadequate in describing these places. Sun City, on the northern edge of Phoenix, had a population of 46,000. Sun City West, which bordered it, had a population of 20,000. Imagine a town roughly the size of Crawley or Harlow, where nobody is under the age of fifty-five. A town where youth was effectively outlawed.

The landscape offered no clue. I drove through mile after mile of drab, featureless suburbia, tract housing thrown up on dusty farmland, shopping malls, desert scrub. I knew I was approaching Sun City when I realised, with a start, that I was overtaking as many golf carts on the road as cars; when I realised that nobody I had seen in the previous 5 miles, walking or driving, could be remotely described as 'young'.

The receptionist in the offices of the Del Webb Corporation, which built and manage Sun City, was a smiling sixtysomething. Other elderly ladies fussed around the lobby with mail and cups of coffee. But Martha Moyer, head of corporate relations, was a surprise. Martha was in her early thirties, immaculately groomed, resolutely corporate, the bright smile on her glossed lips only partially failing to detract from the hard glimmer of suspicion in her carefully mascara-ed eyes. There were Del Webb Corporation Outstanding Achievements lining her wall, and the inevitable plaque on her desk to remind you who she was: Martha J. Moyer.

Martha told me the story of Del Webb, Phoenix builder, visionary, pioneer: how in the Fifties Webb had looked at his grandparents 'sitting around doing nothing' and decided there had to be a better life for oldsters. Sizing up a stretch of cotton and alfalfa fields on the fringes of Phoenix, Webb built five model homes, a golf course, a shopping plaza and a recreation centre, and launched the notion of 'active adulthood'. Some 100,000 people came to the opening ceremony. An industry was born – or, as Martha put it, 'the active adult lifestyle which we market so successfully today.

'Three or four decades ago when you retired, life was pretty much over,' she said. 'Del Webb gave life a new beginning. He gave the active adult an opportunity to challenge themselves physically and mentally.'

The idea spread like bed rash in an old folks' home. Sun City opened in 1960, and Sun City West followed in 1978. There were Del Webb 'communities' in Tucson and Las Vegas, and another under construction in Palm Springs. Other developers had jumped on the bandwagon. Driving into Sun City, one passed huge hoardings advertising other 'communities', showing beaming oldsters, lounging beside swimming pools, swinging golf clubs and gazing expectantly into the future (for the idea that you had a future, not just a past, was the central tenet of marketing in this field).

The corporate handout Martha gave me described Webb as 'quietly colourful, warmly human, inherently honest', with friends from all walks of life, 'from US presidents to common labourers'. Curiously, it made no mention of his friendship with Meyer Lansky, who was popularly (if not altogether correctly) believed to be the chairman of the board of the National Crime Syndicate, the Mafia's banker and, for years, the FBI's public enemy number one. Webb was the builder of the Flamingo Hotel in Las Vegas, financed and run by Lansky and Bugsy Siegel. Webb also owned the New York Yankees Baseball Team. And in 1962 he was *Time* magazine 'man of the year'. He died in July 1974. He never lived in Sun City.

Sun City had two cardinal rules to maintain its purity. In order to buy a house, one person per household had to be over fifty-five. And children under nineteen could visit for no more than three months in the year.

Activity was the key word in the Del Webb prospectus. There

were eighteen golf courses in Sun City and Sun City West; ten recreation centres (membership of a recreation centre was mandatory for all residents, at $125 per annum). There were twenty-seven different community clubs; dozens of churches; libraries and a large theatre where Bob Hope, Andy Williams and Wayne Newton performed.

Martha handed me some literature espousing the remarkable effects of Sun City living. A typical story began: 'At age seventy-one, Amos Childers is at his peak. He rises at 5.30 a.m. each morning for a brisk 4-mile run, and on weekends he's likely to be found winning awards at local amateur running events.' There was the motorbike club; downhill skiing; gambling junkets in Las Vegas; a tap-dance club that had performed in Japan. There was a softball league, complete with its own team of women cheerleaders – the Sun City Pom-Poms.

'They're almost reliving their high school years,' said Martha, smiling her corporate smile and making it sound as if the Sun City Pom-Poms were psychiatric patients.

There was something decidedly peculiar about Martha. Here she was, much younger than I was, intelligent, attractive, almost beautiful in fact, and yet Martha was acting so ... well, *old*. I kept expecting some sort of conspiratorial nod or wink, a sign to let me know that she was simply playing her corporate role – that she didn't really *believe* any of what she was telling me. But it never came. And when I made the mistake of referring to 'elderly people', the smile suddenly dropped, and Martha glared at me. 'We don't call them elderly people. They're *active adults*. When you say elderly you think of little people, hobbling around. That's not *our* people.'

She chirruped on. The telephone directory listed husband's name, wife's maiden name, former occupations and home town. You could phone up somebody and say 'I'm from Akron, Ohio too' and reminisce about the old days. People from all walks of life lived here, said Martha, from all fifty states and from fifty-four foreign countries. She made it sound like a rainbow community, a new world order of senior citizens. But in the time I was in Sun City I saw only one black person, in a shopping centre. This was such a shock that I was tempted to buttonhole him and ask whether he actually lived there. Later, he overtook me on the road leaving town, and I concluded he didn't.

I wondered about children. Weren't children supposed to keep active adults younger? 'Families can come and visit,' said Martha, 'and those who really miss children can volunteer to work in neighbouring schools.'

In the main, though, children weren't thought a terribly good thing. Sun City residents did not pay school taxes. The community had opted out at the request of the local school district, after residents kept voting against bond issues, designed to raise money for the schools. They were a powerful political force, 'as solid, and as blind, a voting block as anywhere in America,' Earl de Berge had told me. And 70 per cent Republican.

Sun City even had its own police force, operating under the jurisdiction of the local sheriff's office. This was called the Sun City Possee, a group of volunteers, some 200 strong, who rode around in squad cars and golf carts. Some of them carried guns. It was all part of the volunteer spirit, explained Martha, 'Giving back the need to feel like you are still contributing.'

Sun City had one of the lowest crime rates per capita in America – possibly the lowest – and it was easy to see why. I imagined an impossible scenario – a nineteen-year-old black kid, bouncing along the streets in a pair of Air Jordans and toting a ghettoblaster, coming face-to-face with a carload of trigger-happy active adult Republicans on their way back from a karate class. He wouldn't have lasted fifteen seconds. It would have taken an entire mobile strike force of delinquents just to steal a car radio.

'This is a very patriotic community,' said Martha. 'The motto round here is Be American, Buy American.' She estimated that 75 per cent of the vehicles in Sun City were made by General Motors. There wasn't a Japanese dealership for miles.

The more Martha talked, the more ineluctably depressing the idea of spending one's twilight years as an 'active adult' became, exclusively in the company of other active adults, tap-dancing, gambling in Vegas or dancing with the Pom-Poms. But Martha was a zealous proselytiser. Still in the bloom of youth herself, it seemed she could hardly wait to grow old to take advantage of it all. 'These people are having such a ball; it makes me excited about my retirement years, when you see how this lifestyle has positively impacted on these people. I'd envisage myself living here, no question.

'We know, just by looking at our people, that they age more *gracefully*. And the nice thing is they are with their peers, so they're not afraid of doing something. We have one woman of seventy-six who turns cartwheels with the Sun City Pom-Poms.'

Silently wondering if this was an accurate description of 'ageing gracefully', I left Martha and drove over to the Sun City West Recreation Centre. The golf carts were pulled up in serried ranks in the parking lot. I swung in next to a small Toyota. The owner had thoughtfully hung a flag, 'I Love America', in the rear window. The centre was built on the model of a pedestrian shopping precinct, with workshops where there would normally have been shops. There was a pottery class; a lapidary; a metalwork class; needlework and knitting; and a gift shop to sell the produce. It was a hive of industry. Nobody was turning cartwheels, but in the swimming pool three people were practising synchronised swimming, vanishing below the water and waving their legs in the air.

In the Model Railway Club, some men were tinkering with a large railway layout, daubing newspaper with paste and laying it over a wooden frame to make a tunnel. Bing Crosby music was percolating quietly in the background. Gus Davis, a rotund man with a red face, dressed in a railway driver's cap, was the club's founder. Since moving to Sun City, he said, he hardly saw his wife, who was out all day at clubs and classes. The Model Railway Club was something to do. There were eighty members in total, and more on the waiting list: oldsters with all the time in the world on their hands. Gus was seventy-five, a retired construction worker, who had moved to Sun City from Massachusetts. 'I think I got more out here than I would have back there, you know? Nobody tells me what to do. You got the weather.'

Did he miss anything, I wondered? Gus looked at me queerly.

'Tyres screaming? Hot rods up and down the street? Teenagers drinking? Miss that? You must be crazy.' He paused, as if trying to summon a memory from the old days. 'I miss girls, though.'

His friend Bud laughed. 'My wife, she says, "I'm going over to see the girls." I say, girls? What girls? I never see any girls,' he chuckled, a happy man who could always see the light side.

We fell into silence for a moment, thinking about girls. 'You get spoiled here,' said Gus. 'We're afraid to go out. With the traffic and all.'

What about bars? I asked.

'Bars?' Gus was remembering bars. 'There's no bars round here.'

'I go out on the posse,' said Bud. 'You see a group of ladies walking along and we pull over and say, don't you know the rules here? Teenagers are supposed to be off the streets by 9.00. That always raises a laugh. They love that.'

Earl de Berge had given me some statistics on Sun City. It delivered the highest number of prescriptions per head of any area in Phoenix, and also consumed the largest amount of liquor. There were no bars in Sun City, but in Durants I had heard tales of high jinks and shenanigans behind drawn curtains. A journalist told me one of those stories that everybody knew, but had gone unreported. A woman had discovered her husband was having an affair with a neighbour; she waited until he was asleep, then Superglued his errant part to his stomach, necessitating hospital treatment. I had wanted to ask Martha whether the story was true, but hadn't the nerve.

I drove around Sun City with a growing sense of disorientation. There was nothing higher than ground level. All the homes were rancho-style bungalows of varying degrees of size and opulence, set in neatly tended gardens of raked gravel, cactus and palm, on neatly tended streets. American flags fluttered along the main boulevards. Blue rinse sparkled in the Arizona sunshine, and the very air seemed perfumed with that peculiarly pungent aroma of talcum powder and lavender water so common to the elderly.

The shopping precincts seemed like somebody's idealised vision of small-town America, skewed 25 degrees from reality. You could park your car without locking it, but risked golf cart gridlock on the way out; you could buy a soup and a sandwich, in a shop offering 'a free ice cream cone on your birthday', without being served by some surly ethnic; but you couldn't cluck indulgently over somebody's baby, or shake your head and cluck disapprovingly at what teenagers were coming to nowadays. The shops weren't right either. How many small towns boasted a hearing-aid megastore?

Driving around the side-streets, I found another precinct: it consisted of a pharmacy, a chest clinic, a colon therapy centre, two hearing-aid sale and repair outlets, and a funeral home. The funeral home looked faintly shocking here – less a matter of discreet necessity than a symbol of flagrant opportunism, a grisly reminder that no amount of early morning jogging, pom-pom dancing and Andy Williams concerts could stave off the final reckoning. In the supermarket of American life, Sun City was the final checkout.

Martha had told me about one of the town's social customs. When a married woman dies in Sun City, a queue of women quickly forms at the bereaved husband's door, bearing food. 'We call it the casserole brigade,' said Martha, her bright, corporate smile contorting into something dangerously resembling a leer, as if to say, aren't these active adults something else?

Perhaps it was the close proximity of death that gave a slightly manic edge to all of Sun City's activities. The directory listed bicycle riding, billiards, choral singing, horseshoe throwing, shuffleboard and square-dancing. I wondered whether peer-group pressure would allow you to do nothing, just sit in the sun and read, think about life. Martha considered the idea with distaste. 'There are people who sit around and do nothing, but I wonder why they're living in Sun City.' She made doing nothing sound like a crime on par with serial murder or buying a Japanese car.

I didn't think I wanted to be a Del Webb active adult, sitting in my Del Webb bungalow on Del Webb Boulevard, taking the occasional stroll to the Del Webb Memorial Gardens, or the recreation centre, waiting for the next funeral. Sun City was a place that nurtured uncharitable thoughts, which turned quickly to misanthropic ones. As I drove up and down those manicured streets, past the raked gravel beds and the gardens planted with cacti, I could feel heads turn, eyes narrowing suspiciously, as if to say '*it's a young person*'. I began almost to feel like a teenager again, a delinquent. I wanted to find the loudest radio station I could, playing the most raucous and obscene heavy metal imaginable, crank it up and wind down the windows and cause a few heart attacks. Sun City had made me capable of murder.

I drove out of Sun City thinking that America wasn't a melting pot after all; it was a bouillabaisse – lots of small pieces floating in the same pot, but each quite separate and distinct from the other. It was a nation of fragments: black, white, young, 'active adult', rich, poor, middle income – I had found nowhere where all these elements had coalesced into one entity you could properly call a community.

The map of any American city could be coloured in by race or income; blacks on the south side, Hispanics on the west, white middle class to the north, and so on. But Phoenix went further; the gradations were more complex, more subtle. It was a city where the science of demographics – that witch doctory practised in the worlds of marketing and advertising, whereby the population is segmented into ever smaller, and more predictive, groups to sell things to – had become a practical fact. Television and press advertisements identified your peer group, and steered you towards it. In the suburbs of Scottsdale there were walled housing estates, with guards at the gate, available solely to young professionals with families; they complemented the communities built for 'active adults' on the other side of town.

All of this seemed utterly contradictory to the American nature, which, to the visitor, seemed always so welcoming, so courteous, so gregarious. Americans sought out strangers with an eagerness, and an openness, that could be disarming to anyone accustomed to the guarded and phlegmatic temperament of the British. Even the programmed courtesies of waitresses, ticket inspectors, the clerks at car-rental desks and airport check-ins – the How you doin's, and Have a nice days – which were so often held up as evidence of fakery, opportunism and a corrupted sensibility, seemed to me rather to be evidence of a more fundamental gentility and consideration. Better bogus pleasantry than genuine hostility.

And yet America's better nature itself seemed in danger of corruption. It had turned inwards, become suspicious and fearful. The success of Sun City was surely predicated as much on a fear of the outside world, as on the dubious attractions of an institutionalised 'active adulthood'.

Sun City and the new 'lifestyle' developments of Scottsdale seemed to echo with some atavistic yearning to rediscover, and recreate the old ideas of 'neighbourhood'. But it was hard to be neighbourly in Scottsdale: you would need to negotiate a brick wall, a security guard, another wall, a locked gate ... It made me nostalgic for Hollis, where there were no fences, no walls; where people could walk out of their back doors and talk to neighbours and be bothered by children and noise; where people greeted you with openness and friendliness (I kept remembering Dub Nell's words about his father – 'Daddy, he never met anybody who was a stranger'; in other words, everyone was his friend, a phrase that seemed perfectly to describe Dub himself).

'People in Scottsdale wonder why there's no community spirit,' said Earl de Berge, shaking his head over a beer one night in Durants. 'They work in a high-rise downtown, drive home, shut themselves off with people who share and reinforce exactly the same ideas and opinions they have. No wonder there's no community spirit. These people claim to be protecting themselves, but they're actually shutting themselves off from the world.'

Sun City had made me feel like doing the same thing myself. I took the road to Carefree, 25 miles north of Phoenix, where the desert met the mountains. Beside the road, cactus grew up to 12 feet high, like a lightly forested wood. Every acre of desert carried a 'for sale' sign – the sign of a real-estate business that had ground to a halt.

Carefree was designer desert living. The houses were built in wood, adobe and local stone, and looked as if they had grown from the desert organically. This was the most rigorously protected and planned neighbourhood in Arizona. What kind of people live here? I asked the woman in the real-estate office. 'Rich ones,' she said, without missing a beat.

I drove on, up into the foothills of the mountains. The road narrowed, twisted and climbed; mountains loomed on both sides. The view was untamed and achingly beautiful. A high wind was blowing. An eagle drifted on the air currents, dipped and was carried out of sight. I thought, I could live here. It was wild and free, and too far for the golf carts to travel.

I remembered a conversation that I had overheard, sitting in a House of Pancakes in downtown Phoenix, working my way through a chocolate chip special. It was an earnest young couple, getting to know each other. 'I like history because I wasn't there,' said the boy. The girl had pulled a face. 'Nah. Me, I'm a today kind of person.' At the time, I wasn't sure what it meant, but now I thought I understood. Phoenix was a today kind of city.

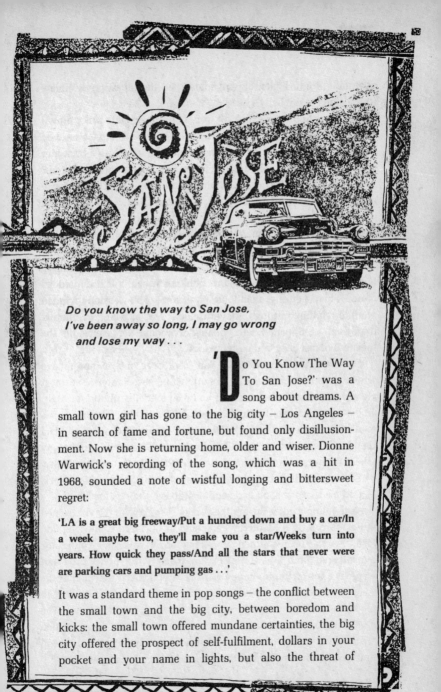

Do you know the way to San Jose,
I've been away so long, I may go wrong
and lose my way . . .

'**D**o You Know The Way To San Jose?' was a song about dreams. A small town girl has gone to the big city – Los Angeles – in search of fame and fortune, but found only disillusionment. Now she is returning home, older and wiser. Dionne Warwick's recording of the song, which was a hit in 1968, sounded a note of wistful longing and bittersweet regret:

'**LA is a great big freeway/Put a hundred down and buy a car/In a week maybe two, they'll make you a star/Weeks turn into years. How quick they pass/And all the stars that never were are parking cars and pumping gas . . .**'

It was a standard theme in pop songs – the conflict between the small town and the big city, between boredom and kicks: the small town offered mundane certainties, the big city offered the prospect of self-fulfilment, dollars in your pocket and your name in lights, but also the threat of downfall. 'Bright lights, big city,' lamented the blues singer Jimmy Reed, 'Gone to my baby's head . . .'

The plane to San Jose took off from Los Angeles into a sky brown with pollution. Los Angeles is a city that breeds a desire for escape.

I had spent the previous afternoon waiting to talk to a rock star who was having her photograph taken. My appointment was for 2 p.m. The studio was in the photographer's house, set back on a road winding up into the hills from Sunset Boulevard, and filled with ugly, overpriced works of art. There were platters of unusual cheeses and five kinds of fancy beer spread out on a table, replenished by a Mexican housemaid. The rock star threw back her long, blonde hair and struck poses, while a posse of assistants, hair-stylists, make-up artists and flunkies teased, billed and cooed around her, pouring unctuous platitudes. The session dragged on interminably through the afternoon. My appointment finally happened at 5 p.m. I left wishing irrational vengeance on the business of celebrity and all its works.

'Do You Know The Way To San Jose?' was one of those songs whose essential charm lay in its sentimental associations. For me, it always carried recollections of a youthful summer, pining for a girl who was, of course, infatuated with someone else. The song was another from the prodigious writing team of Burt Bacharach and Hal David, who wrote a string of hits for Dionne Warwick – and many others, of course, through the Sixties, including '24 Hours From Tulsa' – and when I talked to Hal David about it at his home in New York, he told me that the song had sentimental associations for him too.

As a young soldier during the Second World War, David trained at Fort Ord on the Monterey Peninsula in northern California; San Jose was the nearest town for recreation. 'I was very young', he remembered, 'and I had a lot of fun, met a lot of pretty girls and went to a lot of funny, happy bars. It was a place that had really good memories for me.' Twenty-five years later, when Burt Bacharach played him the provisional melody for the song, David recalled, 'The music seemed to speak to my unconscious. I could have written "Santa Fe", or any other place that scanned, but it was the good times I'd had in San Jose all those years ago . . . it just came back.'

San Jose was a small town when Hal David had been whooping it up there during the war years. 'It seemed to me like the idealised place where a small-town girl, or a small-town boy for that matter, would come from.' Now, San Jose was the third largest city, by population, on the West Coast of America, the eleventh largest in the nation.

It was quite the *neatest* American city I had seen. It had something of the bright, clinical efficiency of a Zürich or a Stuttgart. It was a college town, with all that suggests: a plenitude of eating places, art cinemas, jazz clubs, newspapers crammed with advertisements for mountain bikes and pine frame futons. The café selling *cappuccino* at $2.80 a cup (around £2) was as pretentious, and as expensive, as anything you would find in New York or Milan. It felt modestly proportioned, livable. Around the university campus were handsome Victorian frame houses, within walking distance of offices and shops. There was a light railway that buzzed back and forth across town. Policemen patrolled the streets not in prowl cars but on horseback.

San Jose stood at the southernmost end of the Santa Clara Valley, marked at the opposite end by the tip of the San Francisco Bay. The Valley covers an area of some 170 square miles. Before the Second World War, the Valley had been principally agricultural. With postwar peace and prosperity, however, a new industry took root – electronics. Stanford University in Palo Alto, at the northern end of the valley, was the seedbed: the defence industry was the catalyst.

By 1971, the conurbation of electronics and engineering companies that had sprung up along the valley, from Palo Alto to San Jose, was sufficiently developed for an electronics magazine to christen it 'Silicon Valley'. A myth was born. Silicon Valley was the crucible of the future: a place where computer-smart kids could dream up ideas that would revolutionise the modern world, and turn themselves into millionaires in the process. The story of Steve Jobs and Steve Wozniak, who built the first home computer in a garage in the suburb of Cupertino, and went on to found Apple, was a heroic archetype. Hewlett-Packard started in a garage too; ROLM in a prune shed.

A pamphlet from the San Jose Chamber of Commerce listed the things Valley residents had invented, or to which they had made 'a major contribution'. They included: the Transistor Computer; the Semi-Conductor; the Engineering Work Station; Aerobie; Gene Splicing; the Hydrogen Bomb; Flame Throwers; Polaris; Poseidon; Armoured Personnel Carriers; Transportable Baby Incubators and, mysteriously, the One-Handed Basketball Shot. People spoke of Silicon Valley in mythical terms; as the first model of the post-industrial age, 'the greatest incubator of entrepreneurial endeavours the world has ever seen.' Some 1,500 of the 2,500 largest electronics firms in America were based in Silicon Valley, along with half the leading venture capital firms in the world. People even likened the Valley's topography to computer circuitry: flat, symmetrical, the research labs and business parks sitting on top of it like silicon chips.

Much had changed in the twenty years since the phenomenon of Silicon Valley had been christened. The manufacture of silicon chips had been substantially farmed out to other parts of America, to Taiwan and to the *maquillardos* of Mexico. Nowadays, the Valley specialised mostly in 'R&D'. There were some too, who said the boom days had passed: that the whizz kids who had transformed their one-shot companies into corporations had either sold out or burned out, and that the recession was chipping away remorselessly at the rest. But even so, the Valley still felt like the very summit of the American technological and entrepreneurial dream, with all the feelings of vertigo that implied.

'This is still probably the most competitive place in the world,' Michael Malone told me. Malone was a brash and bullish man in his thirties, a local writer and television documentary maker, but, above all, an indefatigable enthusiast for the vicissitudes of life in Silicon Valley. 'It can be the most exciting place in the world,' he said, 'but it wears people out. If you're not ambitious then the parade will leave you behind. You don't grow old in Silicon Valley.' Nor, it seemed, did you find peace of mind.

While the great age of computers and entrepreneurialism was

incubating at Stanford University in the early Sixties, another, very different, revolution was also under way in Palo Alto. Ken Kesey was a graduate of Stanford, a writer who had based his first novel, *One Flew Over The Cuckoo's Nest*, on his experiences while working part-time as an orderly in a local mental hospital. It was during this period that Kesey had begun experimenting with the drug LSD, then legal and used extensively in psychiatric practice. In 1964, Kesey and a group of friends, calling themselves 'the Merry Pranksters', painted an old school bus in Dayglo colours and set off on a psychedelic journey across America, to meet that other great evangelist of LSD, Timothy Leary, at his home in Millbrook, in upstate New York – a trip (in every sense of the word) which was later chronicled by Tom Wolfe in his book, *The Electric Kool Aid Acid Test*.

The driver of the bus was a man named Neal Cassady. A decade earlier, Cassady had been immortalised under the pseudonym of Dean Moriarty, the hero of Jack Kerouac's *On The Road*. Kerouac's book gave shape to the 'Beat Movement', and defined a particular facet of American mythology, with its theme of frantic, restless movement back and forth across America in search of enlightenment and kicks – a state of 'beatitude' – through what Kerouac called virtuous poverty. Published in 1957, *On The Road* inspired a generation of young American backpackers to set off in search of America and themselves. Its culmination would be seen twelve years later, at Woodstock – although Kerouac, by then, was drunk and embittered that the legacy of what he had imagined as a holy quest should have degenerated into what he regarded as mindless hedonism.

Though his name was scarcely known, Neal Cassady was their model; the prototype American cowboy bohemian. Cassady was born in Denver, and grew up in flophouses in the haphazard care of an alcoholic father. In and out of reformatory schools, he was obsessed with wheels and speed. By his own estimate, Cassady had stolen (in his term 'borrowed') more than 500 cars by the age of sixteen. He had scant formal education only, yet could recite screeds of Proust and Dostoevsky from memory, and was a prolific writer, although he was never published in his lifetime.

Cassady was the maverick, unfettered spirit devouring life as if it might be snatched from him at any moment, lionised in prose by his friends. Kerouac saw in him the perfect expression of the instinctual freedom he craved for himself; to Allen Ginsberg, Cassady was both freedom personified, and the object of his own homosexual longings. In his epic poem *Howl*, the first salvo of the Beat Movement to win broad public attention, Ginsberg wrote of 'N. C., secret hero of these poems, cocksman and Adonis of Denver'.

But even as Kerouac and Ginsberg were being fêted as harbingers of a new literary style and intellectual freedom – and damned as moral degenerates – Neal Cassady was struggling to live the life of the good bourgeois in San Jose with his wife Carolyn and three children, working on the Southern Pacific Railway as a brakeman. Cassady described San Jose as 'nowheresville'.

'Life so simple, good and easy here,' he wrote to his friend Jack Kerouac, 'that it's actually unreal seeming like a joke or dream, no reason for worries . . .' Until the siren call of the road sounded once again, and Cassady left his wife and children, took up with Kesey's Merry Pranksters and piloted the bus across America, under the nickname 'Speed Limit'. He died in 1968, at the age of forty-one, after collapsing beside a railway track in Mexico from a combination of drugs and alcohol.

'He is the mover,' wrote William Burroughs of Cassady. 'Compulsive, dedicated, ready to sacrifice family, friends, even his car itself to the necessity of moving from one place to another. Wife and child may starve, friends exist only to exploit for gas money. Neal must move.' One reads from this a very American hero; torn between the work ethic and the hunger for self-gratification; the need for home, and the urge to move, infatuated with the road and the power of the automobile and the possibilities of flight – from job, family, responsibilities – which it offered him.

It was fitting, of course, that Cassady should have ended up in California, for if America was a country whose very essence was compounded of movement, the search for place, after California there was nowhere left to go – nowhere, that is, other than on more subtle and complicated journeys into the inner self. Kerouac and

Cassady had sought it through experience and 'virtuous poverty';
Leary and Kesey through LSD. And California now was the
spiritual heartland of 'New Ageism', with its trappings of channel-
ling, crystal-gazing and cosmic psycho-babble. California was the
edge of the known world; the place of final reckoning.

'Spiritual search?', Neal Cassady's long-suffering wife Carolyn
would note wrily, many years after his death. 'All Neal and Jack
ever really wanted was a house with a white picket fence and a
station wagon in the drive.'

There were lots of white picket fences and station wagons in the
drives of San Jose as I drove out through the suburbs to meet John
Cassady, Neal's only son. He lived in a single-storey frame house,
on a street of identical houses, each with a sloping drive, a back
yard and a basketball net attached to the garage door.

John's full name was John Allen Cassady. He had been named
after Jack Kerouac and Allen Ginsberg. Every time John wrote his
name, there was the history of the Beat Movement, right there. John
was in his early forties, with a shock of unruly white hair and a
scraggy white beard. He was an immensely likeable man, with a
manic, fast-talking gusto – mimicking accents from Groucho Marx
to True Brit – that might have come from his father. He worked in
– what else? – computers, for a company that had developed a
magic wand which passed over typed documents and fed the
information directly into a computer. 'People ask me how these
things work. I tell 'em it's all a matter of PFM,' John chuckled. 'Pure
fucking magic.'

John talked of his job with an ironic detachment, work rather
than a vocation. He wasn't the corporate type. The back room of
his house had been turned into a 'music room', with guitars, ampli-
fiers, and an old piano on which he would hammer out blues songs
when everything got too much. His girlfriend Vimula had studied
Hindu philosophy at the Naropa Institute and made jewellery out
of silver and turquoise.

We took a drive to Los Gatos, a short distance from San Jose,
where the Cassady family once lived. In Neal Cassady's time, the
road would have run past fields; now it ran past suburbs. Then,

Los Gatos was a small, sleepy town set amid fruit orchards. Now the town bore the unmistakeable patina of gentrification; most of the fruit orchards had made way for housing developments; the old school house was a themed shopping centre with expensive gift boutiques. But Los Gatos was a lovely place still, with elegant Victorian timber houses on tree-lined streets, which wound up into the hills, through lush redwood and pine woods to bring you to a commanding view across 'the ditch' of Silicon Valley.

Los Gatos had always been middle class – Neal Cassady bought his home, a modest bungalow, with a settlement from an accident working on the railways. In the intervening years it had become simply rich, home for the Silicon Valley whizz kids and the new heroes of the entrepreneurial age. Steve Wozniak, the founder of Apple, lived here; and Gary Dahl, the man who 'invented' that quintessential symbol of disposable income, the Pet Rock, a common or garden rock that the owner was supposed to treat with the affection of a family pet.

We meandered around the hills and eventually came to the old Cassady home. We were less than 5 miles from where John now lived, only 2 from where he worked, but he said he had not visited the house in years, and seeing it stirred old memories; how they would go on family outings in the car, with the radio turned up loud, Neal jerking the car from side to side in time to Chuck Berry's 'Nadine', while the children rocked and squealed delightedly in the back seat.

John pointed out a neighbour's house where as a child he had 'borrowed' a soapbox go-cart while his friend was out. The neighbours had returned to find not John, but the middle-aged Neal careering down the hill in the soapbox, whooping joyfully.

It was hard for him to get a perspective on his father now, he said; hard to separate his personal memories from what he had read and been told, the myth of Neal, the last American cowboy, 'Speed Limit', 'the fastest man in America'. His speed carried him away from the family too often, and for so much of John's childhood his father had been a mere rumour, working on the railroad, off on a spree. When John was twelve, Neal left the family altogether, to live in San Francisco, although he would come home again from time to time, when the craziness got too much. 'I guess he was kind of torn,' said John. 'Neal was an intelligent, logical man and it actually drove him mad that he had these impulses towards sex and drugs. People got the wrong idea and thought that's what Neal and Jack and Allen were all about, but they weren't about that at all. I think Neal wanted to taste as much life as he could, but he wanted to explain life too.'

John remembered a day in Los Gatos – he would have been fifteen or sixteen – and a crowd of people milling around outside a bookshop. John pressed forward to see what was going on. Outside the shop was a piece of psychedelic sculpture, and there beside it was Neal, a ruler in his hand, pacing to and fro around the sculpture, rocking and rolling, gesticulating like a crazed college professor while he delivered an impromptu lecture on the sculpture's form, structure and meaning – the famous Cassady 'speed-rap' where philosophy, history, literature, metaphysics, hipster-speak and gobbledegook conjoined into a surreal, bamboozling stream of consciousness. The crowd were laughing and pointing, unsure whether they were watching a genius, a madman or a clown. 'I was embarrassed, you know,' John remembered, 'seeing your own father doing this. I kind of hung back on the edge so he wouldn't see me, but then he looked over and caught sight of me, and he shot me this look as if to say 'I'm sorry, son.' That was what John remembered when he thought of Neal.

A Mercedes and a Volvo were now parked in front of the old Cassady house, where Neal and Jack Kerouac had talked literature and philosophy and the creed of virtuous poverty long into the night. The house was owned by a Korean family.

Poverty – virtuous or otherwise – appeared to have been banished under some obscure public ordinance. San Jose had the highest number of upper-income households of any 'metro area' in America. It was the highest-ranking area in household income, after tax, in the country; its population was among the most highly educated. It seemed rich in everything except for contentment.

'San Jose is post-modern living at its very best – or very worst,' Bob Glenner, a professor in sociology at San Jose State University, told me. If Michael Malone had been the most ardent champion of San Jose's entrepreneurial spirit, Bob Glenner was San Jose's harshest critic. Glenner had the air of a liberal idealist whose time had come and gone. 'There's no sense of community here,' he said; 'everything is spread out, atomised. People spend enormous amounts of time commuting. You have a tremendous fragmentation of lifestyle; just to afford to live here everybody needs to work ludicrous hours; family life suffers. The prevailing feeling here is of life going too fast for anyone to keep up. And it's getting worse – just little things, like the way people cut each other up at freeway exits. You noticed that?' I had. The previous night I had been caught in a cloud burst on the freeway and been swept past my exit by the stream of traffic ploughing recklessly through the sheeting rain, refusing to let me cross lanes. But this was hardly unusual. Freeway driving was an arena for personal idiosyncracies and solipsistic whim; one minute you could find yourself engaged in gladiatorial duels with thundering semi trucks; the next trapped for miles behind three cars strung across the freeway, all driving at 35 miles per hour, refusing to move over to let you pass. Freeway formation driving was one of America's more bizarre pastimes.

People in the Valley worked hours 25 per cent above the national average. The Valley had the highest divorce rate in the country, along with one of the largest disposable incomes per capita in America. In 1985, a local newspaper estimated that the illegal drug bill in Silicon Valley was $500 million a year; another local survey reported that 35 per cent of respondents in the computer industry 'frequently' or 'occasionally' worked under the influence of cocaine or marijuana (44 per cent admitted they frequently or occasionally worked under the influence of alcohol). The drugs fad had somewhat faded in the purgative atmosphere of the late Eighties. 'The softies – the guys who work in software making up all this magical stuff no one else can understand – they're still into pot,' one computer technician told me. 'But middle management are drinking carrot juice and pumping iron.'

There was also, Bob Glenner told me, 'a lot of angst about bonding.' Everywhere I went I kept catching fragments of other people's conversations: 'I don't know who to trust any more.' 'I'm giving relationships a rest.' One Sunday afternoon I sat in a restaurant, watching two girls pick their way through a plate of oysters. 'Why can't I find anyone who isn't just interested in themselves?' 'It's a shame I missed him – he'd have been a real catch . . .' They looked affluent, chic, and gloomy.

Everybody seemed to have been divorced at least once and to have nightmarishly complicated personal lives. No one offered a better perspective on all this than Rand. She worked in real estate, selling property to the people who had made their fortunes in computers, selling it again when they hit their first divorce, nervous breakdown or financial crash. 'San Jose is money, greed, all pervasive superficiality . . .', she said. It was flip, but it contained more than a germ of truth. Yet perversely all this angst gave a bracing quality to the air. It made people feel like survivors. There was nothing else to do but be cynical.

'It's a land beyond guilt,' said Rand. 'There's no accountability, because your roots are somewhere else.'

Rand was middle-aged, divorced with grown-up children, vivacious, a chat show host waiting to be discovered. 'This is California rancho, this is *faux* . . .' – she was thumbing through her brochure of available properties, an alternative map of the psyche of San Jose – 'this is nice, this is nowhere . . . '

The brochure gave way to her photo album. 'This guy's independently wealthy. He made a fortune with Apple. He doesn't do anything now except drugs.' A man was smiling blearily into the camera. He was wearing a novelty shop Groucho Marx nose and moustache. Rand turned the pages. There was her mother; her father; her daughter; somebody she had been sailing with in Sausalito; friends; neighbours; a dog. They were all wearing Groucho Marx masks.

'That's my friend. He's fifteenth in rotation. I try to get my men in rotation, so I don't see too much of them. You'll notice he's drinking out of my famous Mickey Mouse cup.' Dave was wearing a Groucho Marx mask too.

'And this is Jack Kerouac Park . . .' It was a photograph of the memorial to the writer, in his home town of Lowell, Massachusetts. Rand came from Lowell too. 'I blame Kerouac for the whole mess we're in now,' she said with a sigh. What mess, I asked. Rand smiled, as if to say, isn't it obvious? 'The if-it-feels-good-do-it philosophy of the Sixties. It's corrupted everything that's decent about America,' she said. It was hard to tell if Rand was being serious. This was a woman, after all, who put her men on rotation; who photographed people wearing Groucho Marx nose and moustache sets. She had made a decision, she said. 'I'm going back to grad school to put some structure in my life. That's what everybody here is after now – structure . . .'

The great earthquake of October 1989, in which 273 people lost their lives, had given everybody pause for thought. The epicentre had been only 20 miles from San Jose, and in Los Gatos some of the most handsome Victorian houses were still slumped at awkward angles, as if they had been punched by a giant fist, or were jacked up and in the process of reconstruction. 'The quake really shook people up,' said Rand, 'made them aware of their mortality. It made people reassess. It brought neighbours together for the first time, erased boundaries. Suddenly everyone was talking about how many champagne glasses had broken . . .'

To the casual observer, the hi-tech of Silicon Valley seemed to have all but eclipsed the high times of Neal Cassady – but not quite. A few weeks before I arrived in San Jose, Ken Kesey, the orchestrator of the acid test, had also passed through town, driving a replica of his painted psychedelic bus, *Furthur* (sic), en route for the Smithsonian Institute in Washington, which had requested it for its collection of Americana. (The original bus stood rotting on Kesey's Oregon farm, and the Smithsonian subsequently refused the replica.)

There was a new generation of psychedelicists in Northern California – a sort of 'hi-tech underground' that was the antithesis of corporate computer culture, built around the development of computerised 'virtual reality' and the so-called 'smart drugs' – legal (and some illegal) substances designed to have quite specific psychotropic and neural effects. It was a movement with its own literature (much of it, of course, on floppy disk rather than in print) and its own jargon: 'cyberspace', 'virtualphobia', 'memory fuel', 'yogatronics'.

An advertisement in *Metro* – the Santa Clara Valley weekly newspaper – announced that Timothy Leary would be among the lecturers for a seminar at Stanford University on the subject of 'Psychedelics – the past, present and future'. Leary now made his living lecturing, writing and designing computer software programmes. Thumbing through the computer journals in the Computer Literacy Bookshop I came upon an article which Leary had written describing the computer screen as 'both interactive and inter-personal . . . a tool for amplifying the consciousness of individuals and for facilitating the interpersonal relationships between human beings.'

The Computer Literacy Bookshop claimed to stock the largest selection of computer books in the world, and I could well believe it. I was looking for a book called *Behind The Silicon Curtain*, by Dennis Hays, which Bob Glenner had recommended as required reading on the ills of Valley life. It was not exactly burning up the bestseller lists. I had had to telephone five major booksellers before I could find anyone who had even heard of it. Like almost every commercial transaction in America, from buying an aspirin to checking the oil in the car, actually buying the book entailed an interminable journey to a shopping mall on the other side of town. I drove past mile after mile of modern, low-slung office buildings, grimly featureless, crouching furtively, it seemed, behind banks of shrubbery, chain-link fencing and security cameras. They carried a distinct air of menace – these crucibles of gene-splicing, napalm and aerobie. It was disconcerting to think that behind the shrubbery and the security cameras, people were hunched over electronic work-stations, plotting the future.

It was hardly surprising that nobody stocked *Behind The Silicon Curtain*. Hays' book painted a picture of Silicon Valley as a grim dystopia of passive, supine, exploited corporate drones, addicted to work and seeking respite from their alienation in compulsive shopping, physical fitness and drug abuse. Once computers had promised a vision of paradise, Hays wrote; now they were tools of corporate enslavement and unscrupulous profit-making.

The Computer Literacy Bookshop had one copy, filed at the back of their sociology section. It seemed to have been there some time. With its clinically functional lay-out, its air of quiet, humidified industriousness, the Computer Literacy Bookshop somewhat resembled a computer 'clean room'. The customers were mostly Asian students. They were scrutinising the texts on networking, software engineering and DOS systems with the rapt concentration of archaeologists deciphering hieroglyphics. This was San Jose's temple of wisdom, where today's seekers after enlightenment were to be found.

Bob Glenner told me that two-thirds of the 15,000 students 'majoring' in engineering and electronics at San Jose state were Asian – Chinese, Vietnamese, Korean. Walking around the campus I had been struck by its air of industriousness; students hurrying along the corridors between classes, bent studiously over textbooks in stair-wells. In the late Fifties, Jack Kerouac contributed a definition of the 'Beat Generation' to the American College Dictionary. It read: 'Members of the generation that came of age after World War Two–Korean War, who join in the relaxation of social and sexual tensions and espouse anti-regimentation, mystic disaffiliation and material simplicity values, supposedly as a result of Cold War disillusionment.' It was not, I fancied, an entry that was much read or heeded at San Jose state. 'Mystic disaffiliation' seemed a concept which nobody here looked much interested in – a luxury nobody would feel they could afford. But then I had met nobody of college age in all the time I had been in America who had read On The Road, or even heard of Jack Kerouac. His ideas were as much ancient history as the Roman Empire or the Beatles.

Engineering and computer sciences were attractive to Asian students, said Glenner, because they did not depend on language skills, and led to jobs that immediately lifted you into the professional classes, in much the same way as law and accountancy had appealed to an earlier generation of Jewish immigrants from Europe. They were a way of getting on.

Some 16 per cent of San Jose's population was Asiatic; 55 per cent was Anglo-White; 25 per cent Hispanic, and only 4 per cent black. Santa Clara Avenue – coincidentally, the street where Neal and Carolyn Cassady lived when they first moved to San Jose – was lined with Vietnamese and Korean supermarkets, restaurants, garages and workshops. These immigrants from the Pacific Rim were the new Americans, and they brought with them not only the traditional immigrant virtues of close familial ties and a willingness to work hard, but also a certain style.

One night I had a drink in the Fairmont Hotel – a grandiose establishment in the centre of San Jose, newly refurbished with an imposing marbled entrance hall and a luxurious piano lounge. The lounge was filled with people quietly drinking cocktails, largely indifferent to the music. But when the pianist struck up 'Begin the Beguine', an oriental couple rose from their seats and swept elegantly across the floor in an ostentatious display of precise ballroom dancing. When they finished, the lounge erupted into applause.

'The Vietnamese and Koreans are a thrilling injection into the Valley,' the writer and broadcaster Michael Malone told me. 'No past, all future. They want to make it.'

Malone took a phlegmatic view of the vicissitudes of life in the Valley. He was the most fervent champion of social Darwinism, the survival of the fittest, I had met since Eustace, the Ugandan refugee, back in Chattanooga, all those weeks and thousands of miles ago. Life in the Valley might be stressful, said Malone, it might lead to broken marriages for some, broken lives for others, but what the hell ... it was the very essence of the American Dream – the new gold rush, the ultimate entrepreneurial challenge. 'What's always been at the heart of this valley is that great leap of faith,' Malone said. 'But the big question now is, does it poison itself? For a while, this was the most expensive part of America. There is terrible traffic pollution. Prices are sky-high. If people can't afford to risk leaving their jobs because the house payments are too high; if zoning laws become too rigid, then you risk killing entrepreneurship.

'With entrepreneurs, you never know what they're going to come up with. They have no community constituency, because they're not that kind of person. They become self-interested; their objective is to acquire power and influence. It enforces a meritocracy. This isn't a racist place at all. There's not so much time for that kind of social stratification; people get rewarded on results. And if you can't keep up, you'd better clear out.

'As a rule, the key firms have a ten-year stretch. So if you want to bet on the future you have to bet on a bunch of guys sitting around in a coffee shop some place with their dreams. But maybe these guys don't exist now, in which case Silicon Valley is already dead. This place could be paradise, or it could be Gary, Indiana – a dying, anachronistic city.'

Having spent the last fifteen years writing about and commenting on the fever of entrepreneurialism, Malone himself was now joining in. His mornings were spent with a couple of friends, sitting in coffee shops, chewing over an idea for a new business. Of course, he wouldn't tell me what it was. 'This town is the ultimate example of what freedom looks like,' Malone enthused. 'You drop your old life and pick up a new one. You can do what you want. But if you fail, no one's going to pick you up. It's thin ice.'

It took me back to something Bob Glenner had said. 'Nobody has time for talking about the *meaning* of existence any more. Where's the essence? Where are we going? Is this seriously the pinnacle of Western civilisation, this mess we've got ourselves into? Nobody asks those questions. Here, meaning revolves around material success. It's very personalised. It's not seen in terms of community or society.'

Nor were the ethical questions that had preoccupied people in the Sixties being raised any longer, Glenner said. More than 500 firms in Silicon Valley worked directly on military contracts, and hundreds more worked indirectly for the Pentagon under subcontract. Glenner had conducted a survey among students in the university's engineering department and been alarmed to find that the majority of them would have no qualms about using their talents to make bombs.

'A lot of these younger people will be the first generation in three to be downwardly mobile from their parents. They want careers.'

The great attraction of California was always its possibilities of freedom. 'This was where you could be whatever you wanted to be, without people hassling you.' So if it had once meant freedom, I asked, what did it mean now? Glenner gave the question some thought. 'Insecurity . . .', he said at last. 'Fear.'

On Sunday I followed the weekend traffic, out through the mountains to the coastal town of Santa Cruz. It had rained in the night, and the trees were lush, renewed, the aroma of pine and redwood cutting through the asphalt and exhaust smell of the freeway.

It was a beautiful day, too cold to swim, but some hardy souls in kayaks and on surf boards were paddling out to catch the breakers, a quarter of a mile from shore. At the end of the pier, sea lions were basking on the steel girders and honking for food. You could buy small pots of fish from the souvenir stall, and children were running back and forth, dangling over the edge of the balustrade, squealing delightedly and throwing morsels to the sea lions below.

America had never seemed more ordered, more at peace with itself. The green hills rolled away behind the town, to vanish in the shimmering afternoon haze. Along the headland, traffic had slowed to watch the surfers, bobbing perilously in the swell. One after another, a figure would rise up out the foam, their body thrown into relief against the wall of water, as they chased the wave into the shore – momentarily triumphant – to be silently swallowed up in its soapy blue-green diamond maw.

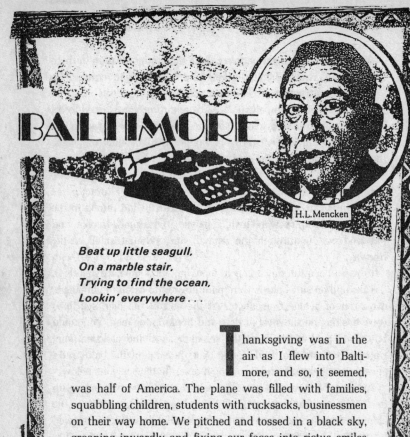

H.L. Mencken

Beat up little seagull,
On a marble stair,
Trying to find the ocean,
Lookin' everywhere...

Thanksgiving was in the air as I flew into Baltimore, and so, it seemed, was half of America. The plane was filled with families, squabbling children, students with rucksacks, businessmen on their way home. We pitched and tossed in a black sky, groaning inwardly and fixing our faces into rictus smiles as the plane hiccuped in and out of turbulence.

We touched down in time for the evening rush hour, and the heavens opened. Traffic on the freeway slowed to a standstill. Thanksgiving itself was still three days off, but in my hotel there was a palpable holiday mood. I ate supper to the accompaniment of a muzak tape of nauseatingly jaunty Christmas songs. 'Four more weeks I gotta put up with this shit,' said the waiter under his breath.

The two celebrations, it seemed, had fused into one, as if Thanksgiving was simply a rehearsal – a mere preparatory overture – for the orgy of gluttony and consumption that Christmas would bring. Advertisers offered special holiday sales of everything from automobiles to vacuum cleaners, as if the blessing of the holiday was somehow incomplete without the personal indulgence of over-extending one's credit line. TV anchorpeople hyped-up the Thanksgiving dinner as if it were the Superbowl, turning to each other at the end of newscasts with syrupy smiles, smacking their lips theatrically and making remarks about each other's turkeys that seemed rich in double entendre. 'Got that bird in the oven yet, Tammi?' 'Mmmm, the bigger the better for me, Todd.'

The first Thanksgiving dinner was eaten by the Pilgrims some time between 21 September and 9 November 1621, a feast to give thanks for the successful harvest of the native corn crop, after a winter of terrible hardship and deprivation which had followed their landing in the *Mayflower* at New Plymouth in December 1620. The Pilgrims' feast is believed to have lasted for up to nine days, and included oysters, eel, corn, bread, goose, venison, watercress, leeks, plums, berries, turkey, of course, and 'popped corn', brought to the feast as a gift by members of the native Wampanoag tribe.

By comparison, the modern American managed to cram in his Thanksgiving meal of turkey, ham, sauerkraut, roast potatoes, chocolate cake and pumpkin pie in a mere six-hour sitting. (And nowadays the popcorn came in cartons.) The average American consumed 2.8 pounds of food on Thanksgiving Day – this in a country with a population of 240 million people. America put on some 300,000 tons weight in an afternoon. And the next day people waddled and groaned, told each other their ice boxes were working overtime, their microwaves busting a fuse and swore not to eat for a week.

I sat in my room and watched *Avalon*, the director Barry Levinson's retelling of his own family history. Levinson grew up in Baltimore, and most of his films have been autobiographical essays on his own upbringing. *Diner* was about his own teenage years; *Tin Men* about his father. *Avalon* tells the story of Sam Krichinsky (a character based on Levinson's grandfather), a Russian Jew who arrives in Baltimore in the early part of the twentieth century to join his brothers in the wallpapering business. It is Thanksgiving, and Sam wanders wide-eyed along the streets of the city, as fireworks explode around him. It is an epiphanous moment of deliverance, optimism and hope: an emblem of so many entwining American myths about family, community, the promise of redemption and freedom in the new world.

The very idea of America was based on all these communities finding a shared focus in these aspirations, a consensus that over-ruled ethnic or racial differences. It was a heroic ideal. And yet travelling across America one had been reminded time and again how insuperable a task holding together this fragile consensus had become.

Baltimore was one of America's oldest cities, the most European of any in America I had visited. It had crescents and squares of Georgian homes that reminded you of Cheltenham or Gloucester; imposing marble-clad public buildings and, in the working districts, terraces of row houses, which resembled the Victorian working-class areas of Salford, Bolton or any other northern English industrial city.

Baltimore was a port; traditionally a centre of industry and traffic, on the cusp of the north and the south. Compared to southern cities, it seemed fast; compared to northern, it moved slow. Its dichotomy was echoed in its very speech. To southerners it sounded northern; to northerners it sounded southern – the faintly nasal twang, the drawled consonants. Local people lived in somewhere called 'Bawl'more'.

Randy Newman's song about the city, 'Baltimore', sounded a plangent tone of decay and loss; a city past its sell-by date.

Hard times in the city/In a hard town by the sea/Ain't nowhere to run to/ There ain't nothing here for free.

Newman describes vignettes of a city in decay:

Hooker on the corner, waitin' for a train/Drunk lyin' on the sidewalk, sleepin' in the rain/And they hide their faces, and they hide their eyes/ 'Cause the city's dyin', and they don't know why

The singer dreams of escape, taking

my sister Sandy, and my little brother Ray,

and heading off in a station wagon to the country

Where the mountain's high/Never comin' back here 'till the day I die.

Randy Newman had made something of a speciality of writing about cities. His song 'Birmingham', about the state capital of Alabama, was a droll paean of praise to the redneck capital of America. 'I Love LA' a crudely energetic celebration of the vulgarity and hedonism of that benighted city. By comparison, 'Baltimore' was an exercise in studied sobriety. It was hardly a surprise to learn that Newman had never been to the city before writing the song. (There was no reason he should have been: Hal David had never been to Tulsa; Joni Mitchell had been stuck in the traffic outside Woodstock: not having been to a place seemed like the perfect qualification for writing about it.)

'I'd been through it in a train,' Newman told me, when I spoke to him at his Los Angeles home. 'And I'd read about it in the *National Geographic* magazine. But it was about the biggest city in America that I'd never stopped in. It had this reputation as the quintessential dying city, and I was fascinated by the look of it from the train – all those endless row houses, all that marble. At a time when everything in America is becoming so homogenised, Baltimore seemed to have its own character.

'There's no place that looks like Baltimore. I've played there since, and I've seen a bit of it. Actually, they were very angry at me for writing the song, because the city's not dying. It was hardly the image they wanted. So they were pretty mad. There was a local politician who replied by writing poetry in the local newspaper – 'Randy Newman is not human . . .', that kind of thing. And when I played the Lyric Theatre they had Miss Baltimore come up on stage and give me a bunch of letters from people, complaining about what I'd written. When I played there it was the worst snowstorm they'd had in a hundred years. Still, I got a good house.'

Newman wrote and recorded 'Baltimore' in 1977 (it appeared on the album, *Little Criminals*), at a time when the city, and its reputation, was undergoing rehabilitation.

In the Sixties, Baltimore had been a byword for inner-city decline

– a place, Antero Pietila, a city affairs writer on the *Baltimore Sun* told me, 'which felt permanently dismal about itself'. Nothing made it more dismal than its harbour. Once one of the busiest on the Eastern seaboard, the coming of containerisation, and the decline of Baltimore's industry had turned the harbour into a desolate zone of scabrous warehouses and abandoned industrial workings. Millions of dollars had been poured into restoring the area, not as a working harbour but as a tourist playground, with shops, restaurants, an aquarium, a collection of historic sailing vessels. Baltimore was hailed as a model of restoration. A showcase city. The Mayor, William Donald Schaeffer (who subsequently became the governor of Maryland), was a showboater who puffed and flattered the city's ego with slogans. 'Baltimore Is The Best.'

'Everyone knew it was an outright lie,' said Pietila with a chuckle, 'but it still made them feel better. The late Sixties and early Seventies were a period of great hope and energy in Baltimore. But that energy has gone now. Now people feel awful about the city.

'The harbour front is wonderful, of course. The quality of life in the city has improved if you measure it by restaurants and gift boutiques. But measured by education, health, employment, crime, housing standards . . . in all of these ways it has declined, absolutely in all cases and relative to other cities in America.'

In twenty years, the population of Baltimore had fallen from 970,000 to 740,000. Thirty years ago, the biggest employer in the city was Bethlehem Steel – the world's largest steel producer – which employed 35,000 people; 6,000 worked there now. Baltimore was a manufacturing city on the skids.

Like St Louis, like almost every city of any size north of the Mason-Dixon line which had experienced similar problems, Baltimore had tried the customary ploys of inner-city regeneration – a new ballpark in the centre of town; the selective rehabilitation of particular areas; an urban pioneer scheme – the 'dollar housing' policy by which abandoned homes were sold for a dollar to anyone willing to rehabilitate them. But Baltimore had no corporate headquarters, no downtown department store – the subtle indicators of commercial prosperity.

'We fool ourselves,' said Pietila. 'We talk about gentrification and reclamation, but for every one person moving into the city, three more are moving out into the counties. The white middle class has largely gone, and the black middle class is following them.'

It was Saturday, unseasonably warm, and I took a walk by the harbour. There had been a parade – Americans love parades – and children were running around with flags and balloons and the expression of flushed excitement that comes from having witnessed something wondrous and larger than life. Like so many monuments to American civic planning, the harbour had been hemmed in behind a six-lane highway, making any sort of pedestrian assault at ground level a hazardous, not to say suicidal, enterprise. Instead, a 'skypath' had been built, which cunningly carried visitors into the harbour through an enormous food complex where they could scoop up burgers, giant cups of popcorn, crab cakes, squelchy hot dogs, cartons of French fries, slices of pizza the size of portable television sets and cans of liquid sugar – all the things which nobody seemed able to go for more than half an hour without.

I passed an elderly black man seated on a bench, holding an enormous piece of cardboard bearing a crudely stencilled message that began: 'My daughter caught fire and she has a three-year-old daughter and another one nine months . . .' It was the most complicated plea for help I had ever seen, a complex explanation of tragic circumstances, moving on to exhortations to righteous behaviour, complete with Biblical references, and ending with a poignantly optimistic promise, 'Show mercy and you will get help on the other end'. There was something touching about this, a man reduced to begging, offering a complete religious and philosophical justification for charity with the promise of remuneration for the charitable at the end of it – as if no decent American could turn down a transaction which offered eternal blessings as a reward. Let's make a deal: I get the money, you go to Paradise.

But as a sales pitch it was truly hopeless. You had to stop in your tracks and read it – really *study* it – and nobody did. He was a toothless man, rheumy-eyed, a baseball cap skewed sideways on his head. 'Bad wire,' he said when I asked about the house. 'No insurance.' He raised his voice at passers-by, 'People – help me out!'

By night, the mood of the city changed. The streets emptied, and the centre of Baltimore took on the habitual air of abandonment and desolation of all American cities.

I had met up with some friends, John and Eileen, and we went to a late showing of the film *Cape Fear*. We were the only whites in the theatre. The audience were more unnerving than the film. Nobody would keep still; groups of young men moved from one part of the cinema to the other, slumping in seats, moving again, as if engaged in some cryptic, unfathomable business. At moments of high psychological tension, people whooped and roared with laughter. In the seats behind us, a group were loudly discussing some family business. I felt very English, very white.

John was my oldest friend. We had grown up together, closer than brothers: first scrapes; cigarettes furtively shared; first girlfriends; first mohair suits. He had lived in Venezuela, then in California. Now, at the age of forty, he had married Eileen, who came from a Baltimore Jewish family.

Eileen's mother had lived alone since the death of her husband in an apartment block in Park Heights, a comfortable, middle-class Jewish neighbourhood. The Eisens were a close-knit family. Her brother and sister lived in the same block. Two of her three children still lived in the city. Mrs Eisen's family had arrived in America from Odessa at the turn of the century. This awareness of knowing where your family came from, remembering why they had come, increasingly struck me as the very essence of being an American.

Mrs Eisen was an elegant woman in late middle age. We sat in her immaculately appointed apartment and she talked about being Jewish in Baltimore. Her husband, she told me, had been a member of the Lions – a charitable organisation – and she remembered being invited to a fellow member's house for dinner. 'And as we arrived they said, "These are our Jewish friends, the Eisens." They'd introduce you like that so nobody would make anti-Semitic remarks at dinner, you see?' She shook her head at the sadness of this. And now, she said, some friends were worried because a house nearby had been bought by a family named Johnson. A common black name.

The Jewish population of Baltimore was around 90,000. One quarter of them were Orthodox. Baltimore had the largest population of Orthodox Jews by percentage of any city in America – greater even than New York.

German Jews began arriving in the city as early as the eighteenth century. The Bremen Line made its business by shipping emigrants to the new world, coal back to the old. The pogroms of the nineteenth century brought two and a half million Jews from Russia and Eastern Europe to Baltimore. New York processed its immigrants at Ellis Island. Baltimore's equivalent was Locust Point, off the southern tip of the city.

The newcomers settled in the east of the city, fanning out from the point of disembarkation at the old harbour of Fells Point. The centre of the Jewish community was Lombard Street, Baltimore's equivalent of New York's Hester Street, a warren of row houses and tenement blocks, a bubbling soup of human activity. Its centre-piece was the Lloyd Street synagogue, the heart of Jewish religious life – and, therefore, all life – in the city.

The great diaspora had long since flung most of the Jewish population north-west, to the suburbs. The row houses around Lombard Street had been demolished, and replaced by project housing, and the population now was predominantly black. But the Lloyd Street synagogue still stood, transformed into a Jewish Heritage Centre, with a library and a permanent exhibition of Jewish life in Baltimore.

On a Sunday morning, the car park outside the synagogue was full of people, coming back to the place of their heritage, bewildered pilgrims, glancing nervously from side to side as they stepped off the bus. The exhibition chronicled the birth and development of the Jewish community through sepia photographs, letters, scraps of official documents; the Jewish schools, hospital, benevolent associations, the Hebrew Free Burial Association.

Much of it was given over to a history of the Jewish clothing industry in Baltimore. About 70 per cent of Jewish immigrants had worked in 'the needle trade'. There were items of clothing on tailors' dummies – a simple linen dress, a gentleman's suit; advertising cards and brochures from the Twenties and Thirties, and heartbreak photographs of tailors and sweatshop seamstresses, simple faces, the pride and expectancy shining through their worn, frozen expressions. And there, nestling like a viper, a pre-war advertisement for the Swastika Realty Company of Baltimore, advising prospective customers, 'You can buy a home site in Frederick and ... you are sure your family will have desirable neighbours. The kind of people you are glad to meet anywhere.' The kind of people, in other words, who weren't Jews.

I sought out the archivist. Edward Sandler was a small, wizened man with a face like a wrinkled berry, mournful, deeply sunk eyes and an agitated manner. Above his forehead, his pate glistened and shone like an eggshell. Ed's father had arrived in Baltimore from Lithuania in 1897; his grandfather had been in the leather business (a sandler is a shoemaker). Respectable people, doyens of Lombard Street, there in the human soup.

'But then what happens is this,' he said. 'People better themselves.' The Jewish migration outwards, he said, had been controlled by a system of restricted covenants, which prevented Jews and blacks renting property in desirable areas, and which operated in the city until they were declared unconstitutional in 1948.

The Jewish population had been 'channelled' into the north-west part of Baltimore – the areas of Pikesville, Randallstown and Stevenson. It was here that the vast majority of the city's 90,000 Jews lived, and where the majority of synagogues were.

'I've never lived next door to a Gentile in my whole life,' said Ed. 'From the time I was a little boy. Four or five times I've moved. And that's the history of the Jewish people.'

Listening to Sandler I was reminded of *Avalon*, which portrayed so well the gradual fragmentation of family life over the course of three generations. The disintegration of the old values in the face of the new. The film's recurring motif is Thanksgiving, the symbolic centrepiece of the American experience, the moment when the family is at its closest, or when the distance between them is rendered most vividly. It is on Thanksgiving that Sam Krichinsky is reunited with his brothers in the New World. The family gather for the Thanksgiving meal in their home in Avalon – a tenement block in the Lombard Street soup – a warm, chaotic intimacy, parents at one table, children the other.

The family strive and are modestly rewarded. At another Thanksgiving dinner, television is introduced to the family circle. The elderly, sensing its corrosive power, turn away; the children are hypnotised. Time passes. The sons Americanise their names – to Kaye and Kirk – to win acceptability. The migration to the suburbs begins. The city meant virtuous poverty, solidarity, support; the suburbs means dislocation, loneliness, distance. When one of the brothers arrives too late for the carving of the Thanksgiving turkey, the deep bond of the family is finally severed. There are to be no reunions now. Sam's son, Julius, his wife and children, spend Thanksgiving silently around the television set, while Sam's wife dies in hospital. The film closes with Sam's grandson, Michael, visiting the dying Sam in a Jewish home for the elderly with his own son, the fourth generation. They watch the Macey's parade on television. It is Thanksgiving.

'Sure, it's a sad story,' said Edward Sandler with a shrug. 'But the film's a cop-out.' A cop-out? 'It could be about any ethnic group in America,' said Ed. 'You wouldn't even know they were a Jewish family until you see the Star of David in the cemetery. From the point of view of the Jewish Historical Society it was not satisfactory. It hedged it.'

But wasn't that partly the point, I wondered, that the Jewish experience in America was similar to the Italian, the Polish, the Scandinavian, almost every ethnic immigrant group? That the fragmentation the film described was as much a part of the common American experience as hope and unity had once been? The strength of the story was its universality.

'We don't like it,' said Ed, bringing the conversation to a close with a shrug. 'It denies our heritage.' He steered me out of his office and into the bookshop. 'You take a look and see if something interests you. We got a sale on.'

I bought a book on Jewish history. Ed produced a magazine,

containing an article he'd written. 'You can read that if you want.'
Could they make a photocopy, I asked. 'I guess we could do that,'
said Ed. He turned to the lady behind the cash desk. 'How much
do we charge for photocopies?' She raised an eyebrow. 'Just give
the gentleman a photocopy, Ed.'

I took the freeway north, towards Pikesville. The city quickly
melted into suburbs. I took a wrong turning, and suddenly found
myself in the Maryland countryside, gently undulating fields, large
colonial-style houses surrounded by pastures and paddocks. I
doubled back into Pikesville, along leafy streets, lined with mock
Tudor and Spanish-style houses. Park Heights Avenue was lined
with kosher delis, Hebrew bookshops, a synagogue every two or
three blocks. This was the Jewish heartland. 'There may be a
Gentile snuck in there when no one was looking,' Edward Sandler
had said with a smile, 'but I doubt it.'

Ben and Ada Krichinsky lived on a street of neat suburban
bungalows, cars that had been washed and polished to within a
hair's breadth of the undercoat. Ben was a barrel-chested man,
seventy-six years old with a face like a prize-fighter and a voice like
sandpaper. *Avalon* was the story of Ben's life. Sam Krichinsky was
his uncle. 'Matter of fact, he was the only thing I had for a father.
My own father died when I was two years old. He'd come over
from Kiev in 1912. He played the violin, but he got a job working in
the wallpaper section of a department store. He brought his brother
Hyman. Then Uncle Sam arrived. They couldn't speak English, you
know? But all the wallpaper dealers spoke Jewish so they got a job
supplying them.

'East Bawlmore then ... I don't know how much you know
about being Jewish, but if you go to a schull – a synagogue – you're
not supposed to ride; that's the Orthodox way, so every two blocks
there was a synagogue. There was 3 or 4 square miles down there
was mostly Jewish. Everybody was raised with great respect. Good
kids and bad kids. An old man, say my age now, we'd say "Yes,
sir". We'd run barefooted, but we stood close together in them days.

'Now there are many, many multi-millionaires in Bawlmore whose
grandparents came over with nothing. But they worked hard; they

were smart business people. To me, the Jewish race is the most literate in the world, because of the Rabbis. When we were in the old country you weren't allowed to go to school, but the Rabbi would teach. So everybody knew how to read and write, and everybody knew how to count too.

'Everybody wants to make something in life, you unnerstand? So they came to America just to have a chance. They could go to work here. They'd never heard of welfare in those days. But we had our own Jewish societies. My mother, bless her heart, when she was broke in 1929, she wanted to go into the grocery business. She went to the Hebrew Free Loan Society and they lent her $1,000, no interest, to put down the money to buy a grocery store. And after she'd built herself up, for the next ten years she gave them $1,000 a year in donations. You've got to give back, see?'

Ada had brought lemonade and ginger cookies to the table. Ben reached for the picture album. 'This is Uncle Hymie, Sam, Morris, Gabriel, Bertha and Mendel.'

And the little man with the long white beard, wearing a homburg? 'Grandfather Lieb. I was six years old when he came over. All five sons, they bowed to him. We were raised with that kind of respect. He was fifty-four years old when he arrived in America, but he never worked a day in his life from that day on. They all gave him $5 a week each. All day long he'd stay in the synagogue and say his prayers.'

That was back in the Lombard Street days, said Ben. What happened then was just like the film says, the city turned inside out. The Jews started moving north and north-west, out into the suburbs.

'People don't want to live next door to people who hate them.' He took a swallow of lemonade. 'The Jews never ever burnt a cross on a black person's lawn, or threw a stone through their church window. The blacks couldn't go in the Gentile neighbourhoods – the whites, they'd bomb them, stone them, throw them out. If the Jews moved into the neighbourhood – if they were allowed to move in the neighbourhood – Gentiles wouldn't do anything, but they wouldn't get friendly, you unnerstand? But the blacks couldn't live there, so they moved in with the Jews. And what would happen, when the black moved in, the Jews would move out, politely. Never threatening, you unnerstand? But the point is this, see – people wouldn't rent to Jews, not in the south of the city, so we were forced to go north.'

'I remember it,' said Ada. 'There used to be signs on the road to the shore: No Jews or Dogs Allowed. I'll never forget that.'

'Well, yeah.' This seemed to embarrass Ben, the recollection so shocking. I was a Gentile after all. 'But not everybody was like that. And now things are different.'

Ben left school at fifteen. He worked in real estate, and then as a pawnbroker. A good business, until Martin Luther King was shot dead in Memphis, there were riots on the streets of Baltimore, and his business was burned down. 'I lost the equivalent of $1 million, because you could only insure for the equity of the merchandise, not its real value, see? For ten years I was President of the Pawnbrokers Businessman's Association, so when I lost my business a lot of people offered for me to go into partnership with them. I said, wait a minute – I've been in the real estate business and nobody likes a landbroker; I've been in the pawnbroking business and nobody likes a pawnbroker. I was so tired of being in businesses where people look at you like an enemy. So I met a friend and we went in the kitchen business. People look at you friendly in the kitchen business . . .' That was in 1969, he said. And it was in the kitchen business that he stayed until he retired.

To Ben, Jewish life was about family. What happened in *Avalon* – the argument about the carving of the turkey, the way the family broke up when everyone moved to the suburbs – that was all true, he said. And now Ada and he lived in the suburbs too. But that's what happened. There was nothing for Jewish people now in East Bawlmore. Families don't live together any more. Ben and Ada had three children; a daughter married to a builder; a son who was an attorney; another whose business had been sunk by the recession. All lived in Baltimore. And they would be together for Thanksgiving.

'Financially, I did okay,' said Ben. 'I got a nice place here. I got a wife who doesn't make demands – all she wants is to take care of her children. So you know . . .? Life's okay.'

I looked across at Ada, pouring more lemonade. She pushed the plate towards me.

'Have another ginger cookie,' she said.

Later that night, I heard another view of Jewish life in Baltimore when I visited Reuben Kramer. Kramer was Baltimore's most distinguished living artist. Eighty-two years old, he lived alone in his studio in Bolton Hill, a neighbourhood of elegant squares and townhouses in the centre of the city. Wallis Simpson – later the Duchess of Windsor – was born 200 yards away. Kramer was a tall, thin man with long grey hair falling over his forehead, a Charlie Chaplin moustache and sharp, bird-like eyes. His studio had been designed and built to his own specifications; a modernist brick building on a plot of land abutting a Victorian terrace. It was a place for work: a large, circular open-plan space, filled with bronzes of all shapes and sizes in varying stages of completion. Every inch of shelving was stacked with heads and small figures, drawings neatly catalogued and filed. There were more in the basement.

Kramer's father, Israel, was a tailor in the Russian Army, who had arrived in Baltimore in 1889. Reuben was born and raised in the city, and apart from brief sojourns in Europe in the 1930s, he had never left it. Since the death three years ago of his painter wife, Perna Krick, he had lived alone with his cats, seldom venturing out, working methodically from dawn to dusk, as he had always done.

'I never had a vacation in my life,' he said. 'If you see the number of bronzes I'd made nobody would ever believe one person had made them. I haven't been to the movies in over twenty years. I could go. I could buy anything I want, but I got work to do. I'm still working, still casting. I've laid out a fortune in bronze. Nobody's waiting for it, but I have to do it. I don't know why. It's like an alcoholic who can't stop drinking.'

Reuben had another career – in the correspondence columns of the *Baltimore Sun*. For more than thirty years he had been writing letters about everything and anything under the sun: politics, art, society, George Bush, senators' pay, Saddam Hussein – no subject was too big, nor too insignificant for his attentions. He gave vent to his indignation, dispensed wisdom. It was a democratic duty. Sometimes he illustrated his letters with a line drawing, elegantly turned in a still firm hand.

'Once again our dedicated fat cats . . .' He began to read aloud from a photocopy of his latest submission. 'I call 'em fat cats because I think they're disgusting. "Once again our dedicated fat cats decided they needed a raise, so in the dark of night, in secret meetings, they voted themselves a $24,000 addition to their salary. One wonders how these fat cats felt, sneaking home, avoiding the citizens sleeping in doorways . . ." I despise politicians,' he said. 'If they were investigated like the average person is, a quarter of them would be in jail.'

He had always been a campaigner. In the Forties he had taken the Maryland Institute to court for not admitting black students; in 1944 he and Perna Krick had founded the Baltimore Art Centre, the first school in Maryland where blacks and whites could study together. And they had stood together on picket lines outside restaurants and theatres which refused to admit blacks.

'We brought the black singer Marian Anderson here in 1952, and we had to fight to let her sing in the Lyric Theatre. They wouldn't let her in the theatre until 7.30. And, of course, a prima donna should be in the theatre at 5.00.'

There was a note of outrage in Reuben's voice as he remembered this. How stupid, how insane, that something as mean and poisonous and petty-minded as racism should interfere with something as beautiful, as life-enhancing as the art of the prima donna.

'I know about racism,' said Reuben. 'I know about ringing a doorbell and the woman answering and saying, "we don't rent to Jews." That happened to me, here in Baltimore. What a stupid, sickening woman to talk like that.'

This was the past, where things were still vivid. Reuben was his own life's curator. His press clippings, notices, details of his innumerable awards (a yellowing cutting from 1934 announced his departure for Italy to collect the Prix de Rome), his sundry forays into public life, his letters to the *Baltimore Sun* – all had been carefully photocopied and filed for reference and possible distribution. He handed me a photograph. 'Look at the curly hair I had when I was fifteen years old,' he said, as if he barely recognised himself.

He moved slowly around the studio, picking up pieces of sculpture, explaining them – notice the difference in technique between this and that? – replacing them carefully on the shelves. 'Look at this . . .' he paused over a box of cat litter. A turd lay on top, and the area around it had turned hard. 'It's new stuff,' he said. 'The piss turns it hard, like concrete, so you don't get that mess at the bottom of the tray. It's better.' He examined it for some moments turning the patch with a stick. 'See? Like concrete.'

He had been married to Perna for forty years, he said. When she was alive, she would sit with him as he sculpted, reading and talking. 'If anything went wrong, she'd turn the blow torch off.' He chuckled quietly. 'If I collapsed now, I'd burn the whole building down.'

Dashiell Hammett came from Baltimore. Edgar Allan Poe died and was buried there. The novelist Anne Tyler lived there still. But there was only one writer in Baltimore who had become a local industry. H. L. Mencken was the most prolific, most famous and most powerful man in the history of American journalism. From the appearance of his first newspaper column in 1899 to the time of the debilitating stroke which effectively ended his career in 1948, Mencken wrote over 10 million words for publication. He wrote newspaper columns, magazine articles, literary reviews; he wrote thirty books and contributed to some twenty more. At the height of his fame, in 1927, the *New York Times* called him 'the most powerful private citizen in America'.

Mencken lived in the same house in Baltimore from the age of three until his death at the age of seventy-six, in 1956, for all but five years when he was married. 1524 Hollins Street was a handsome brownstone overlooking Union Square. In Mencken's youth,

Union Square had been a prosperous, middle-class residential district. It had begun to deteriorate in his lifetime, but Mencken had clung on, refusing to leave the family home. Now the neighbourhood was caught in that twilight zone between decay and rehabilitation. The nineteenth-century town houses were being colonised by professionals. Just a couple of blocks away, was a street lined with abandoned building, storefront churches and fortified grocery stores. But on a warm Saturday, the Union Square market was bustling; bric-à-brac spilled on to the pavement from antique shops and weekend shoppers milled around. Here Baltimore felt very much vibrant and alive.

The Mencken house had been lovingly preserved and refurbished. There were only three visitors: two women – one Irish, one Japanese – and me. We drifted through the house, pausing to admire the stolid Victorian furniture, Mencken's piano, the bookshelves lined with the works of Shakespeare, Nietzsche, Oscar Wilde, Ibsen, Goethe, the *Encyclopaedia of Religion and Ethics*. A battered Underwood typewriter and a crooked newspaper spike stood on the desk in his first-floor study, beside the window from where Mencken could look down on Union Square, the trees turning brown in the late autumn afternoon.

Mencken's grandfather arrived in Baltimore from Germany in 1848. By the time Mencken was born, in 1880, Baltimore was America's fourth largest city, and the German-American community accounted for almost a quarter of its population of 425,000. Mencken's father, Adolphe, was a cigar manufacturer, who hoped his son would follow him into the family business, and the young Henry grew up steeped in the bourgeois values and moral certainties of the German middle class. All his life, Mencken cherished industriousness, honesty, the ease and comforts of middle-class life, and Baltimore middle-class life in particular. A Baltimorean, he would later observe, was a special kind of person. He was not an average man; he was *of* Baltimore in the European fashion of the Middle Ages and the Renaissance, when the best men were marked by adding their geographical locations to their names. In Baltimore, Mencken reflected, 'living is an art, not an affliction.'

Mencken made his start in journalism at the age of nineteen as a cub reporter on the *Baltimore Herald*, 'the maddest, gladdest, damndest existence ever enjoyed by mortal youth'. But it was his weekly columns for the *Baltimore Evening Sun* that made Mencken's reputation. He wrote on everything within the periphery of his vision: music, literature, education, politics, executions, the sewerage system. Photographs of Mencken taken in middle age show a small, portly man, conservatively dressed, of somewhat florid complexion, a plump, well-scrubbed face, a cigar jutting from the corner of his mouth adding a waggish, somewhat cavalier air, to an otherwise bland and inscrutable countenance.

Certainly, there is nothing to hint at the potential for withering scorn and savagery, which lay below the surface. For Mencken's Monday columns for the *Sun* became a byword for cynicism and vituperation. His enemies, and there were many, regarded him as a petty-minded, vindictive man who goaded for the sake of goading. But it was precisely this waspishness, his reluctance to suffer fools or cant gladly that made Mencken such a devastating commentator.

It seemed true to his character that Mencken had not passed quietly into history. Indeed, he had become an industry. There were already a dozen biographies extant, and more on the way – collections, anthologies, forgotten scraps of writing republished. Forty-odd years after his death, he was still capable of provoking an argument. In 1989, the *Baltimore Sun* ran a lengthy article resurrecting the accusation that Mencken was racist and anti-Semitic, provoking a heated exchange in the paper's correspondence columns.

Mencken's defenders had rallied to the cause. It was pointed out that one of his most contentious pieces, 'The Eastern Shore Kultur', was written in response to the lynching of a black man in Salisbury, Maryland. The Eastern Shore, Mencken wrote, was the 'Alsatia of morons' and the lynching 'a public obscenity worthy of cannibals'. And his very last piece for the *Baltimore Sun*, written in 1948, was an attack on segregation in Baltimore parks, after blacks and whites had been arrested for playing tennis together. 'So few men are really worth knowing', he wrote, 'that it seems a shameful waste to let anthropoid prejudice stand in the way of free association with one who is.'

Perhaps the simple truth about Mencken was that he did not discriminate in his savagery: black, white, Jewish, Gentile; to Mencken, idiocy was idiocy and he wasn't going to hedge his opinions for anyone.

'He was the most eloquent exponent of America's adversary culture,' said Vince Fitzpatrick, a curator of the Mencken archive at Johns Hopkins University, and the author of *H. L. Mencken – A Short Critical Biography*, which had been savaged in the *Jerusalem Post* for not being quite critical enough.

'He didn't care what people said about him. A lot of us say that, but not a lot of us mean it. He said what he thought, and didn't worry about making himself unpopular.'

Mencken was a Jeffersonian liberal, said Fitzpatrick, who believed that the government is best which governs least, a believer in individual freedom and *laissez-faire* capitalism. He hated reform movements. Social workers. Do-gooders. He was vehemently opposed to Prohibition, or to any whiff of moral rearmament.

Ever the self-satisfied bourgeois, what Mencken wanted most of all was for things to stay exactly as they were. He cherished the charm of turn-of-the-century Baltimore – its home-owning populace, its plentiful supply of seafood from the Chesapeake Bay; its southern politesse; its conservatism. Politicians who promised to make Baltimore bigger, and more prosperous, by developing industry – ravaging the city that Mencken loved – were 'boosters and boomers'. Moral reformers were 'wowsers' and 'smut hounds and snouters and virtuosi of virtue'. Shortly before his stroke, he wrote fondly of a time 'when people could spend weeks, months, and even years without being badgered, bilked or alarmed ... The human race had not yet succumbed to political and other scoundrels who have been undertaking of late to save it, to its infinite cost and degradation. It had a better time in the days when I was a boy ...' But then, of course, it always has.

Mencken's *bêtes noires* were Franklin D. Roosevelt – the architect of the New Deal, and probably the greatest reforming American president of modern times – and William Jennings Bryan, the populist orator and religious fundamentalist. Perhaps Mencken's most splenetic hour was his coverage of the Scopes Monkey Trial in Dayton, Tennessee, an event that Mencken saw not simply as a conflict between religion and science but between superstition and reason – the pathological ignorance and credulity of rural America against the learned sophistication and urbanity of the city dweller. Mencken described the events in Dayton as 'a universal joke'. And his contempt for Bryan was bottomless. When Bryan died, immediately after the Scopes Trial, Mencken wrote his obituary, describing him as 'a poor clod like those around him, deluded by a childish theology, full of an almost pathological hatred of all learning, all human dignity, all beauty, all fine and noble things. He was a peasant come home to the barnyard.'

More than sixty-five years later, these words still carried a sting. Richard Cornelius, the professor at Bryan College in Dayton, had spoken of Mencken with the withering disdain the devout usually reserved for the anti-Christ. To Mencken, the Scopes Trial was as much about social ideas as religious ones. Darwinism was not only a scientific rebuttal to what he regarded as the dangerous, superstitious nonsense of the biblical creationists but 'social Darwinism', which equated natural laws with economic ones and was frequently used as a way of explaining divisions of class and race, provided Mencken with a justification for his own comfortable caste.

'My attitude to the world and its people', he explained, 'is and always has been that of the self-sustaining and solvent class. It requires a conscious effort for me to pump up any genuine sympathy for the downtrodden, and in the end I usually conclude that they have their own follies and incapacities to thank for their troubles.' Any attempts at social or political reform were bound to fail, he believed. Visionaries were 'misguided, wasteful . . . and your attempts to restructure American society are doomed because you cannot restructure the nature of man.' Mencken, one couldn't help thinking, would have been very much at home in George Bush's America.

And yet one wondered too what he would have made of the

legacy of that social Darwinism in his beloved Baltimore; the way the city had cracked and buckled at the edges; the unedifying squalor that characterised the worst areas of the city, the racial tensions that still coursed below the surface.

It was easy to be sickened by so much of American life. The relentless messages to consume, which could seem like harmlessly amusing diversions one minute, but the most insidious and poisonous brainwashing the next; the jarring contradiction, within the space of half-a-dozen city blocks, between extreme wealth and poverty. The appalling dereliction of its inner cities, tinderboxes waiting to ignite. The utter cynicism of the political process that ensured power would always devolve on those who could afford to buy it. The way in which a substantial proportion of the population – what were called the underclass – had been allowed to fall behind, and were now hopelessly beyond any reasonable aspirations for self-improvement. American democracy had been built on the notion that by industriousness, ingenuity and fair play anyone could make something of themselves. But while a president might once have come from a log cabin, it seemed that none could ever come from the ghetto.

A palpable sense of disillusionment seemed to underpin almost every sphere of American life; a disenchantment with its institutions and with government; a sense of the great machinery of the American Dream – with its self-perception of power and justice at home and abroad – afflicted by entropy; a decline measured between two acts of violence: 'victory' in the Gulf War, and bloodshed on the streets of Los Angeles, and expressed in the thoughts of the Washington columnist George Will. 'Never in this Republic's history', he wrote, 'has there been a mood-swing as severe as that in the fifteen months between the bombing of Baghdad and the burning of Los Angeles,' when America had passed from 'giddy triumphalism to equally disproportionate angst'.

The election of Bill Clinton as President, with his promise to heal the divisions and build a Re-United States of America, was clearly a response to this angst; the mark of a nation in search of a vision.

*

The Baltimore Yellow Pages contained six pages of hospitals; thirteen pages of car dealers and forty-four pages of lawyers. Lawyers were the most despised, the most derided, professional group in America, held, it seemed, in almost universal contempt. Fat cats committing corporate crime; violent criminals with the spoils of cocaine deals in their back pockets – these walked free while the little man paid the price. Who was to blame? Lawyers. People affected to despise them, and yet business boomed because lawyers held the key. They had shoehorned their way into almost every crevice of American life, made themselves indispensable navigators of its madness. They were expert climbers through loopholes, exploiters of the quarter-chance; alchemists in Italian suits, driving German cars; magicians with brass name-plates who had created a whole industry for the purpose of making themselves rich, which nobody but lawyers could understand but everybody knew was patently ridiculous.

'Why don't sharks eat lawyers?' ran one of any number of jokes. 'Professional ethics.' Stanley, who told me this joke, was a lawyer himself – a lawyer with a speciality. Rear-end whiplash; knee sprains; shooting pains in the arm; a dull throbbing in the head; a thousand and one nebulous, indefinable industrial ailments. 'We chase ambulances,' said Stanley with a smile. Stanley's antidote to public contempt was to brazen it out with chutzpah. He had been among the first lawyers in America to advertise his services on television. Now everybody was doing it. The former assistant state prosecutor of Maryland, good heavens, was advertising as a champion of malpractice suits.

Nobody could deny that the damages claim was, in theory, a just and useful thing. People who had suffered physical harm because their employers were negligent in their duties and responsibilities should, of course, be compensated. People who suffered accidents as a result of other people's carelessness rightly felt a sense of grievance and expected recompense. Yet these modest principles had been used to inflate malpractice law into an industry of ludicrous proportions. Damages claims offered a particularly piquant expression of how the dynamic of American life had resulted in its complete antithesis of paralysis.

Privatised medicine had created an adversarial relationship between doctor and patient. The middle classes complained about the cost of health insurance; the cost of treatment was astronomical, and patients wanted satisfaction for their money. A doctor might earn $3,500 for a hip replacement operation, but risk a malpractice suit costing thousands more in the process. But the same doctor could earn ten times as much, without the risk, for writing out 'negative prognoses' for industrial insurance claims. Lawyers had a whole roster of doctors who could be relied upon to provide medical information to insurers. 'If somebody came to a doctor and says they've got a pain and can't work, how can a doctor argue against that?' said Stanley.

But where was the incentive to honesty, integrity? Stanley looked at me as if to say, are you seriously asking that question?

He invited me to his home. It was a private gallery, of paintings, objects and artefacts picked up on world travels. There was an exercise room, a sauna, a studio, a Jacuzzi and, in the basement, a fully equipped workshop. 'My life's work,' said Stanley. On the bench was a meticulously constructed model of his own house, each room crafted exactly to match its real equivalent. Furnishings, decor, carpets, kitchen equipment and bathroom fittings. Minute artworks hung on the walls, microscopic magazines were thrown on miniature coffee tables. It was a work of complete and all consuming devotion. It was where Stanley retreated each evening, to forget neck braces, arm strains, gashed limbs. An act, one suspected, of catharsis and redemption. Out there might be chaos, hypocrisy, greed. Here in the workshop, Stanley's life was totally under control.

On Saturday night, John, Eileen and I went for a drink in Fells Point. Fells Point had been Baltimore's oldest working-class community. German Jews had been the first to settle in the area; then Czechs, Ukrainians, Poles, Irish. The two principal sources of livelihood for the area were shipbuilding and canning – at one time Baltimore was the centre of one of the biggest cannery industries in America. The work was uncomfortable and exhausting; the area teeming, overcrowded, families compressed into small terraced houses. In the nineteenth century, the population of Fells Point was decimated by a series of yellow fever epidemics. By the Sixties, Fells Point was in advanced state of decay, worn out, surplus to commercial requirements. In the Seventies, the city council planned to drive a freeway through the area. Residents fought against the proposals, and in the early Eighties the old harbour was designated as a historic district, sparing it from the wrecker's ball, and consigning it instead to gentrification and rising prices. The rows of small brick houses had become bijou residences: the grocery stores had become boutiques, and there were bars on every corner, masquerading in 'authentic' (which is to say bogus) heritage style, as sailors' haunts.

'Doing Fells Point' was a weekend institution for Baltimore's students and young professionals. The streets were thronged with groups in sweat shirts and baseball caps; the bars crowded with people bawling each other out while the inevitable folk-singer struggled manfully with the inevitable Don McLean and Simon and Garfunkel songs. These were people with too much drink inside them, and a none too subtle line in small talk. 'Nice ass, lady,' leered a man built like a truck, as Eileen, John and I shouldered our way out of one tavern, 'but I don't think much of the faggots you're with.'

The Port Mission was almost the last surviving relic of the old Fells Point; an anonymous building set on the main square, completely ignored by the trippers who came to Fells Point to drink. The Mission had been founded a hundred years before by a group of Christian businessmen, to minister to the moral welfare of visiting seamen. But the port had moved; the seamen had long since stopped coming, and the Port Mission had turned to 'rescue' work instead, ministering to the needs of those local people who had been pushed to one side in the gentrification of the area.

It was a plain hall with wooden chairs laid out in rows, a lectern on a stage and an old upright piano. There was a smell of stale vegetables and body odour, and the hymn books were sticky from years of handling. The walls were decorated with admonitions to righteousness in foot-high letters: God is Light, God is Love, God is Just, Be Sure Your Sin Will Find You Out; and The Soul That Sinneth,

It Shall Die. There was no sign that the Mission was soft-pedalling on the morality question to boost its congregation. There were perhaps fifteen people in the hall, mostly elderly, in varying stages of neglect and attentiveness. An old man dozed peacefully through the message. Another held his hymn book upside down and mouthed a song in his own head. Two visitors had come from a local Presbyterian church; a man with pink cheeks, dressed in self-consciously casual clothes, played the piano, while a woman sang a hymn in the sort of deliberate, piercing voice usually reserved for recitals in more comfortable surroundings than this, for more appreciative audiences. The congregation snored and shifted uncomfortably in their seats, well aware that the price of a meal was a pretence of piety. Afterwards they shuffled as quickly as seemliness allowed to an adjacent room where the tables had been set for dinner.

Bill Stivers, the director of the Mission, took me upstairs to his office. He was in his early forties, with his hair brushed forward and trimmed neatly over his ears; a plump, well-manicured, but kindly face. Bill worked for the Defence Department; his directorship of the Mission was voluntary.

In the old days, he told me, families would rent houses in Fells Point for $15 a week. Now you would have to pay between $250,000 and $300,000 for a small, terraced row house. 'Only the wealthy can afford that. There's been a lot of turmoil here; as the tax assessments have gone up, people who've lived in the neighbourhood for years can't afford to pay the taxes on their own houses.' Bill's congregation were mostly elderly, single people, he said; living in one room, or even sleeping on the streets; poor, untidy, probably unwelcome in the chic bars and boutiques that had proliferated in the area.

'We give 'em the time of day. Some of them aren't pretty to look at any more. Nobody else would give them the time of day. But we realise they're precious human beings that need to be loved.'

But even in rescue work, it seemed, there was a surfeit of services in this part of Baltimore. The Helping Up Mission and the Baltimore Rescue Mission were both within walking distance, and both offered dormitory facilities. The caravan of desperation had moved elsewhere in the city.

'One of the reasons we have our service early,' said Stivers, 'is so they're out of here by 5.30, so they can get signed in for the late services at the other Mission. They have to sit through the service there so they can get a meal and a bed. You have to sing for your supper. That's the price you have to pay.'

On the wall there were photographs showing the Mission in an earlier, busier time. A picture taken in 1941 showed the dining room packed to capacity with seamen sitting for Christmas dinner, their faces turned to the camera with that curiously haunting expression of innocent jollity and bravado such pictures always convey. These were men who had been thankful for a hot meal, companionship, a kindly word a long way from home.

Bill wondered what the Mission could be doing to minister to the new Fells Pointers – the affluent brokers and professionals who hung fishing nets and weights in their windows, and displayed old brass lamps on their mantelpieces.

'Now we're trying to deal with people who think they have it all,' he said, 'and the last thing they think they need is the gospel.'

There had been some thought, he said, that a change of name from 'The Mission' might do the trick, something less resonant of old time charity, less reminiscent of the saviour of lonely seamen and lost souls. Bill talked of introducing discussions about issues 'relevant' to the new Fells Point populace – abortion, education, health care. 'It's going to be tough,' he said, 'it really is. We're going to bring in people who can speak on an intellectual plane – graduates and so on. We're going to turn this thing around.' There was no doubting Bill's commitment, but in all charity it was hard to think, even with the introduction of intellectuals, what the Port Mission could possibly offer to the Fells Point newcomers.

In the dining room, the rag-tag congregation were hoovering up the plates of food. The visiting Presbyterians had declined the invitation to eat. Looking ill at ease, glad to be leaving the smell of cabbage and body odour, their work done, they were backing out of the door. Tomorrow was Thanksgiving.

*

The Eisens had invited me for Thanksgiving dinner. It was a family affair. Grandmother, uncles, aunts, cousins, some fourteen in all. Two tables had been pulled together in the dining room; the food stood steaming on plates and serving dishes in an adjacent room, and we circulated it like ravenous vultures, umming and aahing in unison, because it really did smell so good, and promised to taste even better. Don had spent all day cooking it. We carried the food to our tables, rolling our eyes, breathing deeply, making gurgling noises in the back of our throats, saying 'oh my' and 'this looks good' while Don carved the turkey like a craftsman, looking kind of proud and abashed and quietly heroic under the circumstances.

We ate diligently, silently, purposefully. There was a lot to deal with. And when we'd cleaned our plates, we went back for more. 'Is that your third? Don't worry, we're not counting.' 'Is that your fourth?' In between there was conversation about the kids and how's work going, and it became obvious who got on and who didn't. The usual strains and tolerances, which is what families are about, after all. It occurred to me that it was my presence that had brought those moments of silence and awkwardness to the table; a stranger among the family. And I was touched again by the fact that I had been invited to join them.

I asked Uncle Bob if he'd seen *Avalon*. He pushed back his chair, stretched his legs. The food was taking its toll. 'I don't like these movies with messages. Who needs messages? I used to like cowboy movies. John Wayne . . .'

'Tom Mix . . .' said Uncle Mel.

'Tom Mix I like,' said Uncle Bob.

I went out on to the verandah for fresh air, and was joined by a cousin, shaking his head and saying, 'Families, man, like, don't they drive you nuts?'

At 9.30 the more elderly people began drifting away, and Don said, no, don't worry about the washing-up, you're a guest, and sit, sit.

The TV came on, for the kids. It was 'Beverly Hills 90210'. And we sat in silence around its flickering light.

NASHVILLE cats

Nashville Cats, play clean as country water
Nashville Cats, play wild as mountain dew . . .

Two vignettes in the restaurant of the Holiday Inn, Nashville. A black family visiting from Louisiana sit down to eat supper – parents, a grandmother, and a gaggle of children. After the meal, the eldest son, a grave-looking teenager, rises from the table and starts talking to the Iranian waiter. The parents look somewhat awkward. Is he creating a scene over the service? No, he is simply asking the whereabouts of the nearest mosque. They exchange salaams, expressions of brotherhood. The family leave, and the waiter clears the table.

The next morning at breakfast, the black maître d' bows deeply to a Japanese businessman and greets him in his native language. The Japanese man has brought his breakfast to the table from the buffet, he picks up a video camera and starts filming the contents of his plate, talking into the microphone. 'Wheat toast. Blueberry pancake . . .'

John Sebastian wrote the song 'Nashville Cats' in 1966, a paean from a young pretender in the pop world to the *éminences grises* of country music. 'I was living on Long Island,' Sebastian remembered, sitting in his home in Woodstock. 'The Spoonful were beginning to get a door in music, and Zal (Yanovsky – a fellow member of the group) and I were always talking about these guitarists we'd hear out of Nashville.

'The subtext of the song was there was a sort of irony we were noticing of being twenty and having all this attention, playing poorly a version of something which all these forty- and fifty-year-old guys could play while they were napping.'

It was, Sebastian acknowledged, a performance of the barest competence. 'I met a pedal-steel guitar for the first time in my life, two hours before the session began; a two-pedal Fender that had been left over from the previous session. I came to understand it, but I still couldn't move on the thing. So I played all the licks that were just the pedal-steel chordal motions – five or six tones, moving up and down from one chord to another; and Zal played all the single-line stuff, which a pedal-steel player would be playing in between these licks. It was really apparent to us what novices we were, so it was somewhat of a homage.'

A somewhat inaccurate one too, as Sebastian admits – the 'yellow Sun records' mentioned in the song were produced in Memphis, not Nashville, 'But it was a homage to this whole Tennessee source.'

It was a song that had served him well, he said. It was even now part of his repertoire, still popular with audiences, and it had always opened doors in Nashville. 'I've been down there in Fan Week, when the town is stuffed full of people; I would say my name at a hotel desk and somebody would say "Hey now! You wrote that 'Nashville Cats' tune, didn't you?" And sure enough a room would materialise. That has happened more than once. I've ended up in a room reserved for Loretta Lynn when she's in town.'

'There's 1,352 guitar pickers in Nashville,'

wrote Sebastian in the song,

'and they can pick more notes than the number of ants on a Tennessee

ant hill. Yeah, there's 1,352 guitar cases in Nashville, and any one of them packs his guitar can play twice as better than I will.'

'I did the "Nashville Now" television show a while back and they'd researched the number of session players working in '66 when I wrote the song, and I was within fifty on the number of guitar players in Nashville. It was just a guess. But the thing was how *nice* those guys themselves were about the song.

'Both the musical and the social style of Tennessee is very self-deprecatory, and a lot of these guys who could run rings around you, they'd always be the most modest about their playing. It seems almost like the better these guys play, the harder it is to brag about themselves. The first story they have is about the guy that cut them last week down in the bar.'

When John Sebastian first visited Nashville in 1967, shortly after the song had been an American hit, it was, he remembered, 'a small, sleepy, music town.' Twenty-five years on Nashville was still a music town, but it was no longer small, no longer sleepy, and country music was riding on a peak of unparalleled popularity.

Country had been a periodic fashion in American music, of course. In the Seventies rock performers like the Byrds, the Flying Burrito Brothers and the Eagles had paid homage to their country sources. What was once seen as hick became hip as singers such as George Jones and Dolly Parton were taken up by young performers, in much the same way as blues singers had been a decade earlier, and 'country rock' enjoyed a vogue in the American charts. The Seventies had also seen the popular success of the 'Outlaws'; singers such as Willie Nelson and Waylon Jennings, whose long hair and noncomformist stance made them attractive to a generation of rock fans who had always seen country music – and not without good reason – as a bastion of reactionary attitudes. Through the Eighties, the popularity of country music on a national scale had waned somewhat. But now it was once again pressing its case as the national music of America.

A new generation of country stars had emerged; singers such as Garth Brooks, George Strait, Randy Travis and Clint Black, characterised by their clean-cut, well-groomed appearance, and their shared fondness for large ten-gallon stetsons. These were the 'Men in Hats' – so called 'neo-traditionalists', combining an old-time simplicity in their songs and arrangements with sophisticated production techniques.

In 1991, *Ropin' The Wind* by Garth Brooks had made music history by becoming the first album to enter both *Billboard*'s country and pop charts at number one, outselling Guns 'n' Roses, Prince, U2, and Hammer.

In truth, neither Brooks, nor any of the Men in Hats, had produced music that was any better – nor any worse – than anything else that had come out of Nashville in the past thirty years. But it was favoured by a particular combination of musical and social circumstances. In New York and Los Angeles, traditionally the twin capitals of the music industry, dance music and the screaming migraine of heavy metal reigned supreme. Neither were genres that nurtured and encouraged the art of songwriting. Country, it was said, was the only kind of music where you could hear songs any more. More and more singers and songwriters were gravitating from the West Coast to Nashville, to take advantage of the session musicians, the more economical studios, the ambience of the city. The borders between pop and country were dissolving; 'Shameless', a number single from *Ropin' The Wind*, had been written by Billy Joel, by no definition a 'country' songwriter.

'It's the centre of middle-American mono-culture,' said Vic, a writer friend of mine. 'Country music is the only place people can go now to hear melodies and stories – stuff that's basically telling them their boring lifestyles are worth while.' Vic was somewhat jaded with Nashville. He had moved here to the city to 'get away from the New York madness', and was now thinking of moving on somewhere else, 'to get away from the Nashville madness'.

'In the North, people are less affable, but their belief systems are more flexible,' he said. 'In the South, people are more affable, but their belief systems are more rigid. You take your choice.' Vic was thinking of moving West.

*

Nashville was originally settled as Fort Nashborough in 1780. It was renamed Nashville in 1784, and became state capital in 1843. In 1897, at Nashville's centennial exposition, the city's famous monument, the Parthenon, was unveiled. It was a symbol of grandeur – Nashville styled itself as the Athens of the South – and of rebirth. The South had suffered humiliation in the Civil War. Now was the time for reconstruction.

That was the ancient history. For the purposes of modern history, Nashville was founded in 1925, when the National Life and Accident Insurance Company launched radio station WSM (it stood for 'We Serve Millions') as a medium for advertising its services. The programme director of WSM, a man named George D. Hay, was one of life's showmen, who hit on the idea of presenting a radio revue based on a country barn-dance, and featuring popular folk and hillbilly performers of the day (the term 'country music' had not yet entered common usage). The programme was broadcast live, each Saturday night from the Ryman Auditorium, a handsome, turn-of-the-century opera house in downtown Nashville. There were other country music programmes springing up throughout the South, in Fort Worth, Texas, Atlanta – even Chicago. But in Nashville, there were complaints that a programme of hillbilly music was not befitting 'the Athens of the South'. When WSM announced that the barn-dance might be discontinued it was inundated by requests from listeners for a reprieve. By 1927, when Hay christened the programme 'The Grand Ole Opry', it was established as one of the most popular radio shows in the South. Sixty-five years on, it was the longest-running programme in the history of American radio.

From the outset, performers were encouraged to dress for the part, as picturesque caricatures of rural types, in bibs, braces and straw hats. Hay himself, as master of ceremonies, played the part of a stock figure of the American rural scene, 'the Solemn Old Judge'. The Opry was playing with a view of America that was nostalgic, even then. But Hay displayed a shrewd understanding of the Opry's appeal. 'The Grand Ole Opry', he said, 'is as simple as sunshine. It has a universal appeal because it is built upon goodwill and with folk music expresses the heartbeat of a large percentage of

Americans who labour for a living.' Hay had coined the first truism of country music: that it was the voice of the common man; the music for people with dirt under their fingernails.

I discovered all this about the Grand Ole Opry walking around the Country Music Hall of Fame, a museum which charts the rise of country, and honours its greatest stars. The Museum was an impressive mixture of music scholarship and theatre, delineating the different strands of country music – Honky Tonk, Western Swing, The Singing Cowboys – in informative audio-visual displays, alongside the inevitable collection of artefacts, instruments and stage costumes.

The Museum was crowded with visitors, and I noticed that the history of the Grand Ole Opry seemed to be the most popular exhibit of all, where people paused the longest, examining the photographs, reading the stories, almost as if they were examining their own family album. A couple of days later, I was given a press release from Opryland USA, the company which now owned the Grand Ole Opry, detailing their holdings – of a size so staggering I jotted them down, as an example of how folksy acorns grow into corporate oak trees. 'Opryland, a musical theme park; the Grand Ole Opry, a live country music radio show; TNN: The Nashville Network, a cable television network available throughout the United States and Canada; the Opryland Hotel; the General Jackson Showboat; the WSM AM and FM radio stations; Gaylord Sindicom, a television program syndication concern; and Opryland Music Group, a division devoted to songwriting, music publishing and recording.' It was Nashville's own version of the old adage, where there's dirt under the fingernails, there's money.

I was reminded of something Vince had said. 'Nashville isn't a yahoo country town at all. It's the corporate centre for yahoo countryism.' You realised this as you walked around Nashville. The people in cowboy boots and stetsons weren't from Nashville at all. They were tourists, living out an idea of how you were expected to behave in the country music capital of America. In Italy, travellers go to Venice intent on finding the 'real' Venice, that secret centre of the city untainted by tourism or self-consciousness. They soon discover there is no 'real' Venice; that there is no choice but to become a tourist. Nashville was like this. It was the country music capital of America, and, by implication, the centre of some idealised notion of the American heart. This was an onerous responsibility, to which the city had responded in fitting style: by transforming itself into an enormous theme park. I had never been in a city so singlemindedly dedicated to a single idea. There was nothing else to be in Nashville but a tourist.

The heavens had opened, drowning Nashville in warm, incessant rain. It poured down gutters, and bubbled out of storm drains. There were flash flood warnings on television. Some 14 inches of rain had fallen on nearby Pulaski in one day. In Memphis, 150 miles away to the West, the temperature was 38 degrees Fahrenheit. In Nashville it was 70 degrees. There was something unnatural about it, spooky, as if the Apocalypse was due at any moment.

The Country Hall of Fame was on Music Row, the centre of the Nashville music industry. In fact, there were two Music Rows: the business end, a quiet and unassuming neighbourhood, no more than six blocks square, of old frame houses and low-rise office buildings, accommodating music publishers, record companies and studios – and the tourist end, a long row of buildings housing restaurants, western clothing stores and gift shops, many of them bearing the names of important country singers. The street was crowded with tourists, ducking from doorway to doorway to avoid the rain.

For the country star, premises on Music Row were clearly an imprimatur of arrival. There seemed to be two alternatives. One was to open a gift shop with museum attached – the option favoured by George Jones, George Strait and the group Alabama. The other was to open a museum with gift shop attached; the Barbara Mandrell and Hank Williams Jnr route. In truth, there was no discernible difference between the two approaches. The basic constituents of both were a display case or two, full of awards, guitars, costumes and photographs, perhaps a desk or favourite chair with the star's name picked out in poker-work – George/ Hank/Porter/Roy – alongside rows of T-shirts, jackets, caps, guitar-shaped ashtrays, kitsch toilet accoutrements, china bells, small porcelain animals: objects whose connection to country music seemed tangential at best.

Mixing with the crowds on the pavement, one could get some idea of the relative popularity of the different stars. ('Norman!' cried a large woman in a plastic mac, corralling her errant husband. 'You wanna go down to Elvis?' 'You ain't nothin' but a hound dawg,' said Norman under his breath, trudging reluctantly behind her.)

The size of these establishments seemed to vary in direct proportion to the magnitude of the artists' record sales and egos. The George Strait gift shop was about the size of a corner tobacconist, hidden in a warren of souvenir shops. Barbara Mandrell World, on the other hand, was the size of a supermarket.

Mandrell was the most artful exponent of snake-oil sincerity. Stepping across the threshold you were greeted by a video presentation of the artiste, explaining that, 'Because you made all this possible, I wanted to share it with you'. $4.50 effected entry to an exhibition of her personal effects, and film of the interior of her home – 'things only my closest friends can see'. Sharing your bedroom with your fans was a tradition long practised in the music business, of course, but here it was raised to new heights of popularism: the museum was packed.

There was something nauseating about this – this gimcrack sentimentality sold so unashamedly as honest feeling – but also something curiously touching. Between the rows of cheap souvenirs and the trophies of success, one could read a deeper story. At a time when America was fragmented, seemingly spinning inexorably out of control, country music was a touchstone of more reassuring times. Country music was about creating a community for working-class white people in the way that soul music had been for blacks. It was a buffer, and a consolation, against the giddying uncertainties of modern life, embodying a vision of an America of unchanging and dependable values. There was a reassuring simplicity in the songs about loving, cheating and drinking too much – everyday human frailties and emotional dilemmas whose very familiarity offered a kind of comfort in itself.

Its moral code was malleable, but essentially traditionalist. There were no 'politically correct' country songs, no explicitly feminist ones. There were no gay country stars, or none who would admit to it. Country stars were expected to lead lives of ordered domesticity, expected to embody the values of family, hearth and home – this was the image projected in the 'museums' of Music Row. But to err was only human. And if their marriages were, in fact, numerous and chaotic; their drinking problems and their drug overdoses spectacular; their spending habits profligate and their bankruptcies ruinous, this would be forgiven, for these things were proof of their humanity and frailty, understood by their audience.

Every country star was a Horatio Alger story, the boy or girl from the boondocks who had risen by honest endeavour, the sweat of their brow, and who celebrated their success unashamedly in a riot of sequinned Mr Nudie suits and pink Cadillacs. This was perfectly acceptable, expected even, but so too was a tempering appearance of humility and gratitude. What they must never do was get above themselves.

Margaret Mitchell, the author of *Gone With The Wind*, the epic evocation of the South during the Civil War, and the world that had vanished with it, once described it as a book about 'gumption'. Gumption was the thing that distinguished those who survived from those that didn't. Gumption was what every country singer was supposed to have.

The Grand Ole Opry was no longer broadcast from the Ryman Auditorium. In recent years, it had relocated to the Opryland complex, 10 miles from the centre of town. The amusement park and attractions were closed for the winter; the car park all but deserted. As I parked, a Winnebago van pulled up beside me, weather-beaten, dirty, bearing Oregon plates; pilgrims who had travelled more than 2,000 miles to the shrine. Walking around Opryland, I was struck by how it appeared to have been modelled on an idealised small-town America, a village of clapboard buildings and cottages, but in this case housing not a hardware or feed store, but the inevitable gift boutiques.

The auditorium where the Grand Ole Opry was staged was in the middle of this village, and next to it was a modest family home, behind a white picket fence. There was a mailbox outside – one of those mailboxes you see in Thirties' films – with the name Roy Acuff written on it. Acuff was the grand old man of country music. He made his first appearance on the Opry in 1938, and he was appearing still, presenting the show on Friday and Saturday nights. And here he was, living less than 100 yards from the theatre. He was to die shortly after I visited Opryland, but the fact that he had lived barely two minutes' walk away from the theatre in the middle of the theme park – 'This way he can just walk out of his front door and on to the stage,' someone explained with startling logic – seemed a vivid demonstration of the intimacy between stars and fans, real or imagined, that was central to country music. The idea of stars secluding themselves behind high walls and barred gates was anathema, almost a perversion. 'Country stars', a woman explained, 'are some of the warmest, down-to-earth, reaching, touching people you will find. They adore their fans. A lot of rock and roll stars, from what I can see, they're afraid of their fans.'

At Country Music World, I joined a queue of people outside Twitty City, the home of Conway Twitty. Country Music World was a thirty-minute drive from Nashville, another complex of museums and attractions clustered around the gates of Twitty's home. Twitty had been a country star for almost thirty years, a success that virtually obliged him to open his house to the public. I imagined the events that had followed this, the other attractions clustering around it, like squatters at the gate of a castle, to take advantage of the passing trade. And from this, a small nation state had grown; another of Nashville's dream arcades.

A Twitty Museum had been built away from the house, and here we were ushered into a darkened room. A film was projected on to the wall, Conway Twitty singing 'I Am The Dreamer, You Are The Dream' – one of his hits. We were led past a diorama showing chapters in Twitty's life: his childhood in a wooden shack beside the Mississippi, the son of a riverboat captain (cue song 'Many Years Ago In Days Of Childhood'); how the radio in this shack would be tuned to the Grand Ole Opry; how he made his first public appearance at the age of twelve. These scenes were presented with the tweeness of Biblical parables being told to a Sunday School class, and I began to feel irritated that someone who was, after all, only a mediocre country singer, should have mythologised their own life in this way. We continued past the Walk of Gold, representing all his number-one records; past the inevitable Cadillac, and the life-size model of the Twitty tour bus, where each of his musicians was singled out for praise, and we were told the band was 'like a family'.

We were led out of the hall, and into the garden. It had been decorated for Christmas, with giant lollipops and stuffed animals, and seasonal music percolated out of loudspeakers set in the trees. The house was modest enough, comfortable but not ostentatiously furnished. The tour was confined to the ground floor: a lounge, a den, a master bedroom. I thought it seemed odd to find a bedroom on the ground floor, and the guide confirmed my suspicions: Twitty toured eleven months of the year; he was almost never here, and when he was he lived in the rooms upstairs, which were roped off from public view. This story, from humble origins to wealth beyond imagining, was a familiar one; a fable of possibilities. The message was designed to be reassuring, inspirational, and yet the people around me walked away from Twitty City, as they walked away from the gift shop/museums of Music Row, with a palpable shadow of disappointment passing across their faces, as if the promised communion with the stars – with the meaning of stardom – had somehow failed to materialise. It was as if 'The World's Only Mermaid' had been revealed as just another piece of flimflam, designed to dupe them, after all.

There was something almost touching in its fraudulence. The empty garden strung with Christmas lights, the cheery, ridiculous songs playing in the drizzle; the way in which you had to exit through the gift shop, filled with exactly the same cheap, meretricious rubbish to be found in every singer's gift shop, but with Twitty's name instead of theirs.

On the other side of the car park was another museum, dedicated, said the sign, to Willie Nelson and his Nashville Friends.

Nelson's was a salutary life. He had come from Texas to Nashville in the Sixties and enjoyed enormous success as a writer with such songs as 'Funny' (a hit for Joe Hinton) and 'Crazy' (sung by Patsy Cline). In 1971, Nelson's house in Nashville burned down and he returned to Texas, gradually rebuilding his career as one of 'the Outlaws'. By the late Seventies, Nelson had become just about the biggest selling singer in country music; he toured incessantly; was taken up by Hollywood; became a national idol – a grizzled, long-haired maverick, who finally attained the apotheosis of outsider status when the Internal Revenue Service stuck him with a tax bill for $17.5 million. The true Outlaw, Nelson responded by taking out a lawsuit against his accountants, Price Waterhouse, alleging that between 1977 and 1983 they had mismanaged his income by investing in tax-shelters that the government had decided were not tax-shelters after all.

The Museum was run by a petite but tough-looking blonde in a shell-suit and sneakers, named Jeannie Oakley. She had known Willie for thirty years, she said, and worked for him for fourteen. She had assembled the contents from the bits and pieces of Nelson's life which had been seized by the IRS, and which she had bought as a single job-lot the day before they were to be sold at public auction. Money from the Museum would go to help pay Nelson's tax bill. In the meantime, Nelson himself was moving to Branson, Missouri, where he was building his own theatre so that he could perform regularly to pay off the balance of his debts. (Branson, people said, was 'the new Nashville'. Boxcar Willie and Roy Clark already had dinner theatres there; and there was talk of opening a branch of the Grand Ole Opry in the town.)

One room in the Willie Nelson Museum had been recreated as his study, with desk, chairs, Indian rugs and hangings, a table set for dominoes. The other room was somewhat more bizarre. There was a pile of exercise equipment, a pool table, a refrigerator and a cooker, simply standing there, looking pretty much like anybody else's exercise equipment, pool table, refrigerator and cooker. In fact, it looked like a storm clearance sale. I tried to figure out what this random collection of domestic appliances was supposed to be telling me about celebrity. Was it some sort of demotic symbol; a way of forging a common bond between Willie Nelson and me — the fact that he had a refrigerator, just like mine? Or was the message in the assemblage itself? That even the famous could not escape death or taxes? All I knew was I had paid $5 to look at Willie Nelson's refrigerator, and I couldn't for the life of me understand why.

A doorway led from the Willie Nelson Museum into another, lesser establishment dedicated to Willie's 'friends'; minor country stars who, for one reason or another, did not merit a museum of their own. This was a museum of tenuous connections, of fame by association. Johnny Darell, Mel Tillis, Johnny Frazier — most of the names meant nothing to me, and there was something rather sad about this collection of fading record sleeves, cowboy suits, guitars and golf clubs.

A man had been sitting behind a counter, with a display of turquoise jewellery, as I came in. Now he saw me making notes and came over. He was in his late thirties, with a pompadoured helmet of black hair and a full moustache, pulling at the corners of his mouth. There was an aroma of aftershave and something insinuating in his manner as he held out his hand. 'James Marvell,' he said, beaming expectantly.

Clearly, I was supposed to recognise the name.

'The Country Cavaleers . . .' I had never heard of them. He led me to a display case. There was a photograph of four men with d'Artagnan hairstyles, wearing capes, Zorro hats, embroidered waistcoats and flapping trousers with satin inlays. Frankly, they looked ludicrous.

James told me his story. Inevitably, it was a hard luck one. How he had once been a member of a group called Mercy, which had enjoyed a number two hit in 1970 (try as I might, I could not bring it to mind). How he had come to Nashville and founded the Country Cavaleers, 'a group before their time' — and how he was now biding his. 'Take this. I'd like you to have it.' He handed me a video and a folder of press clippings. 'You might find it useful,' he said.

The video was called *Criss Cross*. 'James Marvell,' it read, 'lead singer of the chart-topping pop sensations Mercy, and later with the trailblazing "long hairs" of country music The Country Cavaleers now offers you a video chocked full of unprecedented musical memories. James Marvell demonstrates his incredible talent and ability to crisscross the lines separating the musical styles ... and as a special bonus there is even a Spanish ballad, Flower of My Life.'

'It's just $19.95,' said James. I handed it back to him.

Among the press clippings was an article from the *Hendersonville News Examiner* telling in greater detail how James and his friend Buddy Good had risen from obscurity in Tampa, Florida, to hit paydirt with Mercy; how they had toured with the Association and the Beach Boys, fatefully turning down a chance for national television exposure on the 'Ed Sullivan Show' because of 'conflicting schedules' (I detected the voice of James in the narration). 'Unfortunately,' the article noted, 'Sullivan passed away before the group could reschedule.'

The saga continued: how James and Buddy had come to Nashville as the Country Cavaleers, but had been rejected by the country music establishment. They were, it seemed, a legend awaiting rediscovery. In the meantime, the article concluded, 'Buddy Good has found happiness as a salesman at Regent Dodge Madison and at his own Buddy Good's Auto Sales next to McDonald's.' And here was James Marvell, demonstrating his incredible talent and ability to crisscross the lines of daily existence, selling turquoise jewellery.

An elderly couple had strayed into the Museum, and now found themselves trapped at the counter. 'I'll surprise you on the price of this.' James was making a pitch on a turquoise bracelet. 'This for your son? He'll really go for that. It's only $29.95, and I'll sign a form saying you're one of the first hundred purchasers – that'll make it even more valuable, see.'

I walked past without saying goodbye. Outside, the rain was still falling. It felt like tears.

Curiously, country music was not the biggest industry in Nashville.

The printing of Bibles was. Nashville claimed to be 'the Buckle on the Bible Belt' (Dr Cornelius, I remembered, had said the same thing about Dayton; it was evidently a hotly contested claim in the South. But I had never seen so many churches as I saw in Nashville). The predominant faith was Southern Baptist. I wanted to go to church, but I was unsure about which one to go to. I picked one at random from the Yellow Pages: the Bluegrass Southern Baptist Church in Hendersonville.

Naively, I had half-expected something folksy, primitive, romantic – hillbilly music, fire and brimstone, snake handling perhaps – a tourist's misconception of the South. But Hendersonville was a dormitory suburb, fanning out from a shopping strip, comprising a Kentucky Fried Chicken, a Jiffylube, a Blockbuster video and a 'professional building' where dentists, chiropractors and lawyers' offices clustered, as if for mutual support. The Bluegrass Church was on a road lined with trees and spacious ranch-style houses, a neat, modern building in an affluent middle-class neighbourhood, with a congregation smartly dressed in their Sunday best. Nor was the sermon quite as hell-raising as I had expected. The Church was playing host to a visiting missionary from Venezuela, who spoke at some length about the vicissitudes of spreading the gospel in Caracas. 'So you came all the way to Hendersonville to learn about Venezuela?' someone enquired genially at the end of the service. These were friendly people, anxious to welcome a stranger in their midst.

The pastor, Dr Leonard Markham, invited me home to lunch with his wife Deborah, and their two teenage sons. Over lunch Dr Markham talked about the conflict in the Southern Baptist church (he pronounced it 'Bab-dist'). The Baptists were a 'born again religion' he said, and probably 50 per cent of Dr Markham's congregation were converts from other denominations, such as Methodists, Presbyterians, Episcopalians. They were evidence of the trend towards conservatism among the true believers, although the church overall was in decline. This Dr Markham attributed to internal politics, and the row within the Southern Baptists between fundamentalists and moderates.

The focal point of the Baptist faith was the Southern Baptist Convention, which met each year to decide church policy. For some thirty years, said Markham, a row had been simmering over one single article of faith: 'whether the Bible is truth without any mixture of error for its matter'. Of course, this was an argument that had been raging in varying degrees of intensity and rancour among theologians since the time of the Scopes Trial and William Jennings Bryan's declaration that Jonah had indeed been swallowed by the whale. But within the Southern Baptist church it had developed into a fight to the death between fundamentalists and moderates. At stake was the very heart and soul of the Southern Baptist faith.

Markham described it as a battle between 'the educated and the uneducated. There are educated people on the side of the uneducated, but that's where their power-base lies. They're using the Bible as a club to beat people down. They don't want scholarship, investigative research; they just want people to follow their doctrine.

'They are teaching creationism; that the Bible is literally true. They tend to be conservative politically. They advocate government vouchers for education, incentivising parents to take their children out of the public school system. If you go to some of these churches, you'd think you were at a Republican political meeting, and that has serious implications for this country. You've got 15 million Southern Baptists in America.

'Baptists have always advocated a separation between church and state. We've always said that when the church and the state get married it's the church that gets raped. We've stood for religious liberty and freedom. But that's not true today. These people are saying that you don't have the right. They'll be forcing people to pray at school, football games, every place. And that's not right.'

The Fundamentalists were the energetic people; they packed out the National Convention, and they had taken over the Baptist Seminaries and institutions. 'They fight,' said Dr Markham. 'The moderate temperament is not to fight; it's to love other people, accept them. That's why we're losing.' He said the word with some emphasis. Dr Markham believed the division was now irreparable. 'The divorce will take place; it just hasn't happened yet.'

It was an argument, he said, which had made the Baptists 'the laughing stock of America. People don't want any part of this.' Clearly, by the standards of many Southern Baptists Dr Markham was a liberal – if not a dangerous radical. 'I would describe myself as a Fundamentalist,' he said. 'But I don't believe in the creationist line. But a lot of these people are just mean-spirited. I believe in a more tolerant interpretation of the Bible.'

Dr Markham was forty-three. He had grown up in Knoxville in East Tennessee, in a family of Southern Baptists. He was eighteen when he decided to become a pastor. 'I was in a church service at high school and I had this overwhelming sense that God was calling me. I didn't understand it at the time, but now I do believe that people are called, to be preachers, or missionaries or doctors. From a psychological perspective, in the environment in which I was brought up that's pretty normative for most people.'

His congregation in Hendersonville were mostly professional people: lawyers, doctors, management people. (Barbara Mandrell had been a member, but moved away.) In Knoxville, where he came from, the congregation was made up largely of people who had been born or grown up there. But here in Hendersonville there were people from Ohio, Minnesota, Indiana.

I said I thought it was interesting to hear all this in Nashville, the country music capital, because country music and its resurgent popularity had struck me forcefully as a symbol of America struggling to keep in touch with the old values, the old certainties, the old sense of community. 'I don't know too much about country music – I never listen to it myself,' said Dr Markham with a laugh. 'But certainly there have been great changes in this country in the families and the home, and the South has felt those changes like anywhere else.

'We find our church has become the substitute family for a lot of people,' he said. 'People come looking for community, fellowship, warmth, acceptance. You find people put a lot more emphasis on holidays, thinking about decorating the church now for Christmas and so on. Because their real family is some place else, they regard the church as their family.'

And in the meantime, the church was tearing itself to bits with ideological arguments. 'That's true. One of the big problems is that congregations don't really understand what's happening. Most people have enough worries of their own – they're out of work, getting a divorce, their son is in psychiatry; they would say those issues are more important than what's happening in the Southern Baptist Church, and I'd agree with them. But to me, what's happening is like being kicked out of your own home.' He toyed with his meal awhile. 'I've been a pastor for twenty-three years, and now I feel I'm being evicted.'

The Nashville Songwriters' Association International listed more than 1,100 writers/members. But according to Roger Sovine there were probably upwards of 5,000 people in Nashville who would call themselves songwriters. Less than 1,000 of those made any money, and fewer than 500 actually made a living. Songwriting was to Nashville what acting was to New York. There were no waiters in Nashville; they were all putative songwriters.

Roger Sovine was head of the Nashville office of BMI, the largest performing rights society in America, responsible for collecting 'mechanicals' – the publishing royalties songs earned from being played on radio and television. Roger was the son of Red Sovine, a country singer who, in the Sixties and Seventies, had enjoyed a string of hits with songs about truckdrivers, including 'Phantom 309' and 'Teddy Bear', an excruciatingly sentimental song about a crippled boy, a teddy bear and a truckdriver. But Roger was as far from truckdriving as could be imagined: a smooth-jowled man with an affable, laid-back manner, dressed in a Ralph Lauren shirt, a club tie and blazer.

Sure, musicians were important, said Roger; of course, the singer was vital. But in Nashville, it was the song that counted most of all. 'Everybody's success depends on that,' he told me. 'And everybody knows it.'

Songwriters came and went. But there was one who had defied

time, the fickle whims of public taste and industry caprice – possibly gravity itself. Harlan Howard had been at the top in the songwriting field for more than thirty years. He had written some 4,000 songs in all. More than 1,000 of them had been recorded. Sixty had been number-one country hits. His songs included: 'I Fall To Pieces', sung by Patsy Cline; 'Heartaches By The Number' by Guy Mitchell; 'I've Got A Tiger By The Tail', by Buck Owens; 'Busted', which had been a hit for both Ray Charles and Johnny Cash; 'The Streets Of Baltimore' by Bobby Bare and 'No Charge' by Tammy Wynette.

His songs had been recorded by Kitty Wells, Waylon Jennings, Conway Twitty, Brenda Lee, Nanci Griffith, and sundry Men in Hats. He had recorded several albums himself, and had a top forty American hit with a song called 'Sunday Morning Christian'. In 1961, he won a record number of ten BMI songwriting awards. BMI continued to show its gratitude to Howard each year by hosting the Harlan Howard Birthday Bash in their car park. Like Harlan Howard himself, it had become a Nashville institution.

Harlan Howard's 'office' was a corner stool at the bar of a restaurant called Maud's Courtyard. Roger drove me over in his Cherokee Chief. Like so much of the Nashville that was nothing to do with tourists, Maud's was a surprise. I expected a steak house tricked out like a frontier bar-room, with raucous honky-tonk music. Maud's was quiet, decorous, with an expensive à la carte menu.

Harlan was at the bar: a tall man, stooping somewhat, dressed in a denim shirt and jeans, a snow drift of hair brushed forward into a fringe. I liked him immediately – the sparkling button eyes, the grin which creased his face. It was 11 o'clock in the morning and he was already nursing a vodka and chocolate milk – what Harlan called 'a milkshake'.

We settled ourselves at a corner table and Harlan and Roger started exchanging shoptalk. It quickly became apparent that it wasn't enough for a writer simply to write songs. He or she had to know how to play the Nashville game.

'Let's say there's six record labels in town that count,' Harlan explained. 'Each label has thirty albums a year. So that's 180 albums a year that I could maybe get a song on. If someone's just done cutting an album, then as far as I'm concerned they're dead in the water. But when it gets down to two months before they cut another one, then they get looking. That's when I gotta be ready. They call up all the publishers and that's when everybody tries to get in on it.

'Say George Strait needs ten, twelve songs. His people'll get a stack of cassettes, most of them shitty. They'll probably listen to 1,000 songs, narrow that down to maybe twenty. And the ones that pass the screen go to George's ranch out in Texas. Then his secretary will call up – hold that song. I had two on his last album like that.

'See, someone like Clint Black, it took him thirty years to write his first album. Then he has nine months to write the next one. That's why in the end they all turn to the old classics, or look to writers like me. But you've got to be good. Garth Brooks – he's writing wonderful songs, and if you want to even try to kick his ass you've gotta write wonderful songs too.

'Every album has maybe five great songs, and five fillers. Those are the things that may be a good performance, good production, but they're only mediocre songs. Now I'm not going to get one of those songs on an album – that's political.'

Political?

'What I mean is, a singer isn't going to do just a pretty little song that I've written; he's going to do his own – throw in that filler shit, because he's still going to get the publishing on that. The thing he wants from me is a Grammy, Oscar, Emmy – something that'll make him sell platinum albums. Hit singles attract attention and you hopefully sell a shitpot full of albums. So we have to get one of the five that's a killer.

'And we don't get any favours. "Let's do old Harlan's song; he ain't had a hit in a while . . ." – nobody thinks shit like that about me. I've had hits for decades. I started in '59, and the first week in '91 I had a number-four record with Glen Campbell. Now that impresses people. They will make appointments, listen to your songs. But you've got to earn that. You still gotta have a song that smells like money.

'I'm just a sixty-four-year-old fart; I've been doing this shit for the past thirty-one years. I'm hot and I'm cold, I'm in and I'm out, but I'm true blue traditional fucking hard core — horses, poontang, drinking, all the important things in life. I'm into all that shit. I'm earthbound. I write about things people do whether they should or not. Goddamn it, I write about realism. I'm a happy guy who knows to write sad songs. Man, that's all I can tell you.'

He sat back in his chair, beaming contentedly and took another swallow of his milkshake.

His was not a country music background, Harlan said. He came from Michigan, not from Texas or Kentucky or some place where country writers are supposed to come from, although his parents had been born in West Virginia. 'Daddy moved up north, but between the factory and the house were a lot of bars, and he was a hillbilly boy. He had trouble getting home with his paycheck. My mother would give him a bunch of bullshit; he'd slap her around — that macho thing — and she left him. And he deserved it.'

Harlan drained his glass and called for a refill. 'It's a sad story, except that's a real background for someone who wants to write sad love songs. For some reason I had this love as a child for country music. When I heard Ernest Tubb singing "I wonder why you said goodbye ..." it fucking blew my mind. For some reason I was given this gift. Long before I could get over my shyness to speak to women ... it was the perfect gift for me. I was lonely, ugly, rejected, big nose, two teeth knocked out in front, but I could write. If I'd had the perfect life, finished college, nice family — it wouldn't have worked for me. But I'm from blue-collar USA, Michigan. They make fucking cars up there. They're not selling too well, but they make 'em ...'

He had been a paratrooper. He had worked as a bookbinder and as a forklift driver. When he first arrived in Nashville in 1960, he said, there was a change in the air, from singers writing their own songs — like Hank Williams and Lefty Frizzell — to looking to others to write songs for them. 'In other words, we're talking about the birth of Tin Pan Alley in Nashville. You had all these wonderful singers who didn't write and needed songs from people like me. I'd get six to twelve records a week: I was big … *humungous* – I was writing two or three songs a day; I made a lot of records – a lot of them were mediocre, album cuts, but no backsides of big hits. I never had a backside in my life. So these weren't all great songs, but out of quantity came quality.

'You hear guys sometimes saying a song took 'em fifteen minutes to write. I disagree. I say, my lifetime plus fifteen minutes. I write from the heart, matters of the heart. I don't write anything I don't see. I don't make up anything. I want the truth of a deal between a man and a woman – and the children. Families, love – it's the whole thing that makes our world important. Our love and need for hang-out buddies; a shoulder you can cry on, a pal you can depend on. Once in a while you need an unpaid shrink who won't blab it all over town. I'm not a psychologist, but I know this. Today's big event will recede – unless it's terminal cancer or something . . .'

The waitress stopped by for our order. Roger and I ordered soup and a sandwich. Harlan ordered another drink. Outside, the rain had started falling again, and people were coming into the restaurant with more fuss than they normally would – shaking the rain off themselves, exchanging comments about here it comes again and will it ever stop.

'The other thing I know is, if you're in an unfavourable love affair, get the fuck out,' Harlan was picking up the thread of his conversation. 'You'll be a better and smarter person for it. You cheat on a woman and lose her, maybe you won't cheat on the next one. Life's a series of lessons. I've been married five times – beautiful ladies, no sluts. And I've probably fucked up all those relationships. I'm a happily married man now, I've got me a beautiful child-bride and I intend to keep her.

'Shit, I hang out here and I love waitresses and bartenders – women – cute little bastards; and I flirt and talk trash with them. I do it when my wife's with me. It's not a lecherous thing. But I draw this energy from them – all their bullshit and stories. They're raising two kids by themselves and their fucking man's in Oregon or off scuba-diving – to me, they're stories and they're real. The fucking divorce rate's 50 per cent. I know that. I know about this quest for love.

'See, this is the deal. No matter what your gift is, no matter what you do, you get this money, mansion on the hill, limos but – and this is where country music comes in – *you don't want to live in a mansion by yourself*. You want a lady, and yet from childhood you're born enemies, because you're opposite sexes; you feel totally fucking different about everything. So your total quest in life is to find this mate; this is just talking about normal, natural people, you understand; not people who are fucked up, or faggy or whatever. But it's got to be the right person, and the problem is finding that person. Goddamn it man, it's tough. She could be 80 per cent, and that other 20 per cent will fuck you up, make your life unhappy.

'This goes back to Charlemagne. It's nothing new. We start out hating each other; then we fuck their brains out, have a great time and they get pregnant. But men, we're not really concerned about that. You're pregnant? Here's 200 dollars, find a doctor . . . Man, our attitude is so shitty. But you hear that mating call, and that gets us in a whole damn lot of trouble. That's what leads to most of these country songs – fucking for pleasure.'

As we talked, people stopped by at the table, to shake hands, trade greetings and friendly insults – fellow songwriters, music publishers. 'I'll tell you what, son,' said one man with a chuckle. 'You'll be a wiser man after talking to Harlan. You'll be wise enough to know never to do it again.'

A big man in a suit loomed at the table. He was white-haired, with a face that looked as if it belonged on a box of fried chicken, carrying a stetson hat with a rattlesnake band.

'Say hello to Ned Ray McWherter, the Governor of Tennessee,' said Harlan. There was a flurry of handshakes, affectionate insults. 'He hangs here,' said Harlan, as the governor moved to his table at the back of the restaurant. 'He likes songwriters. Damned if I know why.'

'He's a real good governor,' said Roger. 'What I like about him, he was already rich. He's got a big trucking business. He can't be bought. He spent his first four years just figuring things out. Now he's in his second term; he can't serve again, so he's just going to do all the shit that needs to be done. It's gonna make him real unpopular, but he don't care doodly shit about that.' Roger chuckled. 'Ned Ray ... that's a good old-boy name there, Harlan, ain't that right? Ned Ray.'

'Billy Joe,' said Harlan.

'Joe Bob,' said Roger. He rose from his chair. 'Well, somebody's gotta do some work around here.'

After he'd left, Harlan ordered another milkshake. The waitress had done with bringing one glass at a time, and left a pitcherful instead.

Had Harlan ever known a fallow period, I wondered – a time when the hits wouldn't come; when he couldn't write at all?

'I had a seven-year drought,' he said. 'I was in my forties. I was burned out, I'd been writing for the hit parade so long. This was right around the time I'd written "No Charge". That coincided with a bitter divorce, and the personal stress I'd put on myself, getting up every morning thinking I've got to write a top-ten song.' He leaned forward in his chair, warming to the recollection. 'I had lost the joy of music. I'd lost all my childhood fantasies – all that mystical shit I'd loved as a child. When I was young the moon talked to me, and the stars – I believed in all that shit. But somewhere along the way I'd got a little jaded, cynical – poontang or the lack of it. I'd got involved with this man/woman thing too much and written everything I could.

'My marriage blew up on me. Plus the burnout of thinking I was going to have to go back to the factory and write for the bucks more than for the art. I'd lost sight of that original artform. So I got this divorce over with, went fishing in Florida. Got my life resettled, got married again. I got back my original attitude.

'There's a computer print-out I read some place that says most songwriters last five years. I've seen an awful lot of good writers disappear. Blow their brains out in a motel room for unknown reasons – the stress of a little two-month burnout jag. It's tough to write a brand new "I miss you", or "I need you", after all the thousands that have been written. So I went through this burnout, and I came back and decided I was going to sit around, think, write a little stuff on bar napkins. And at this moment I'm hotter than I've ever been. I'm sixty-four. I don't get up every morning in a frenzy like a shark. I'm studying, thinking. I'm not falling apart if, by noon, I haven't written some classic or something. What the hell's a classic? You don't know you've written one till twenty-five years later.

'It's like "I Fall To Pieces" – when I wrote that it was just a nice little old ballad. I still think it's just a nice little old ballad, but Patsy Cline sang the shit out of it. "I fall to pieces each time I see you again ..." It's simple, direct, see? It's comparable to the Hank Williams song, "Your cheatin' heart, will make you weep". Title first, your cheatin' heart, then you got a question, why will it make you weep? – that the rest of the song's gotta answer. In other words. "I fall to pieces each time I see you again." Why do I fall to pieces? How can I still be your friend when I feel this way about you? No one can write around that, because it's all there in that line. It's so simple, and it worked. It made me a few bucks, and I still make money on it.'

That's what you needed, said Harlan. A title that tied the song together, something the listener would know was real; the bait that would draw them in.

'I get my ideas from everywhere. You watch the language, slang, those flip sayings that come off. One I've heard – it's such a cute little thing, a real hip saying: *I'm outta here* ... You hear that everywhere: on the "Johnny Carson Show", or a guy walks out of a bar. But nobody's written a song on it yet.

'I'm writing it with Pam Tillis – "I'm outta here," and Pam's second line is "I'm outta tears". You're not treating me right; fuck it, I'm gone; there's more to life than this. It's not working, but I got some time left and I deserve to be happy, so I'm outta here ...' Harlan chuckled with satisfaction. 'It's going to be cute as hell, but it's going to be truthful. You could be forty-five, you could be fifteen and it would still be true.'

A phrase came into my mind. The one Randy Sprecher had used back in Milwaukee to describe building up his business. Sweat equity. We built our love on sweat equity? Crying tears of sweat equity? . . . I was imagining it in the *Billboard* charts, with a bullet – I was counting the royalties – almost before I'd said it.

'Sweat what?' Harlan drained his milkshake, and looked doubtful. 'This is the South, Mick. That sounds too northern for folks down here, like it's about shares or brokerage or something. It doesn't sound blue collar to me.'

My new career as a country writer was vanishing as quickly as it had arrived.

A young man was passing by the table. 'Harlan! How are you?'

Harlan smiled blearily up at him. 'Drunk.'

'Well, someone's gotta do it, Harlan.'

'I'm doin' it for you, so you'se can get out safe to your pretty little wife out there in Murfeesboro' . . .'

The young man slapped palms and drifted off to the bar. 'He's a good kid,' said Harlan, leaning across the table. 'A good songwriter. But he's not there yet. What he really needs is a divorce to get him going.'

We started talking about America. Why did he think there were so many songs about towns and cities in American music, I wondered. Harlan thought it was to do with the size of the country, the variety of it: the harshness of Montana, the lushness of the California valleys, the parched beauty of the desert. Every place in America was different from the next, he said. 'But what we're all looking for in this country is an ocean, a warm place. That's why Americans move. They move from city to city every five years. Industries move. The woollen industry left New England and now it's in Georgia. The auto industry is into Tennessee – a lot of people from Michigan are here now. Florida's about to sink with its new population.

'See, there's a problem in America we've got to deal with, and it's called success, and success is as hard to handle as failure. We're too rich. Everybody has got two cars and the roads are so crowded you can't get 'em out of the drive. But we'll solve that. We'll have highways in the sky. The brains and geniuses will work things out for us, because they always do. We're the top animal. We've fixed things. And now we've got freedom rockin' the world. Russia!

China! It'll happen all over. I don't care if it takes 200 years. What's that to the Rocky Mountains? They'll be an inch shorter is all . . .'

Man was a creature of appetites, said Harlan. They drove him, and they damned him. He was enslaved by wanting what the next guy had – that and poontang.

'When you screw up, you pay for it. That's the Lord's way, and I swear it's the truth. I will take all the guilt in my life for the things I did wrong, that led to a lot of honest songs that people have enjoyed, and hopefully led to one or two of them not making the same mistakes. I'm not guessing what I'm writing – I did it! A cheating song – I did it! I'm not bragging, I'm confessing I'm weak. But I don't do it any more. Cheating on nice people is not worth the pain it causes, to you or themselves. You get so you want to quit looking in the mirror shaving and being embarrassed. Because even if you screwed around and she don't know about it, she knows about it. Something's missing, I swear to God. I don't think you can do wrong and get away with it. But if we were angels we wouldn't be here . . . and we sure as hell wouldn't get sinus headaches.'

It was getting late. The morning crowd had long since given way to the lunchtime crowd, and now the lunchtime crowd was giving way to the early evening crowd. I was feeling drunk from just watching Harlan drink milkshakes. It had been a *tour de force* performance.

Harlan offered me a lift. I hesitated. I could easily walk, I lied. Through the window we could both see the rain sloshing down. It was falling in gallons, beer to drown the tears.

'You ain't walking,' said Harlan. Could he drive? 'Hell, yes,' his tone was wounded, but the smile as genial as ever. 'I've been in this town so long the car drives itself.' His Cadillac was in the car park. He slotted a cassette into the tape deck and turned up the volume. It was raining so hard that you could barely see through the windscreen. We lurched into the road, Harlan beating on the dashboard and raising his voice in cheerful song.

I knew the gods were with us. Harlan had already written the song anticipating his own demise, to be sung at his funeral, scribbled on a napkin at Maud's. It was called 'When I Fall Off This Barstool'.

*

The next day I went to a recording studio in Music Row where Harlan was producing some demo-tapes of songs written by his protégé, a young writer named Jackson Leap. These were not for public release, but demonstration records, samples to be pitched to singers and producers, to work the system.

Harlan's wife Melanie had organised the session, and had contracted the standard Nashville line-up for the morning's work: drums, guitar, bass, piano, steel guitar, fiddle. The musicians ran through the songs together, talking in the jargon of their trade. 'You play the first twelve, I'll take the next sixteen ...' Nashville musicians have their own idiosyncratic way of arranging music, a system whereby all the musical chords are numbered. The players simply read the numbers, adding 'head arrangements' – a lick here, a filigree there – on the spur of the moment.

Harlan rocked back in a big leather armchair, nodding, cajoling, shouting encouragement. 'That's good. I wanna make sure it's Texas.' And 'Make it lonesome ...'

'That sound too corny?' said the steel guitar player, rehearsing a lick. 'Sounds good to me ... Hey Denis, can I get you to play that piano left-hand real heavy, kinda hold everything together. Be real fun ...'

Denis, a heavy-set man in jeans and braces and with a sleepy manner, vamped a few chords. 'Like this?'

They were playing a song called 'Upright Piano', a loping, honky-tonk style song about the relationship between a country boy and a city girl.

'I get off on Merle Haggard/My budget's slim and tight/But we make pretty music/When we turn out the lights ...'

'Any macho male country singer could do this,' said Harlan. 'Clint Black possibly, or Doug Stone. He had a hit 'bout a year ago, although he seems to be heading to a Jim Reeves kind of blue blazer thing. But any hard young singer ...'

After each song, Billy, the guitarist and band leader, and one or two of the other musicians would come into the control room and listen to the playback. They worked astonishingly fast; two takes –

three at the most – and the song was finished. And the quality was astonishingly high. Any of the tracks sounded good enough to be released in its own right. Some rock musicians could spend hours, days, in the studio simply deliberating over the drum sound. But these musicians had recorded five tracks in under three hours.

In the Sixties, said Harlan, he would do fifteen or sixteen songs in a session, not even do playbacks. 'The producer'd just say "next" and no one'd even move from their seat,' he laughed. 'Then you had your midnight sessions, out in the boondocks some place, paying the musicians 10 bucks apiece – that was strictly non-union. But I'd never do that. I'm from up north. I'm a union man.'

'Harlan's a traditionalist,' said Jackson with a laugh. 'I bet we're the only people in town cutting with an upright bass.'

'That's 'cause I'm ahead of the game,' said Harlan. 'You know what I think? I think you should give your satellite dish to Mother Teresa; give away your pick-up truck. Get hungry again.'

By lunchtime, the musicians were done with, their instruments packed away, their union dockets signed. Now a back-up singer arrived, to add three-part harmonies where required. He listened just once to each song, attuning his ears to the line in the melody, the shifts in rhythm, the cadences of the music, before adding his voice. 'Doing the ooohs,' Harlan called it. 'Denis here can do all the Jordanaires in an hour. I tell you, Nashville is a town full of geniuses.'

By tomorrow morning the songs would have been mixed. By Friday they would have been pitched to the artists and producers. 'We're selective as hell,' said Harlan. 'We'll be pitching these to Clint, Garth, Ricky Van Shelton maybe – the big stars. But after we strike out a few times we start shotgunning and give it to everybody – people in bars, winos.' He chuckled. 'I tell you, I'm the great white shark. I'm sixty-four years old and I still wanna kick their ass. Everybody in Nashville knows that. I hate to lose.' He put an arm around Jackson's shoulder. 'And this here is my boy.'

The last take was completed. Melanie glanced up from the paper she had been reading. 'Hey Harlan, you want to rent a Christmas tree this year?' she asked.

'Let's just rent a picture of one,' said Harlan. 'Then you don't get all that trash in the house.'

Christmas had crept up quietly. But suddenly there were advertisements in the newspapers for gifts and holidays, announcements of seasonal activities and attractions. And today was the unveiling of the Opryland Country Christmas at the Opryland Hotel.

The Opryland Hotel was a short drive from Opryland itself, out on the freeway under a darkening sky, the drops of rain clouding the windscreen. The hotel had been built to resemble an antebellum southern mansion – an echo of the elegance of the old, pre-Civil War South. Except that this was an inflated version of an antebellum mansion, so big it seemed like a caricature. It was six storeys high. Almost a half a mile long. It had 1,891 guest rooms. It was the biggest hotel I had ever been in – so big that bellboys were stationed in the corridors with maps. There was an oak-panelled entrance, the size of a railway station booking hall, with open fires blazing merrily and an enormous Christmas tree sparkling with lights. There had been a convention of tour operators meeting in one of the hotel's numerous conference halls – representatives of resorts and theme parks hawking their wares to travel agents and bus companies. The delegates wandered the corridors and hallways, decked out with name tags and badges, groaning under the weight of pennants, balloons, carrier bags full of assorted gee-gaws. Some of them were wearing sweaters bearing the legend 'Merry Christmas', which were being sold from little wooden wagons posted along the corridors.

People surged this way and that, inspecting their maps, criss-crossing between bars, restaurants and gift shops. I walked down a corridor, following the tide of people. I looked through a window. On the other side, a man was seated at a desk, talking into a microphone. It was a studio, an outpost of WSM, Nashville's country music station, broadcasting live.

I walked on. In 'The Picking Parlour' a man in a cowboy hat was singing 'Honky-tonk Angels' to an audience made up largely of elderly people, tapping their fingers on the tables. I continued past, and found myself in a tropical rainforest. Paths and elevated walkways ran beside pools and waterfalls, tangled, steaming foliage and gorgeously coloured blooms. Set among the greenery were animated models of gnomes and giant lollipops. The sound of a trio, singing 'Take Me Home, Country Roads' filled the air.

In the very heart of the jungle a screen had been erected, decorated with a Christmas scene – white fields, a smiling snowman, a church spire in the distance. There was a bench where people could sit to have their photographs taken. A family asked me to take their picture. The tropical rainforest vanished in the viewfinder, leaving the family frozen in laughter in front of an idea of Christmas.

On I went, into a corridor lined with shops – expensive ones, selling golf clubs, grandfather clocks, onyx and marble statues, and bottles of something called 'moustache anti-freeze'. The corridor led into a second conservatory, even larger than the one I had left. It was half as big again as a football field, a vaulted ceiling soaring six storeys high. On the ground were a series of restaurants, staggered on terraces, a mosaic of lakes and rivers, bordered by jacaranda, poinsettia and fir trees. A Mexican mariachi band was playing 'The First Noel'.

There was a sense of expectancy in the air. The crowd had grown denser now, drawn it seemed, from all corners of this gigantic building, thronging the paths and crowding the aerial pavements which crisscrossed the largest lake, wielding cameras and portable videos. A hush descended. Now a spotlight danced across the upturned faces, and settled on a small balcony set high in the heavens. A figure appeared, clad in a glittering blue sequinned suit, and took his place behind a golden harp. It was Lloyd Lindroth, the famous country and western harpist.

His fingers made a pass over the strings, sending shimmers of celestial sound soaring upwards into the heavens. Far below him, the lake burst into sudden, wondrous life – fountains of water soaring and dying in precision harmony, as coloured spotlights played across their surface. An involuntary moan of pleasure escaped from the assembled multitudes.

On another balcony, on the far side of the atrium, a choir had materialised, dressed in pink and white satin surplices.

All the way across America I had been conscious of a country disintegrating before my eyes. But here, at last, was the healing. Wholeness. The perfect reconciliation of the most profound atavistic desires, dreams and myths – the Civil War South, country music, the Caribbean holiday, mall shopping. A past that had never been, a present built on illusion. A place with no turmoil, no poverty, no strife, no taxes. And there, in the heavens, a camp angel in blue sequins, playing 'Silent Night'. I had found American heaven.

Index

Acuff, Roy 220
Adams, Henry 76
Alexander, Lamar 44
Anderson, Marian 198
Ani Wang Mo 20
Arcady 8
Avalon (dir. Levinson) 185–6, 192–3, 194, 196
Axton, Estelle 57
Axton, Packy 58

Bacharach, Burt 121, 168
Baez, Joan 10
Bailey, D'Army 66–8
Bailey, Loree 65
Bailey, Walter 65
Baltimore 186, 187–90, 191–2, 194, 199–200, 206–9
'Baltimore' (Newman) 186–7
Barbara Mandrell World 218
Beale Street, Memphis 52–3
Behind The Silicon Curtain (Hays) 179–80
Bell, Al 60
Berry, Chuck 51–2
Bethel 2, 12, 31–2
Black, Clint 213, 230
Boothe, Judy 132
Border Patrols, El Paso 139–41, 143–6
'Bowling Game, The' 112, 113
Brooks, Garth 213, 214, 230
Brown, James 4, 5
Bryan, William Jennings 40, 41–2, 203
Bryan College 42
Burke, John 101–2
Burroughs, William 172
Butterfield, Paul 11
'By The Time I Get To Phoenix' (Webb) 154
Byrd, Jane 8
Byrdcliffe 9–10

Campbell, Glen 154
Carefree 165–6
Carlsbad 133
Cassady, Carolyn 172, 173
Cassady, John Allen 173, 174–5
Cassady, Neal 171–3, 174–5
Chattanooga 35–8, 44, 46–8
'Chattanooga Choo Choo' (Warren and Gordon) 35
Church of Christ, Childress 129–30
Civil Rights Movement museum 65, 66, 68, 69
Clarence Thomas case 96
Clinton, Bill 204
Concordia Cemetery, El Paso 149–50
Cornelius, Richard 42–3, 203
Cortopassi, Al 77, 78, 84
Country Music Hall of Fame 216
Country Music World 220
Cropper, Steve 59
Crudup, Arthur 54, 55
Custer, Donna 114–15
Custer, Gordy 114–18

Dahl, Gary 174
Dahmer, Jeffrey 86
Darrow, Clarence 40–2
David, Hal 121, 168
Davis, Gus 161–2
Day (Rainbow Family leader) 14–18
Dayton 39–40, 42, 43
De Berge, Earle 155, 156–7, 160, 162, 165
Dennis, Dave 67
Deskins, Bobbie 126–7, 129, 130
Deskins, Linton 122, 126–7, 129, 130
Deutsch, Miles 19, 20
'Do You Know The Way To San Jose?' (Bacharach and David) 167, 168
Dooley, Don 87–8
Dozgchen Ponlop Rinpoche 20–1
Dylan, Bob 10, 11, 23

Earp, Wyatt 148
Eileen (friend) 190
Eisen, Mrs 190
Electric Kool Aid Acid Test, The (Wolfe)
    171
El Paso 134–46, 147–51
'El Paso' (Robbins) 134, 148
Eustace (Ugandan refugee) 36, 38, 44

Fagen, Donald 11
Family, The 12–13
Fells Point 191, 206–9
Fitzpatrick, Vince 202
Folk, Joseph ('Holy Joe') 75
Ford, Loretta 103–8

Gallico, Al 89
Garrett, Pat 148
Gelish, Louis, Nicky and June 31, 32
Ginsberg, Allen 172
Glenner, Bob 176, 177, 180, 182
'Going Down To Old Woodstock' (Van
    Morrison) 21
Goldfield, David 74
Good, Buddy 224
Gordon, Mack 35
Graceland 55–6
Grand Ole Opry 215–16, 219
Green, Michael 12
Gross, Father Ralph 103–4
Grossman, Albert 10, 11
Gyalwang Gwyla Karmapa 19, 21

Handy, W. C. 52
Hardin, John Wesley 134–5, 148–9, 150
Hardin, Tim 11
Hartmann, Ray 80–1, 82–3
Hay, George D. 215
Hayes, Isaac 58
Hays, Dennis 179, 180
Hendersonville 225
Henry (Ugandan Refugee) 35–6
Hervey White, Harvard 9
Hollander, Brian 26–9
Hollis 122–9, 130–2
'Holy Joe' (Joseph Folk) 75
Howard, Harlan 229–40

Howard, Melanie 238, 239

Indian bingo 98–103, 107
Indian Community School, Milwaukee
    102–4, 107–8

Jackson, Reverend Alvin 61–4
Jackson, Jack 149–50
Jennings Bryan, William see Bryan,
    William Jennings
'Jewish Alps' 30
Jobs, Steve 169
Joel, Billy 214
Joplin, Janis 11
Juárez 135, 137, 146, 147, 151

Keating, Charles 156
Kerouac, Jack 171, 172
Kesey, Ken 171, 173, 178
Khenpo Kharthar Rinpoche 18
King, Coretta Scott 68
King, Martin Luther 50, 59, 65, 68
King, Riley 'B. B.' 53
Kohl, Tom 113
Kramer, Israel 197
Kramer, Reuben 197–8
Krichinsky, Ada 194, 196, 197
Krichinsky, Ben 194–7
Krick, Perna 197, 198, 199
Krystal Burgers 45

Lang, Michael 12
Lansky, Meyer 158
Leap, Jackson 238, 239
Leary, Timothy 171, 173, 179
Levinson, Barry 185
Lindroth, Lloyd 241
'Lookout Mountain Crowd' 36, 38–9
Lorraine Motel 59, 64–5, 68
Los Gatos 173–4, 175, 178
Lupton, Jack 45, 46–8
Lupton, John T. 45–6
Luther King, Martin see King, Martin
    Luther

McCarty, James R. 128
McWherter, Ned Ray 233–4